GRADE 6

STAAR Mathematics

PRACTICE

Table of Contents

Using This Book

What Is the STAAR Mathematics Assessment?

The State of Texas Assessments of Academic Readiness (STAAR) is the current assessment for students in the state of Texas. STAAR Mathematics assesses what students are expected to learn at each grade level according to the developmentally appropriate academic readiness and supporting standards outlined in the Texas Essential Knowledge and Skills (TEKS).

How Does This Book Help My Student(s)?

If your student is taking the STAAR Assessment for Mathematics, then as a teacher and/or parent you can use the mini-lessons, math practice pages and practice tests in this book to prepare for the STAAR Mathematics exam. This book is appropriate for on-grade-level students.

STAAR Mathematics Practice provides:

- Mini-lessons for assessed Math TEKS skills and strategies
- Word problems for assessed Math TEKS skills and strategies
- Questions for griddable and multiple-choice answer format
- Opportunities to familiarize students with STAAR format and question stems
- Answer Keys available online for access anywhere

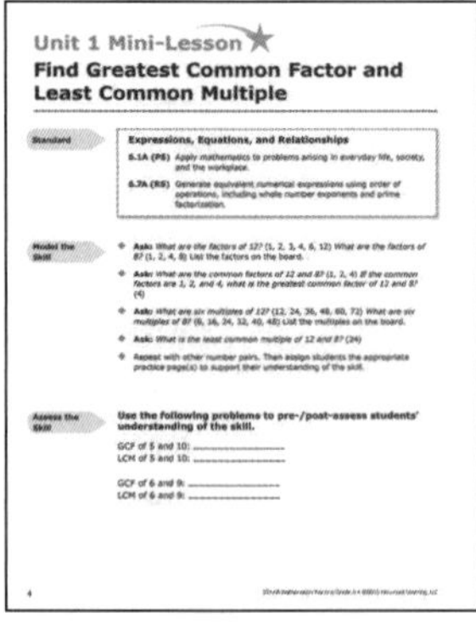

Unit 1 Mini-Lesson

Find Greatest Common Factor and Least Common Multiple

Introduce STAAR-aligned math concept, skill, or strategy

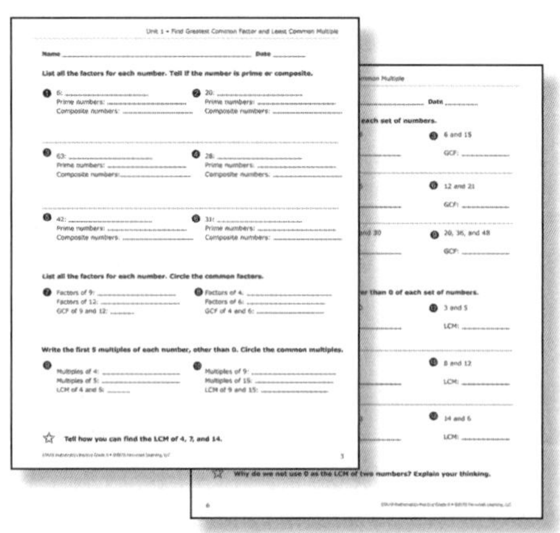

Practice with STAAR-aligned problems

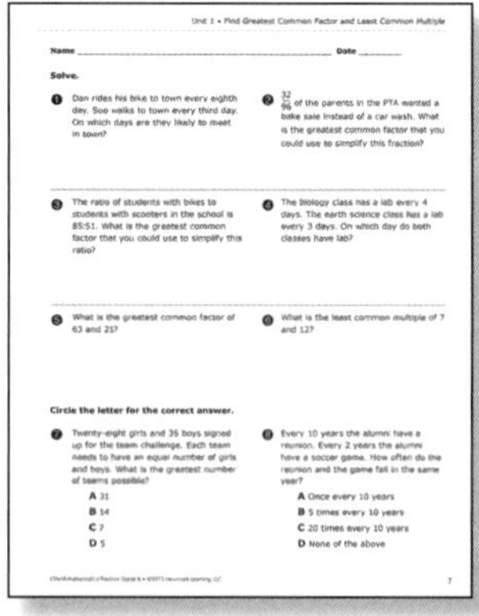

Assess concepts, skills, and strategies with word problems

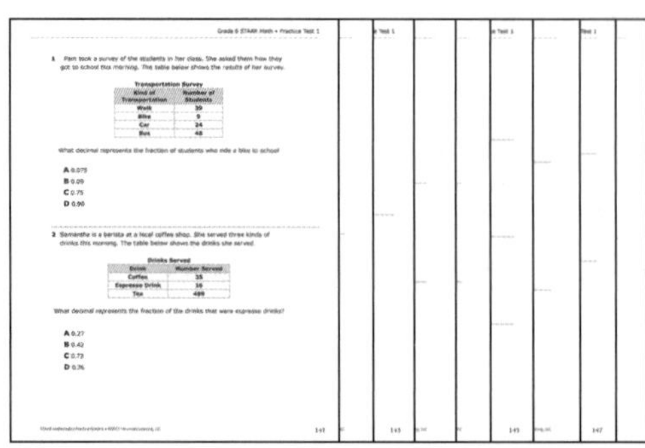

Simulate test-taking with full-length practice tests

STAAR Mathematics Practice/Assessed TEKS Alignment Chart • Grade 6

STAAR Mathematics Practice Unit	6.1	6.2	6.3	6.4	6.5	6.6	6.7	6.8	6.9	6.10	6.11	6.12	6.13	6.14
Unit 1: Find Greatest Common Factor and Least Common Multiple	✔						✔							
Unit 2: Write Prime Factorizations							✔							
Unit 3: Understand Integers		✔												
Unit 4: Use Order of Operations	✔						✔							
Unit 5: Estimate	✔													
Unit 6: Divide Multi-Digit Whole Numbers	✔	✔		✔										
Unit 7: Generate Equivalent Forms of Rational Numbers		✔												
Unit 8: Compare and Order Rational Numbers		✔												
Unit 9: Add and Subtract Fractions	✔													
Unit 10: Addition of Integers			✔											
Unit 11: Subtraction of Integers			✔											
Unit 12: Multiply and Divide Integers			✔											
Unit 13: Use Ratios and Equivalent Ratios				✔										
Unit 14: Use Rates				✔										
Unit 15: Understand Percentages				✔										
Unit 16: Represent Relationships	✔				✔									
Unit 17: Generate Formulas						✔								
Unit 18: Write Equations						✔								
Unit 19: Classify Triangles								✔						
Unit 20: Quadrilaterals	✔													
Unit 21: Locate Points on the Coordinate Plane											✔			
Unit 22: Measure Angles	✔													
Unit 23: Convert Measures	✔			✔										
Unit 24: Solve Problems Involving Measurements	✔							✔						
Unit 25: Estimate Perimeter and Circumference	✔													
Unit 26: Estimate and Find Area								✔						
Unit 27: Estimate and Find Volume								✔						
Unit 28: Use Lists and Tree Diagrams												✔	✔	
Unit 29: Find Probability												✔	✔	
Unit 30: Find Mean, Median, and Mode												✔		
Unit 31: Make and Interpret Dot Plots												✔	✔	
Unit 32: Make and Interpret Stem-and-Leaf Plots												✔		
Unit 33: Display and Interpret Data	✔											✔		
Unit 34: Box Plots													✔	
Unit 35: Debit Cards vs. Credit Cards														✔
Unit 36: Balancing a Checking Account														✔

Unit 1 Mini-Lesson

Find Greatest Common Factor and Least Common Multiple

Standard

Expressions, Equations, and Relationships

6.1A (PS) Apply mathematics to problems arising in everyday life, society, and the workplace.

6.7A (RS) Generate equivalent numerical expressions using order of operations, including whole number exponents and prime factorization.

Model the Skill

- **Ask:** *What are the factors of 12?* (1, 2, 3, 4, 6, 12) *What are the factors of 8?* (1, 2, 4, 8) List the factors on the board.
- **Ask:** *What are the common factors of 12 and 8?* (1, 2, 4) *If the common factors are 1, 2, and 4, what is the greatest common factor of 12 and 8?* (4)
- **Ask:** *What are six multiples of 12?* (12, 24, 36, 48, 60, 72) *What are six multiples of 8?* (8, 16, 24, 32, 40, 48) List the multiples on the board.
- **Ask:** *What is the least common multiple of 12 and 8?* (24)
- Repeat with other number pairs. Then assign students the appropriate practice page(s) to support their understanding of the skill.

Assess the Skill

Use the following problems to pre-/post-assess students' understanding of the skill.

GCF of 5 and 10: ____________________
LCM of 5 and 10: ____________________

GCF of 6 and 9: ____________________
LCM of 6 and 9: ____________________

Name ______________________________ Date __________

List all the factors for each number. Tell if the number is prime or composite.

1. 6: ____________
   Prime numbers: ____________
   Composite numbers: ____________

2. 20: ____________
   Prime numbers: ____________
   Composite numbers: ____________

3. 63: ____________
   Prime numbers: ____________
   Composite numbers: ____________

4. 28: ____________
   Prime numbers: ____________
   Composite numbers: ____________

5. 42: ____________
   Prime numbers: ____________
   Composite numbers: ____________

6. 31: ____________
   Prime numbers: ____________
   Composite numbers: ____________

List all the factors for each number. Circle the common factors.

7. Factors of 9: ____________
   Factors of 12: ____________
   GCF of 9 and 12: ______

8. Factors of 4: ____________
   Factors of 6: ____________
   GCF of 4 and 6: ____________

Write the first 5 multiples of each number, other than 0. Circle the common multiples.

9. Multiples of 4: ____________
   Multiples of 5: ____________
   LCM of 4 and 5: ______

10. Multiples of 9: ____________
    Multiples of 15: ____________
    LCM of 9 and 15: ____________

 **Tell how you can find the LCM of 4, 7, and 14.**

Name ______________________ **Date** __________

Find the greatest common factor (GCF) of each set of numbers.

1. 10 and 25

   GCF: __________

2. 12 and 8

   GCF: __________

3. 6 and 15

   GCF: __________

4. 24 and 60

   GCF: __________

5. 16 and 6

   GCF: __________

6. 12 and 21

   GCF: __________

7. 10 and 30

   GCF: __________

8. 16, 18, and 30

   GCF: __________

9. 20, 36, and 48

   GCF: __________

Find the least common multiple (LCM) other than 0 of each set of numbers.

10. 7 and 9

    LCM: __________

11. 4 and 10

    LCM: __________

12. 3 and 5

    LCM: __________

13. 4 and 6

    LCM: __________

14. 9 and 6

    LCM: __________

15. 8 and 12

    LCM: __________

16. 8 and 3

    LCM: __________

17. 3 and 23

    LCM: __________

18. 14 and 6

    LCM: __________

Why do we not use 0 as the LCM of two numbers? Explain your thinking.

Name ______________________________ **Date** __________

Solve.

1. Dan rides his bike to town every eighth day. Soo walks to town every third day. On which days are they likely to meet in town?

2. $\frac{32}{96}$ of the parents in the PTA wanted a bake sale instead of a car wash. What is the greatest common factor that you could use to simplify this fraction?

3. The ratio of students with bikes to students with scooters in the school is 85:51. What is the greatest common factor that you could use to simplify this ratio?

4. The biology class has a lab every 4 days. The earth science class has a lab every 3 days. On which day do both classes have lab?

5. What is the greatest common factor of 63 and 21?

6. What is the least common multiple of 7 and 12?

Circle the letter for the correct answer.

7. Twenty-eight girls and 35 boys signed up for the team challenge. Each team needs to have an equal number of girls and boys. What is the greatest number of teams possible?

   A 31

   B 14

   C 7

   D 5

8. Every 10 years the alumni have a reunion. Every 2 years the alumni have a soccer game. How often do the reunion and the game fall in the same year?

   A Once every 10 years

   B 5 times every 10 years

   C 20 times every 10 years

   D None of the above

Unit 2 Mini-Lesson
Write Prime Factorizations

Standard

Expressions, Equations, and Relationships

6.7A (RS) Generate equivalent numerical expressions using order of operations, including whole number exponents and prime factorization.

Model the Skill

- **Ask:** *What do you remember about prime and composite numbers?* Remind students that a prime number is a whole number greater than 1 and has only two factors, itself and 1. A composite number is a whole number with more than two factors.
- **Say:** *Every composite number can be written as the product of two or more prime numbers. We call this product prime factorization.* Demonstrate how to find the prime factorization of 8 with a tree diagram by repeatedly dividing until the factors are prime: 2 x 2 x 2.
- **Ask:** *How can we write 2 x 2 x 2 as an exponent?* (2^3) Review how to write an exponent. Have students identify the base and the number of times the base is used as a factor. Continue making factor trees for numbers and finding prime factorization until students understand the process.
- Assign students the appropriate practice page(s) to support their understanding of the skill.

Assess the Skill

Use the following problems to pre-/post-assess students' understanding of the skill.

Write the prime factorization for each, using exponents.

16 18 50 28 81 32

Name ____ Date __________

Write each prime factorization using exponents.

1. 36 = 2 x 2 x 3 x 3 =

____

2. 80 = 2 x 2 x 2 x 2 x 5 =

____

3. 54 = 2 x 3 x 3 x 3 =

____

4. 300 = 2 x 2 x 3 x 5 x 5 =

____

Complete each factor tree to show the number as a product of prime factors. Write each prime factorization using exponents.

5.

24

6 x _____

3 x _____ x _____ x _____

prime factorization is _______

6.

12

2 x _____

2 x _____ x _____

prime factorization is _______

7.

40

_____ x _____

_____ x _____ x _____

_____ x _____ x _____ x _____

prime factorization is _______

8.

27

_____ x _____

_____ x _____ x _____

prime factorization is _______

☆ **Tell how you know if a number is a composite number.**

Name ______________________________ **Date** __________

Use a factor tree to find the prime factors for each number. Write the prime factorization using exponents.

❶ 28

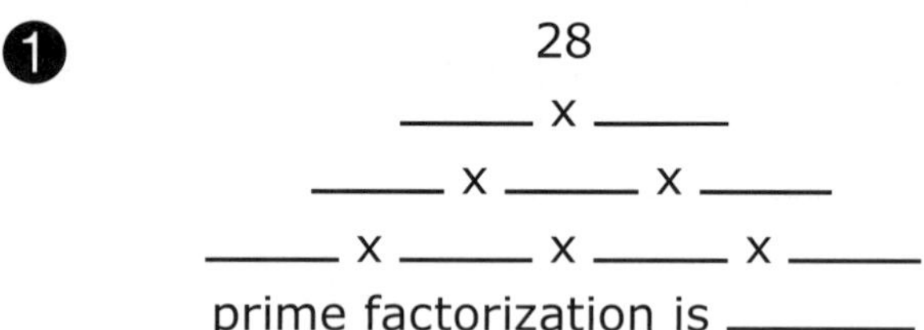

prime factorization is ______

❷ 54

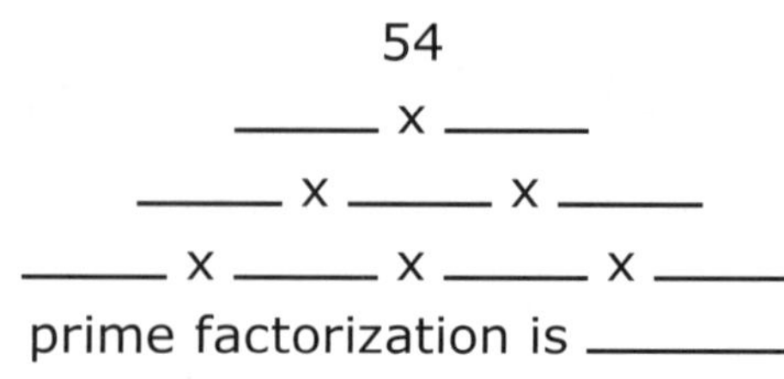

prime factorization is ______

❸ 45

prime factorization is ______

❹ 20

prime factorization is ______

❺ 18

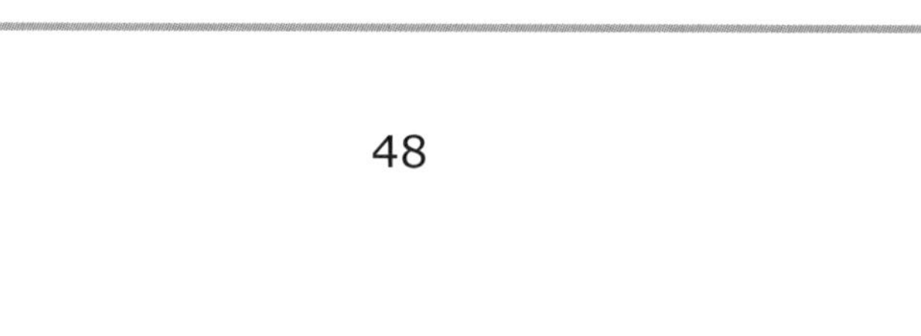

prime factorization is ______

❻ 48

prime factorization is ______

❼ 72

prime factorization is ______

❽ 64

prime factorization is ______

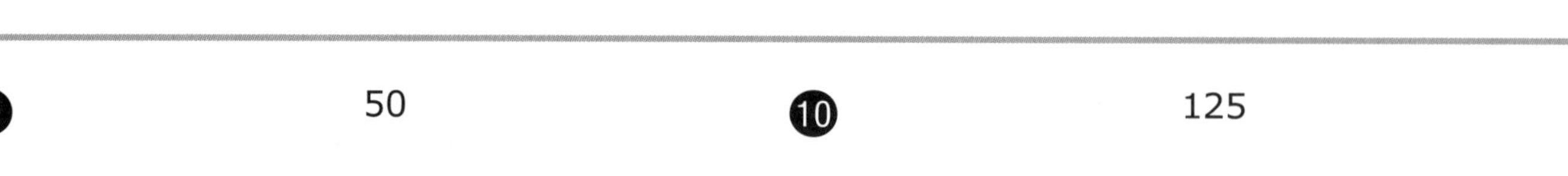

❾ 50

prime factorization is ______

❿ 125

prime factorization is ______

Tell how you find the prime factorization of 125.

Name ______________________________ **Date** __________

Solve.

1. Is 109 a prime or a composite number? Explain how you know.

2. What is the prime factorization of 84?

3. What is the prime factorization of 62?

4. What is the prime factorization of 100?

5. What are the two prime factors in the prime factorization of 51? Explain how you know.

6. What is the exponent needed to complete the prime factorization of 63?

   $7 \times 3^?$

Circle the letter for the correct answer.

7. What number is shown by the prime factorization $2^2 \times 3^2$?

   A 10

   B 12

   C 24

   D 36

8. Which expression shows the prime factorization of 72?

   A 3^4

   B $3^2 \times 2^2$

   C $2^3 \times 3^2$

   D $3^3 \times 2^2$

Unit 3 Mini-Lesson

Understand Integers

Standard

Number and Operations

6.2B (SS) Identify a number, its opposite, and its absolute value.

6.2C (SS) Locate, compare, and order integers and rational numbers using a number line.

Model the Skill

- Draw the following number line on the board.

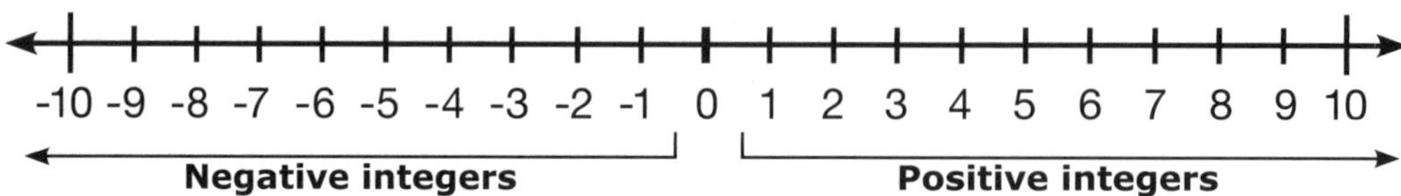

- **Say:** *Today we are going to be working with positive and negative integers. Which point on the number line represents negative 6? How do you know? Which point on the number line represents positive 3? How do you know?*

- **Say:** *The opposite of an integer is its positive or negative counterpart on the opposite side of the number line. So, whatever lies the exact distance from zero on the other side of the number line is an integer's opposite. The absolute value of an integer is the distance of a number on the number line from 0, no matter which direction from zero the number lies. The absolute value of a number is never negative.*

- **Ask:** *What is the opposite of positive 8?* (negative 8) *What is the absolute value of negative 8?* (8)

Assess the Skill

Use the following problems to pre-/post-assess students' understanding of the skill.

integer: _____	integer: –5	integer: 1
opposite: +9	opposite: _____	opposite: _____
absolute value: _____	absolute value: _____	absolute value: _____

Name ________________________________ **Date** __________

Write an integer to describe each situation. Draw a picture to show each.

-10 -9 -8 -7 -6 -5 -4 -3 -2 -1 0 1 2 3 4 5 6 7 8 9 10

Negative integers **Positive integers**

1. 4 stories below ground level
   ______

2. 7 stories above ground level
   ______

3. A temperature 20°C above freezing
   ______

4. A temperature 5°C below freezing
   ______

5. A withdrawal of $75.00
   ______

6. A deposit of $150.00
   ______

Complete. Use the number line at the top of the page to help you.

7. integer: −4
   opposite: ______
   absolute value: |4|

8. integer: −3
   opposite: ______
   absolute value: ______

9. integer: ______
   opposite: +2
   absolute value: ______

10. integer: −5
    opposite: ______
    absolute value: ______

11. integer: 1
    opposite: ______
    absolute value: ______

12. integer: ______
    opposite: −16
    absolute value: ______

13. integer: 107
    opposite: ______
    absolute value: ______

14. integer: −90
    opposite: ______
    absolute value: ______

 **Tell how you find the absolute value of −3.**

Name ______________________________ **Date** __________

Write an integer to describe each situation.

1. A deposit of fifty dollars

   ____

2. A withdrawal of twenty dollars

   ____

3. A decrease in profits of $300

   ____

4. Sixteen degrees below zero

   ____

5. 1,200 meters above sea level

   ____

   56 meters below sea level

   ____

6. A increase in profits of $500

   ____

   A positive charge of 6

   ____

Complete.

7. integer: ____
   opposite: +9
   absolute value: ____

8. integer: +8
   opposite: ____
   absolute value: ____

9. integer: −94
   opposite: ____
   absolute value: ____

10. integer: ____
    opposite: −2
    absolute value: ____

11. integer: −15
    opposite: ____
    absolute value: ____

12. integer: +72
    opposite: ____
    absolute value: ____

13. integer: ____
    opposite: +200
    absolute value: ____

14. integer: +60
    opposite: ____
    absolute value: ____

15. integer: +19
    opposite: ____
    absolute value: ____

What are negative integers? Explain.

Name ______________________________ **Date** __________

Solve.

1. What integer would represent "ten degrees below zero"?

2. What integer would represent "twenty-two hundred feet above sea level"?

3. What is the opposite of 8?

4. What is the opposite of –45?

5. What is the absolute value of –12?

6. What is the absolute value of –674?

Circle the letter for the correct answer.

7. Which of the following is not an integer?

   A 5
   B 0
   C 0.2
   D –2

8. Which integer has an opposite of 9?

   A 0.9
   B 90
   C –9
   D $\frac{1}{9}$

Unit 4 Mini-Lesson

Use Order of Operations

Standard

Expressions, Equations, and Relationships

6.1A (PS) Apply mathematics to problems arising in everyday life, society, and the workplace.

6.7A (RS) Generate equivalent numerical expressions using order of operations, including whole number exponents and prime factorization.

Model the Skill

Order of Operations

1. Simplify within parentheses.
2. Simplify exponents.
3. Multiply and divide from left to right.
4. Add and subtract from left to right.

- Write the equation 6 – 4 = 2 on the board. **Say:** *This is an equation. It uses numbers and symbols and an equal sign.* Write the expression 6 – 4 on the board. **Say:** *This is an expression. How is this different from the equation?* (It does not have an equal sign or an answer.) *Today, we will be evaluating expressions. When you evaluate an expression, you find the solution.*
- Write the expression 7 x 9 – 4 on the board.
- **Ask:** *What do you notice about this expression?* (Possible answer: It has three numbers and two different operation symbols.) *To evaluate this expression, you complete the operations from left to right just as you read words in a sentence. What is 7 multiplied by 9?* (63) *Now you can subtract 4 to finish evaluating the expression. What is 63 minus 4?* (59)
- Assign students the appropriate practice page(s) to support their understanding of the skill.

Assess the Skill

Use the following problems to pre-/post-assess students' understanding of the skill.

- Ask students to solve each problem.

36 ÷ 9 – 3	50 – 12 x 3	26 – 3 x (14 ÷ 2)
42 x 2 – 1	(8 + 17) x 3	(80 – 3) ÷ 11
63 ÷ (9 – 2)	32 ÷ 8 x 4	5 – 51 ÷ 17

Name ______________________________ Date __________

Use the order of operations.
Evaluate each expression.

Order of Operations
1. Simplify within parentheses.
2. Simplify exponents.
3. Multiply and divide from left to right.
4. Add and subtract from left to right.

❶ 5 x (6 – 3)

❷ 24 x (4 – 2)

❸ 32 ÷ (8 – 4)

❹ 28 ÷ (7 – 3)

❺ 7 x (7 – 3)

❻ 56 ÷ (11 – 3)

❼ 3 + (4 x 3)

❽ 40 + (72 ÷ 9) ÷ 8

❾ 23 + (30 ÷ 10) x 4

❿ (24 – 24) ÷ 8

⓫ 32 – 16 ÷ 23

⓬ 22 x 5 ÷ 2 – 1

Tell how evaluating an expression with parentheses affects the solution.

Name ____ **Date** __________

Use the order of operations. Evaluate each expression.

1. (17 x 2) ÷ (16 ÷ 8)
2. (25 − 1) + (7 x 2)
3. (5 x 5) x (6 − 2)
4. 8 x 8 − 9 x 7
5. (22 x 23) − (32 + 7)
6. (2 x 8) − 32 + 7
7. 426 ÷ 3 x 10
8. 183 − 3 x 50
9. 56 + 4 x 6
10. 178 − (3 x 9)
11. 5 x (20 − 3) + 8
12. 72 ÷ 2 + 5
13. 4 x 8 + (42 − 3)
14. 190 ÷ 2 − 2
15. 76 + 14 x 2
16. 24 x 4 ÷ 2 x 3
17. 56 − (52 + 5)
18. 88 − 11 ÷ 11
19. 12 x 5 + 6 x 32
20. 135 ÷ 32 − 23 ÷ 2

Write an explanation of how you evaluated Problem 17.

Name ______________________________ **Date** __________

Solve.

1. Hilary has six times as many apples as James. James has 3 green apples and 4 red apples. How many apples does Hilary have?

2. Kendall has three fewer pencils than Lara. Lara has twice as many pencils as Stephanie. If Stephanie has 10 pencils, how many pencils does Kendall have?

3. There are 13 cars parked in the lot on Wednesday. There are 4 more cars parked on Thursday. There are 5 times that amount on Saturday. How many cars are parked on Saturday?

4. Jaden has 156 baseball cards in a pile. Jaden divides the cards evenly into four albums and then buys 2 more cards to put in each album. How many cards will Jaden have in each album?

5. Brady has 3 dozen eggs. He uses 6 eggs to bake some muffins. Then he uses three times that amount to make omelettes. How many eggs does Brady have left?

6. There are 4 windows in the living room. Each window has 1 set of blinds and 2 panels of curtains. The blinds cost $20 each. Each curtain panel costs $28. How much do the window treatments cost?

Circle the letter for the correct answer.

7. $48 \div 23 - 2 = ?$

   A 2
   B 4
   C 6
   D 8

8. $90 \times 7 - 4 \times 50 \div 2 = ?$

   A 6,750
   B 215
   C 530
   D 3,375

Unit 5 Mini-Lesson
Estimate

Standard

Mathematical Process Standards

6.1A (PS) Apply mathematics to problems arising in everyday life, society, and the workplace.

6.1C (PS) Select tools, including real objects, manipulatives, paper and pencil, and technology as appropriate, and techniques, including mental math, estimation, and number sense as appropriate, to solve problems.

Model the Skill

- **Say:** *Estimation is a very useful test-taking strategy. You can estimate a solution to know if the answer is reasonable.* **Ask:** *What are some other ways we use rounded numbers or estimation?* (for example: in science in interplanetary distances; in history and archeology to know the approximate age of artifacts)
- **Say:** *Let's estimate the solutions to some travel problems.* Write the following information on the board while you speak. *You're going to drive 1,205 miles from Texas to Wyoming. Your car gets 27 miles per gallon. Gas costs $3.27 a gallon. You are sharing the cost with 3 friends. So far, you have saved $493 for the trip.*
- **Ask:** *About how much will gas cost for the trip? What will your share be? If your trip will take about 3 weeks, have you saved enough money for food? About how much money a day (a week, 3 weeks) will you need for food?* Help students estimate by using round or compatible numbers, determining the operation, and estimating the solution.
- Assign students the appropriate practice page(s) to support their understanding of the skill.

Assess the Skill

Use the following problems to pre-/post-assess students' understanding of the skill.

Have students estimate.

2,378 + 5,689 11,540 – 7,702 379 x 11 2,168 ÷ 52

Name ______________________________ Date __________

Estimate the solution to each problem.

1.
```
      25,394 ———>     [    ]
  +   10,705 ———>  +  [    ]
  ----------       ---------
```

2.
```
       3,210 ———>     [    ]
  –      956 ———>  –  [    ]
  ----------       ---------
```

3.
```
     415 ———>     [    ]
  x   23 ———>  x  [    ]
  ------       ---------
```

4.
```
     1,879 ———>     [    ]
  x     11 ———>  x  [    ]
  --------       ---------
```

5. 52)3,628 ———> 50)4,000

Or use compatible numbers
3,500 ÷ 50 = __________

6. 7)665

Compatible numbers
__________ ÷ 7 = __________

7. 475 + 183 + 500 = __________

8. 732 + 151 = __________

9. 82 x 12 = __________

10. 3,140 ÷ 16 = __________

11. Mohit spends $12 each week on bus fare. About how much does he spend on bus fare in one year? __________

12. If the Parks drive at an average speed of 58 miles per hour, about how many hours will it take them to drive 469 miles to Flower Mound? __________

13. Is this calculator result reasonable, 736 x 12 = **1,472** ?
Explain ______________________________

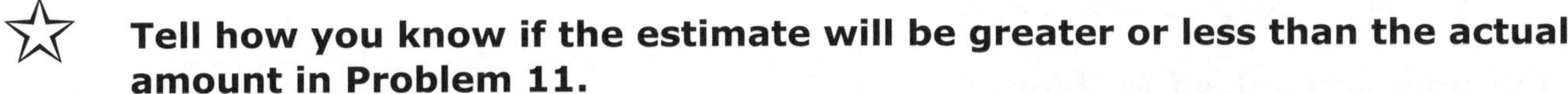

☆ **Tell how you know if the estimate will be greater or less than the actual amount in Problem 11.**

Name ______________________________ Date __________

Estimate the solution to each problem. Tell the method you used.

	Problem	Estimate	Method
1	6,192 + 8,549		
2	\$3,095 x 28		
3	\$589.99 ÷ 12		
4	\$7.83 x 13,098		
5	74,859 – 21,789		
6	25,430,164 + 3,671,277		
7	16,982 – 8,329		
8	37.89 x 6.29		

9. Historic Parker-Cabin in Fort Worth was built in 1848. About how many years ago was it built?

10. Bernard works weekends at the cafe. This weekend he made 83 crepes on Saturday and 129 on Sunday. About how many crepes does he make in a year?

11. This year the Lone Star Chorus concert cost the town \$130,732. Concert tickets were \$24.95 and the town sold 10,018 tickets. About how much did the town profit from the concert this year in ticket sales?

12. Addy's great grandmother was born in 1917. Addy was born in 2002. About how old was Addy's great grandmother when Addy was born?

13. Each football uniform costs \$43. The pads cost \$67 and the cleats cost \$59. If there are 42 players on the team, about how much do the team's families spend on football equipment? Tell how you know your answer is reasonable.

14. Jesse drove from the Alamo to King Ranch in 3 hours and fifteen minutes. If the driving distance between the two sites is 186 miles, about how fast was Jesse driving?

Tell how you solved Problem 9.

Name ______________________________ **Date** __________

Estimate to solve. Use the price list for Problems 1–4.

Parks Landing	
Canoe rental	**$14/hr** **$35/day**
Picnic lunch	**$22/person**
Cabin rental	**$129 per night**

1. The Wilson family rents a cabin for one week and a canoe for three days. About how much will it cost?

2. Eighteen people ordered a picnic lunch. About how much will it cost?

3. Five friends share the cost of renting a cabin for 8 days. If they split it evenly, about how much does each friend pay?

4. Maurice and Dia are staying for 2 days and 3 nights. About how much will it cost for them to rent a cabin, have a picnic lunch each day, and rent a canoe for 3 hours each day?

5. Trevor multiplies 4,278 by 45 and gets a product of 19,251. Is his answer reasonable? Explain why or why not.

6. Timon is making a 2-sided quilt for his grandmother. If he sews about 9 squares a week, and the quilt has 196 squares on each side, about how many weeks will it take him to sew all of the squares?

Circle the letter for the correct answer.

7. Shira exchanged $115 US dollars for Indian rupees. The exchange rate was 57 rupees for each dollar. Which is the best estimate of how many rupees Shira received?

   A 5,000 rupees
   B 6,000 rupees
   C 8,000 rupees
   D 10,000 rupees

8. Pilar is driving 148.4 miles to Palo Alto from San Antonio. If she drives at 52 miles per hour the whole way, about how long will it take her to get to her destination?

   A 20 minutes
   B 3 hours
   C 30 hours
   D 2 hours

Unit 6 Mini-Lesson

Divide Multi-Digit Whole Numbers

Standard

Number and Operations

6.1A (PS) Apply mathematics to problems arising in everyday life, society, and the workplace.

6.2E (SS) Extend representations for division to include fraction notation such as a/b represents the same number as a ÷ b where b ≠ 0.

6.4B (RS) Apply qualitative and quantitative reasoning to solve prediction and comparison of real-world problems involving ratios and rates.

Model the Skill

Write the following problem on the board.

$2{,}552 \div 4$ $\quad$ $4\overline{)2{,}552}$ $\quad$ $\frac{2{,}552}{4}$

- **Say:** *Today we are going to be dividing multi-digit numbers. Look at the problem. Which number is the divisor?* (4) *Which number is the dividend?* (2,552) *How will you divide 2,552 by 4?* Point out connections to place value and to multiplication by showing how to use the divisor to divide each place–first, the hundreds, then the tens, then the ones.
- **Say:** *Now divide 2,552 by 4. Can you tell me the quotient?* (638) Point out how when there aren't enough thousands to divide, you move on to the next place value and try to divide into the hundreds place, and so on.
- Assign students the appropriate practice page(s) to support their understanding of the skill.

Assess the Skill

Use the following problems to pre-/post-assess students' understanding of the skill.

2,901 ÷ 12
4,560 ÷ 40
7,291 ÷ 71
8,600 ÷ 24

Name ______________________________ Date __________

Divide. Write the remainder as a whole number or as a fraction in simplest form.

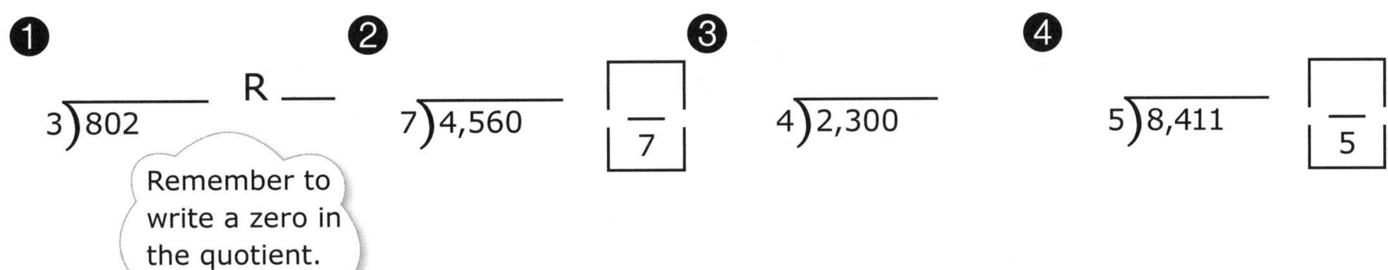

5. 8)2,432

6. 10)3,197

7. $\frac{692}{12}$

8. $\frac{13,604}{16}$

Divide. Write each remainder as a decimal.

9. 4)425

10. 8)538

Remember to write a decimal point and zeros to continue dividing.

11. $\frac{396}{5}$

12. $\frac{2,469}{6}$

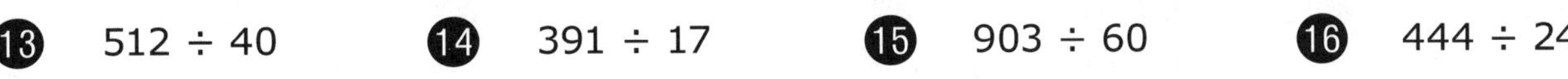

☆ **Look at Problem 13. Tell how you can check your answer.**

Name ______________________________ **Date** __________

Divide. Write each remainder as a whole number or as a fraction in simplest form.

1. $5\overline{)428}$

2. $\frac{812}{14}$

3. $20\overline{)1,365}$

4. $\frac{785}{15}$

5. $512 \div 40$

6. $\frac{282}{5}$

7. $6,984 \div 4$

8. $\frac{5,428}{8}$

Divide. Write each remainder as a whole decimal. Round to the nearest hundredth as necessary.

9. $\frac{250}{8}$

10. $16\overline{)1,526}$

11. $4\overline{)765}$

12. $48\overline{)954}$

13. $9,430 \div 20$

14. $\frac{3,871}{7}$

15. $693 \div 10$

16. $300 \div 16$

Show how you divide $20\overline{)3,005}$. Label each step.

Name ______________________________ **Date** __________

Solve.

1. Sarah earned $114 in 8 hours. How much did she earn per hour?

2. Rafael's grandfather has 126 baseball cards in his collection. If the grandfather gives the same number of cards to Rafael and his two sisters, how many cards does each sibling get?

3. Mike's boat can carry 40 people across the river. Last month 2,504 people rode on Mike's boat. What is the least number of trips that Mike could have made across that river?

4. There are 60 floorboards in the living room. The floor is 14 feet wide. If each floorboard is the exact same width, how wide is each floorboard?

5. Jenna has 300 centimeters of string. She needs 27 centimeters to make a necklace. How many necklaces can she make?

6. The fence is 106 meters long. Each section of fence is 3 meters long. How many sections were needed to complete the fence?

Circle the letter for the correct answer.

7. Anna bought 120 feet of copper wire. She cut it into 16 pieces of the same length. How long is each piece of copper wire?

   A 8 ft
   B 7.8 ft
   C 7.55 ft
   D $7\frac{1}{2}$ ft

8. Oliver buys 258 lbs of rice for his restaurant. He buys 20 bags of rice. How many pounds does each bag hold?

   A 12.6 lbs
   B 12.9 lbs
   C 1.29 lbs
   D 129 lbs

Unit 7 Mini-Lesson

Generate Equivalent Forms of Rational Numbers

Standard

Number and Operations

6.2C (SS) Locate, compare, and order integers and rational numbers using a number line.

6.2D (RS) Order a set of rational numbers arising from mathematical and real-world contexts.

Model the Skill

Write the following equivalents on the board.

$5 = \frac{5}{1} = 5.00$ $\frac{1}{4} = 1 \div 4 = 0.25$ $0.75 = \frac{75}{100} = \frac{3}{4}$

- **Say:** *We can write equivalent numbers using whole numbers, fractions, or decimals. Look at the first set of numbers.* **Ask:** *How can we write a whole number as a fraction?* (Write 1 as the denominator)
- **Ask:** *How can we write a fraction as a decimal?* (Divide numerator by denominator.) Point out that the fraction bar means "divide." **Say:** *Some fractions result in a repeating decimal.* Demonstrate with $\frac{1}{3} = 0.3333...$ Show students how to write a repeating decimal with a bar over the digit(s) that repeat.
- **Ask:** *How can we write a decimal as a fraction?* (Use place value.) Remind students to write the resulting fraction in simplest form, as shown above. Discuss how to use equivalent forms of rational numbers to compare and order decimals and fractions.
- Assign students the appropriate practice page(s) to support their understanding of the skill.

Assess the Skill

Use the following problems to pre-/post-assess students' understanding of the skill.

- Have students write the decimal or fraction equivalent for each number. Then have them write the numbers from greatest to least.

$\frac{2}{5}$ $\frac{3}{8}$ $\frac{1}{6}$ $\frac{9}{9}$ $\frac{9}{1}$ 0.2 0.6 0.50 0.35

Name ______________________________ **Date** __________

Divide. Write each fraction as an equivalent decimal.

1. $\frac{1}{2}$ $2\overline{)1}$ ________
2. $\frac{1}{5}$ $5\overline{)1}$ ________
3. $\frac{1}{8}$ $8\overline{)1}$ ________
4. $\frac{3}{8}$ $8\overline{)3}$ ________
5. $\frac{7}{10}$ $10\overline{)7}$ ________
6. $\frac{1}{6}$ $6\overline{)1}$ ________

Use place value. Write each decimal as an equivalent fraction in simplest form.

7. 0.9 ________
8. 0.4 ________
9. 0.28 ________
10. 0.15 ________
11. 0.75 ________
12. 1.3 ________

Compare. Use >, <, or =.

13. $\frac{1}{3}$ ○ 0.55
14. 0.35 ○ $\frac{2}{5}$
15. $\frac{3}{6}$ ○ 0.5
16. 0.7 ○ $\frac{1}{7}$
17. 0.625 ○ $\frac{5}{8}$
18. $\frac{5}{4}$ ○ 0.6

☆ **Tell where you would place $\frac{3}{6}$, 0.7, and $\frac{2}{5}$ on the number line.**

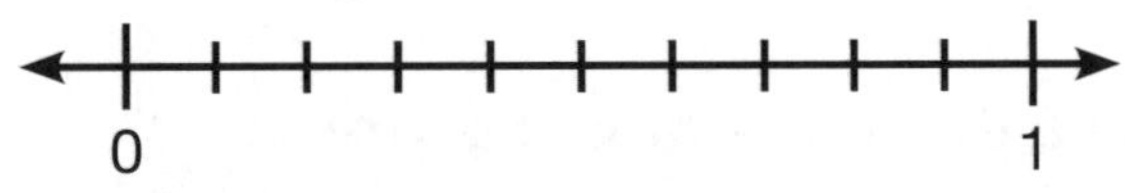

Name ______________________________ **Date** __________

Write the fraction or decimal equivalent for each number. Write fractions in simplest form.

1. $\frac{3}{8}$ ________
2. $\frac{1}{16}$ ________
3. $\frac{4}{5}$ ________
4. $\frac{2}{3}$ ________
5. $\frac{3}{10}$ ________
6. $\frac{7}{12}$ ________
7. 0.3 ________
8. 0.333 ________
9. 0.26 ________
10. 2.25 ________
11. 1.375 ________
12. 0.625 ________

Compare. Use >, <, or =.

13. $\frac{2}{3}$ ◯ 0.75
14. 0.85 ◯ $\frac{3}{5}$
15. $\frac{3}{4}$ ◯ 0.875
16. 0.3 ◯ $\frac{1}{5}$
17. 0.88 ◯ $\frac{7}{9}$
18. $\frac{3}{8}$ ◯ 0.4

Write the numbers in order from least to greatest. Place them on the number line.

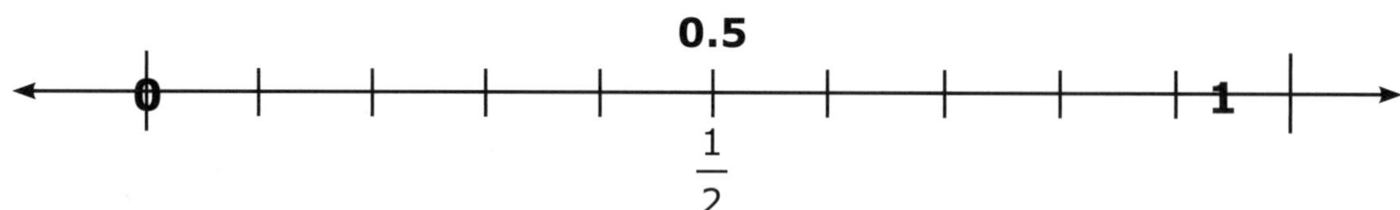

19. $\frac{3}{5}$, 0.25, $\frac{1}{20}$ ________
20. 0.45, $\frac{6}{8}$, $\frac{12}{12}$ ________

☆ **Tell how you compare decimals and fractions.**

Name ____ Date __________

Solve.

1. What fraction is equivalent to the decimal 0.4?

2. What fraction is equivalent to the decimal 0.65?

3. What decimal is equivalent to the fraction $\frac{5}{8}$?

4. What decimal is equivalent to the mixed number $3\frac{5}{6}$?

5. What fraction is equivalent to the decimal 1.375?

6. What fraction is equivalent to the decimal 0.416?

Circle the letter for the correct answer.

Breakfast	Number of Orders
Pancakes	37
French Toast	23
Belgian Waffle	40

7. The table shows the breakfast orders of 100 customers at the Pancake House. What decimal represents the fraction of customers that ordered the Belgian Waffle?

   A 0.37

   B 0.6

   C 0.4

   D 0.23

8. What fraction represents the portion of customers that did not order pancakes?

   A $\frac{2}{5}$

   B $\frac{3}{5}$

   C $\frac{37}{100}$

   D $\frac{63}{100}$

Unit 8 Mini-Lesson

Compare and Order Rational Numbers

Standard

Number and Operations

6.2C (SS) Locate, compare, and order integers and rational numbers using a number line.

6.2D (RS) Order a set of rational numbers arising from mathematical and real-world contexts.

Model the Skill

Draw the following number line and problems on the board.

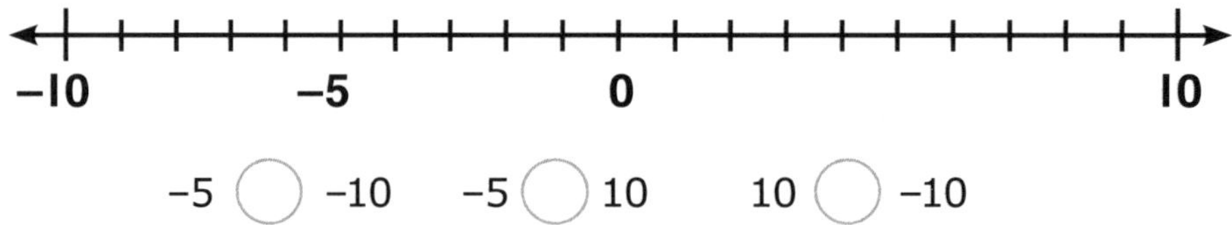

–5 ◯ –10 –5 ◯ 10 10 ◯ –10

- **Say:** *Today we are going to be comparing and ordering integers. Look at the number line. Use the number line to tell which number in each expression is greater. Then place the numbers in order.* (–10 < –5 < 10)
- **Say:** *Now plot the following points on the number line: –8, 7, –3, 6, 2, –1.*
- Assign students the appropriate practice page(s) to support their understanding of the skill.

Assess the Skill

Use the following problems to pre-/post-assess students' understanding of the skill.

- Ask students to use > or < to make each statement true.

–4 ◯ –18 –12 ◯ 6 3 ◯ –3

- Ask students to plot the following points on the number line: –6, 3, 8, –5, –4

–10 0 10

Name ______________________________ **Date** __________

Solve. Then write the integer on the number line.

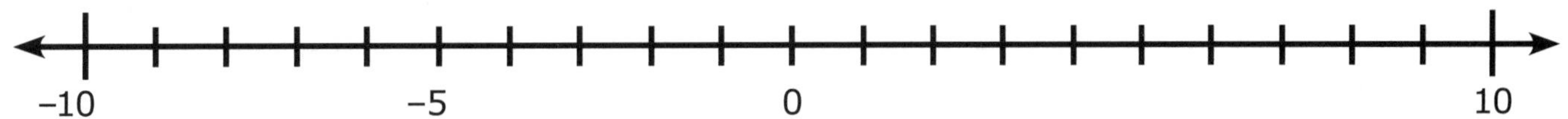

❶ An integer whose opposite is 1 ______

❷ An integer whose opposite is 8 ______

Remember: An opposite integer is an equal distance from 0, but on the opposite side of 0.

❸ Two integers whose absolute value is 151 ______

❹ Two integers whose absolute value is 27 ______

Think: Absolute value is a number's distance from 0 on the number line.

Complete the number line above. Write > or < to make each statement true.

❺ –9 ◯ –7 ❻ –2 ◯ –5 ❼ –6 ◯ –11 ❽ –4 ◯ –14

Remember: Numbers to the right on a number line are greater.

❾ –12 ◯ –8 ❿ –7 ◯ –8 ⓫ –13 ◯ –19 ⓬ –16 ◯ –6

⓭ –5 ◯ –1 ⓮ –3 ◯ –10 ⓯ –6 ◯ 7 ⓰ –4 ◯ –8

⓱ –23 ◯ –25 ⓲ –73 ◯ –15 ⓳ –18 ◯ –81 ⓴ –2 ◯ 5

Fractions and decimals are also rational numbers. Tell where you would place $\frac{1}{2}$ and 3.5 on the number line.

Name ______________________________ **Date** __________

Solve. Then write the integer on the number line.

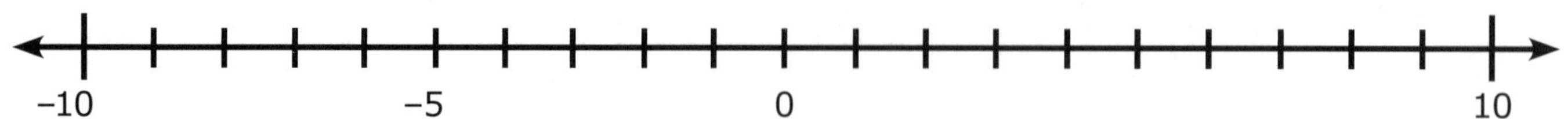

1. An integer whose opposite is 7 _____

2. An integer greater than 7 and less than 9 _____

Solve.

3. An integer whose opposite is 16 _____

4. Two integers whose absolute value is 252 _____

5. An integer whose opposite is –58 _____

6. An integer greater than –10 and less than –8 _____

7. Two integers whose absolute value is 14 _____

8. Two integers whose absolute value is 84 _____

Complete the number line above. Write > or < to make each statement true.

9. –12 ◯ –5
10. –4 ◯ –5
11. –18 ◯ 17
12. –6 ◯ –21
13. –7 ◯ –4
14. –18 ◯ –7
15. –3 ◯ 3
16. –19 ◯ –2
17. 23 ◯ –8
18. –13 ◯ –15
19. –41 ◯ –51
20. –17 ◯ –71
21. –10 ◯ –25
22. –23 ◯ –9
23. –6 ◯ 5
24. –3 ◯ –19

Write how you solved the ninth problem. Draw a picture to prove your answer is correct.

Name ______________________________ **Date** __________

Solve.

1. Which point on the number line is located at –4?

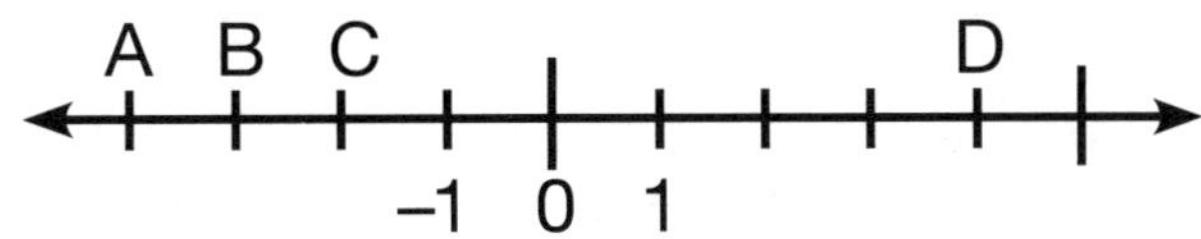

2. Write the integers 4, –7, 5, –2 in order from least to greatest.

3. Which point on the number line is located at 2?

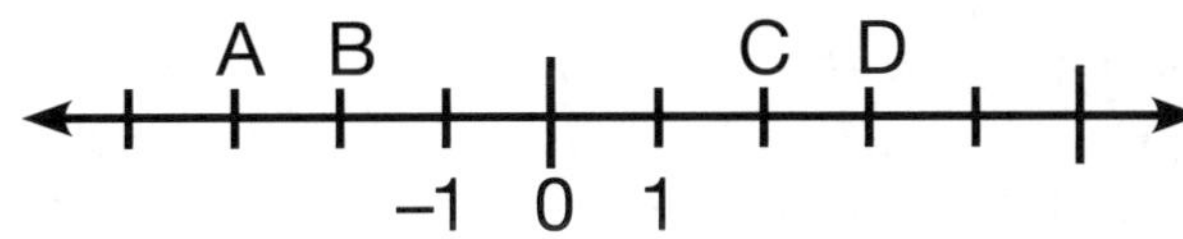

4. Write the integers 12, –14, 10, –20 in order from greatest to least.

5. Which point on the number line is located at –30?

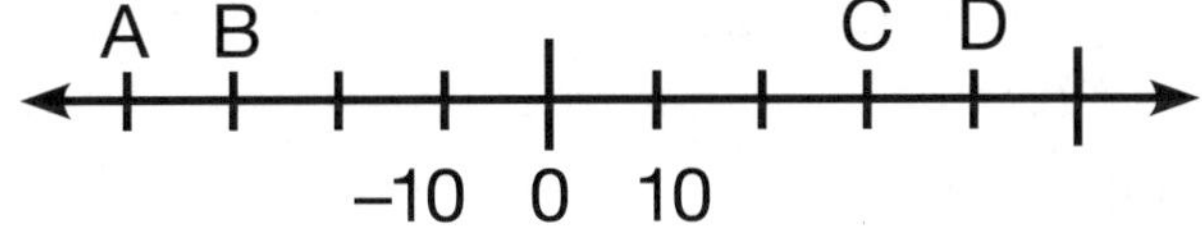

6. Write the integers –143, 125, –118, 60, –36 in order from least to greatest.

Circle the letter for the correct answer.

7. Which statement is true?

   A $-15 > -13$
   B $12 > -14$
   C $10 > 11$
   D $-11 < -12$

8. Which statement is false?

   A $-6 < -12$
   B $-11 < 1$
   C $21 < 22$
   D $-15 < -7$

Unit 9 Mini-Lesson

Add and Subtract Fractions

Standard

Number, Operations, and Quantitative Reasoning

6.1D (PS) Communicate mathematical ideas, reasoning, and their implications using multiple representations, including symbols, diagrams, graphs, and language as appropriate.

Model the Skill

- **Say:** *Today we are going to add and subtract fractions.*

  Write $\frac{1}{5} + \frac{2}{5}$ and $\frac{2}{5} - \frac{1}{5}$ on the board.
- **Ask:** *How do we add fractions that have the same denominator?* (Add the numerators and keep the same denominator.) *How do we subtract fractions that have the same denominator?* (Subtract the numerators and keep the same denominator.)
- **Say:** *Discuss how you would add or subtract fractions that have different denominators.* Write $\frac{1}{3} + \frac{1}{6}$ and $\frac{1}{3} - \frac{2}{6}$ on the board. (Find a common denominator using equivalent fractions.)
- **Say:** *We will use equivalent fractions to find a common denominator.* Help students understand that when one denominator is a multiple of the other denominator, they can simply write an equivalent fraction. Review how to find equivalent fractions by multiplying ($\frac{1}{3} \times \frac{2}{2} = \frac{2}{6}$).
- Assign students the appropriate practice page(s) to support their understanding of the skill.

Assess the Skill

Use the following problems to assess the students' understanding of the skill.

$\frac{1}{2} + \frac{1}{2}$ $\frac{1}{3} + \frac{2}{3}$ $\frac{1}{4} - \frac{1}{4}$ $\frac{3}{5} - \frac{1}{5}$

$\frac{1}{2} + \frac{2}{3}$ $\frac{4}{5} + \frac{1}{4}$ $\frac{5}{6} - \frac{1}{3}$ $\frac{5}{7} - \frac{2}{5}$

Name ______________________________ **Date** __________

Find a common denominator. Add or subtract.

1. $\frac{1}{3} + \frac{1}{2}$ $\quad \frac{1}{2} \times \frac{3}{3} + \frac{1}{3} \times \frac{2}{2} = \frac{3}{6} + \frac{2}{6} = \frac{\;}{\;}$

2. $\frac{1}{4} + \frac{1}{2}$ $\quad \frac{1}{4} + \frac{1}{2} \times \frac{2}{2} = \frac{1}{4} + \frac{2}{4} = \frac{\;}{\;}$

3. $\frac{3}{4} - \frac{1}{2}$

4. $\frac{5}{6} - \frac{1}{2}$

5. $\frac{3}{6} + \frac{1}{2}$

6. $\frac{1}{6} + \frac{4}{8}$

7. $\frac{7}{8} - \frac{1}{4}$

8. $\frac{3}{8} + \frac{1}{2}$

☆ **Tell how you find the common denominator.**

Name ____ **Date** __________

Find each sum or difference. Use symbols to tell if the sum is greater than (>) or less than (<) 1.

1. $\frac{1}{3} + \frac{1}{6}$
2. $\frac{3}{4} + \frac{1}{2}$
3. $\frac{3}{5} - \frac{1}{10}$
4. $\frac{1}{4} + \frac{3}{8}$

---

5. $\frac{2}{3} - \frac{1}{9}$
6. $\frac{1}{5} + \frac{7}{10}$
7. $\frac{1}{8} + \frac{1}{2}$
8. $\frac{3}{4} - \frac{5}{8}$

---

9. $\frac{5}{7} - \frac{1}{5}$
10. $\frac{1}{3} + \frac{7}{12}$
11. $\frac{2}{3} - \frac{1}{5}$
12. $\frac{1}{6} + \frac{6}{9}$

---

13. $\frac{3}{10} + \frac{4}{5}$
14. $\frac{1}{8} + \frac{5}{12}$
15. $\frac{1}{3} + \frac{4}{7}$
16. $\frac{7}{8} - \frac{1}{10}$

Tell how you know if the sum will be greater than 1.

Name ______________________________ **Date** __________

Solve.

1. What is the sum of $\frac{1}{8}$ and $\frac{3}{4}$?

2. What is the sum of $\frac{2}{5}$ and $\frac{1}{4}$?

3. What is the difference of $\frac{3}{5}$ and $\frac{3}{7}$?

4. The chapter is 8 pages long. Kosta read $\frac{1}{4}$ of the chapter aloud. Then Christina read three pages to the class. How many pages have they read so far?

5. Clara ate $\frac{1}{8}$ of the pie. Jacob ate $\frac{1}{4}$. How much of the pie did they eat in all?

6. The tangerine had 12 sections. I ate five sections. Dad ate $\frac{1}{3}$. How much of the tangerine did we eat?

Circle the letter for the correct answer.

7. The inn has ten rooms. One-half of the rooms are reserved for Friday. The rest are vacant. If 2 more rooms are reserved for Friday, what will be the total number of occupied rooms on Friday?

   A $\frac{5}{12}$

   B $\frac{5}{10}$

   C $\frac{7}{8}$

   D $\frac{7}{10}$

8. What is the difference of seven-eighths and one-sixteenth?

   A $\frac{13}{16}$

   B $\frac{14}{16}$

   C $\frac{7}{8}$

   D $\frac{8}{16}$

Unit 10 Mini-Lesson
Addition of Integers

Standard

Number, Operations, and Quantitative Reasoning

6.3D (RS) Add, subtract, multiply, and divide integers.

Model the Skill

Draw the following number line on the board.

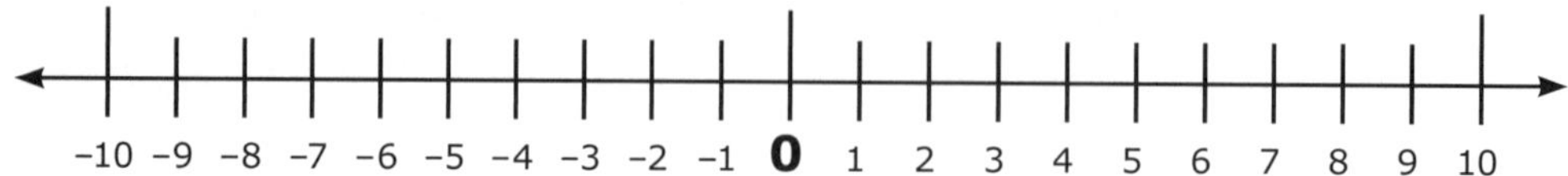

- **Say:** *Today we are going to add integers by looking at some real-world applications and the number line.*
- **Ask:** *How would you represent an elevator that went up 3 floors and then went up 5 floors?* Show students that this could be represented by the integers (+3) + (+5) or 3 + 5.

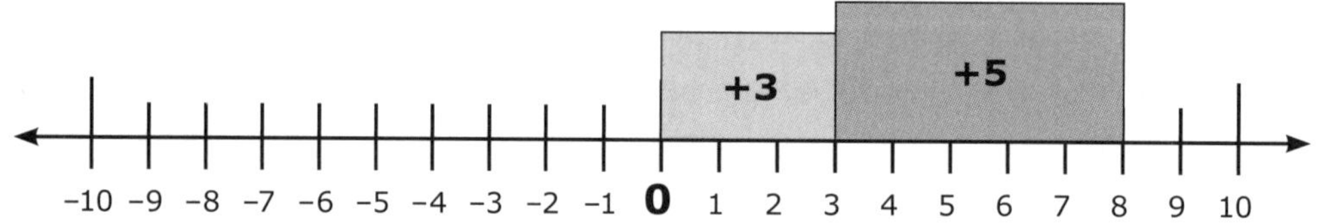

- **Ask:** *How would you represent an elevator that went up 5 floors and then went down 3 floors?* Show the students that this could be represented by the integers (+5) + (–3) or 5 – 3.

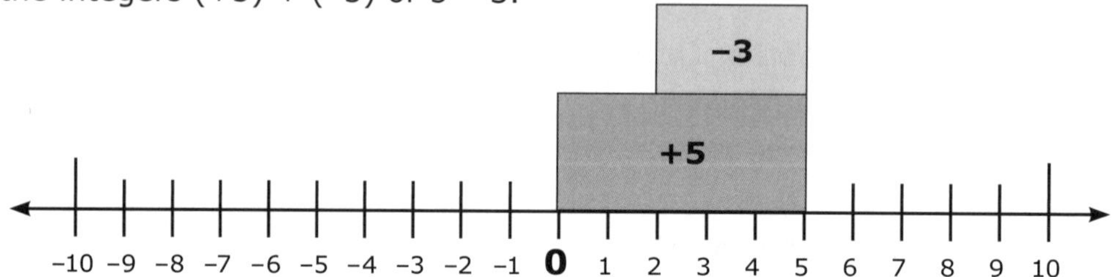

- Assign students the appropriate practice page(s) to support their understanding of the skill.

Assess the Skill

Use the following problems to assess the students' understanding of the skill.

(+4) + (+3) (+9) + (–5) (–4) + (+6)

Name ______________________________ **Date** __________

Complete the table.

Signs	Expression	Solution	Sign of Solution
(+) + (+)	(+2) + (+5)	7	Positive
(–) + (–)	(–2) + (–5)		
(–) + (+)	(–2) + (+5)		
(+) + (–)	(+2) + (–5)	–3	Negative

Add the integers:

1. (+5) + (–2)

2. (–1) + (–5)

3. (–6) + 8

4. (+5) + (–4)

5. 5 + (–8)

6. (–2) + (–6)

7. 2 + (–6)

8. (+3) + (+4)

9. When you add a positive number plus a negative number, how can you tell what the sign of the solution will be?

☆ **When will you have a positive answer?**

Name ______________________________ **Date** __________

1. At 7:00 a.m. the temperature in Houston was 75°F. By noon the temperature had risen 20°F. Write a number sentence that shows the temperature in Houston at noon.

2. On Saturday, golfer Judy shot 2 under par (–2). On Sunday, Judy shot 5 under par (–5). Write a number sentence that shows what Judy shot on Saturday and Sunday combined.

---

3. Starting on the ground floor, the elevator in Marcus's building went up 12 floors. Then it went down 5 floors. Write a number sentence that shows the floor where the elevator stopped.

4. Last winter the temperature was –10°F in the morning. Later that day the temperature had risen 30°F. Write a number sentence that shows the change in temperature and what the temperature was later in the day.

---

5. From the problems above and the two shown below, can you write a rule for adding integers with the same sign?

   (+5) + (+3) = +8
   (–5) + (–3) = –8

   Rule:

6. From the problems above and the two shown below, can you write a rule for adding integers with different signs?

   (+5) + (–3) = +2
   (–5) + (+3) = –2

   Rule:

When will you have a negative answer?

Name ______________________________ Date __________

Add the integers.

1. (+12) + (+15)

2. (–10) + (–15)

3. (–6) + (+8)

4. (+10) + (–12)

5. 45 + 23

6. (–12) + (–17)

7. 25 + (–16)

8. (–36) + (54)

9. 10 + (–15) + 12

10. (–12) + (–20) + (–5)

11. (–14) + (–16) + (20)

12. 56 + (–12) + 24

13. (–25) + (–36) + (23) + (–15)

14. (36) + (–14) + (–5) + 10

Unit 11 Mini-Lesson
Subtraction of Integers

Standard

Number, Operations, and Quantitative Reasoning

6.3D (RS) Add, subtract, multiply, and divide integers.

Model the Skill

Draw the following circles on the board.

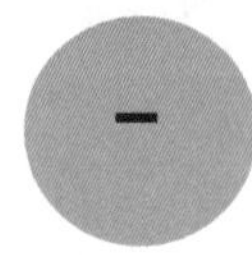

- **Say:** *Let's look at a model problem: −4 − (−3). Use circles on the board. Each circle represents a negative number. There are 4 of them, so the circles together represent the (−4).*
- **Say:** *The problem says to "take away" or "subtract 3 of the negatives" or "− (−3)." Can you do that? What is left?*

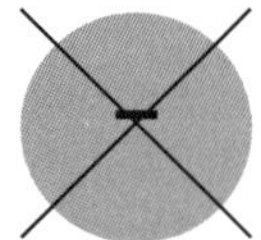
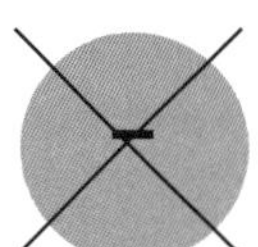
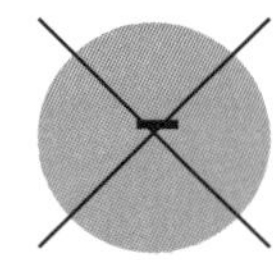
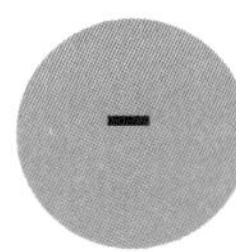

- **Say:** *−4 − (−3) = −1. Let's look at a few more problems to see if you can predict an outcome without using counters.*
- Assign students the appropriate practice page(s) to support their understanding of the skill.

Assess the Skill

Use the following problems to assess the students' understanding of the skill.

Can you give another number sentence that would be the same as −4 − (−3) = −1? What about −4 + 3? Would that equal −1?

Name ______________________________ **Date** __________

Write a number sentence for each model.

1. + + + + minus + + +

Number Sentence: ______________________________

What would this equal? ______________________________

Can you write an equivalent number sentence? ______________________________

2. – – – – – minus + +

Number Sentence: ______________________________

What would this equal? ______________________________

Can you write an equivalent number sentence? ______________________________

3. + + + + minus – –

Number Sentence: ______________________________

What would this equal? ______________________________

Can you write an equivalent number sentence? ______________________________

What happens if you subtract two negative numbers?

Name ______________________________ **Date** __________

Are the following equivalent sentences? Answer *yes* or *no*.

1. $+4 - (-3) = +4 + 3$ ____________
2. $+5 - (+2) = +5 - 2$ ____________
3. $-5 - (+2) = -5 - 2$ ____________
4. $-7 - (-5) = -7 + 5$ ____________
5. Is subtracting a number the same as adding its opposite?
   Explain your answer using examples from above.

Modeling subtraction of integers on a number line can be helpful.

$5 - 3 = 5 + (-3)$

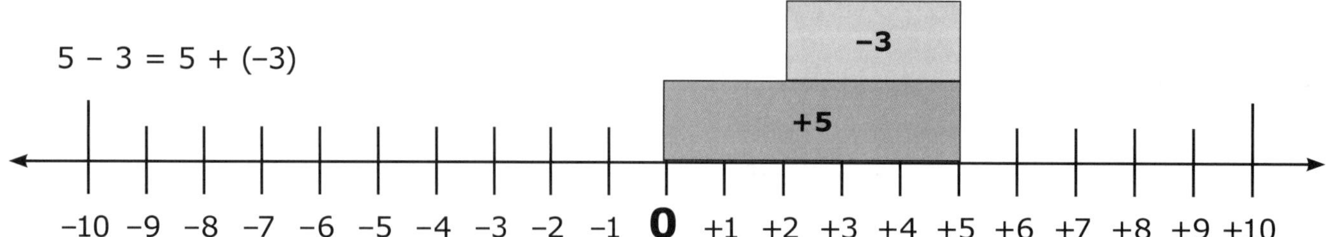

$-6 - 3 = -6 + (-3)$

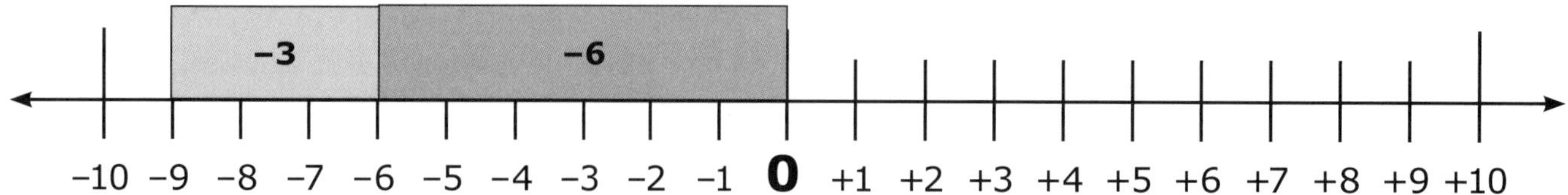

Complete the following.

6. $(+6) - (+5)$
7. $(-8) - (+3)$
8. $(+4) - (+10)$
9. $(-10) - (+15)$
10. $8 - 11$
11. $-15 - 25$

Name ______________________________ Date __________

Write number sentences.

1. Benjamin and Suzanne went scuba diving while on vacation. Suzanne was 20 feet below the surface of the water. Benjamin was 45 feet below the surface of the water. How much farther down was Benjamin than Suzanne? Write a number sentence to represent this situation.

2. In researching the heights of landmarks around the world, Jacob found a mountain in Asia that is 15,765 feet high. He also found that Death Valley is 282 feet below sea level. What is the difference in the heights of the mountain and Death Valley? Write a number sentence to represent this situation.

3. Dakota noted that his town had a record high temperature in December of 92°F. He also noted that the town's record low temperature for December was –10°F. What is the difference between the high and low temperatures? Write a number sentence to represent this situation.

4. While playing golf on Saturday, Watson shot ten under par (–10). On Sunday Watson did not play as well and shot two under par (–2). What is the difference between Watson's score on Saturday and his score on Sunday? Write a number sentence to represent this situation.

Unit 12 Mini-Lesson

Multiply and Divide Integers

Standard

Number, Operations, and Quantitative Reasoning

6.3D (RS) Add, subtract, multiply, and divide integers.

Model the Skill

Draw the following circles on the board.

−5

- **Say:** *Today we will learn how to multiply and divide integers. Looking at the diagram on the board, there six counters that each represent (−5) or (−5) + (−5) + (−5) + (−5) + (−5) + (−5).*
- **Ask:** *What multiplication problem could this represent?* (6 x −5)
- **Ask:** *What do you think the answer would be if the six counters shown above were divided into 3 groups?*

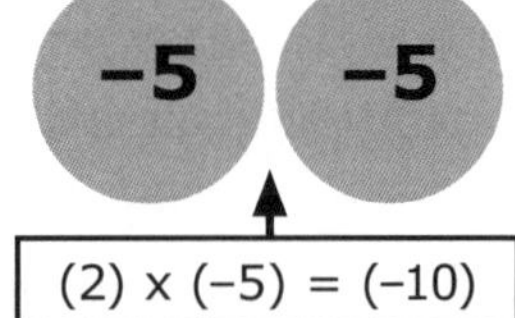

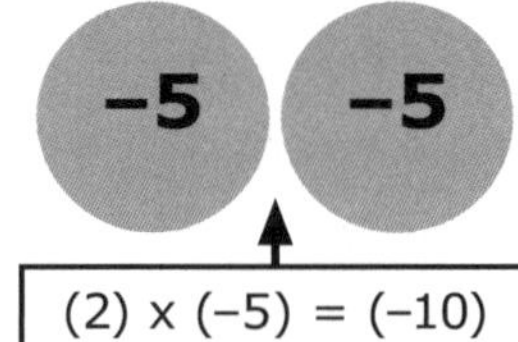

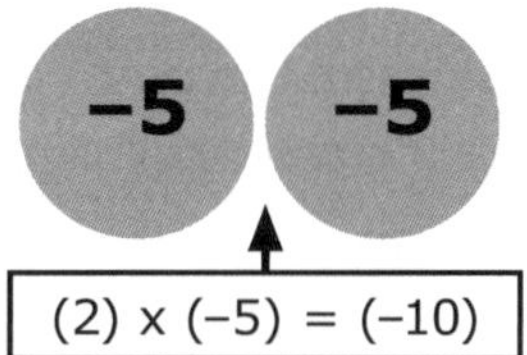

- **Ask:** *Can you explain why (−30) ÷ (3) = −10?*
- Assign students the appropriate practice page(s) to support their understanding of the skill.

Assess the Skill

Use the following problems to assess the students' understanding of the skill.

7 x (−3)   2 x (−8)   9 x (−2)

−10 ÷ 2   20 ÷ (−4)   −25 ÷ 5

Name ______________________________ **Date** __________

Rules for Multiplying and Dividing Integers

Multiply.

❶ The product of two numbers with the **same sign** is **POSITIVE**.

+ 5 • + 3 = +15 | −5 • −3 = +15

+22 • + 4 = ________ | (−22) • (−4) = ________

+12 • + 6 = ________ | (−12) • (−6) = ________

❷ The product of two numbers with **different signs** is **NEGATIVE**.

+5 • (−2) = -10 | (−5) • +2 = −10

(−6) • + 11 = | +10 • (−3) =

(−8) • + 5 = | +12 • (−8) =

Divide.

❸ The quotient of two numbers with the **same sign** is **POSITIVE**.

+6 ÷ +3 = +2 | (−12) ÷ (−4) = +3

+16 ÷ +4 = ________ | (−25) ÷ (−5) = ________

+14 ÷ +7 = ________ | (−30) ÷ (−6) = ________

❹ The quotient of two numbers with **different signs** is **NEGATIVE**.

+8 ÷ (−2) = −4 | (−12) ÷ +6 = −2

+49 ÷ (−7) = ________ | (−100) ÷ +20 = ________

(−21) ÷ (+7) = ________ | (+81) ÷ (−9) = ________

☆ **When will your answer be positive?**

Name ________________________________ **Date** __________

Multiply or divide the following integers.

1. (15) (6) = ______________
2. (–30) (+4) = ______________
3. (–12) (–6) = ______________
4. (+15) (–9) = ______________
5. +100 ÷ +10 = ______________
6. (–49) ÷ (–7) = ______________
7. (–20) ÷ +2 = ______________
8. (–99) ÷ +11 = ______________

Give the missing information.

9. __________ • (–5) = –35
10. +36 ÷ __________ = –9
11. (–10) • __________ = +50
12. __________ ÷ + 5 = –20
13. (–3) (–3) (–3) = __________
14. (–1) (+5) (–3) = __________
15. (–10) ÷ (–2) • (–3) = __________
16. (+3) • (–6) ÷ (–9) = __________

☆ **When will your answer be negative?**

Name ______________________________ Date ________

Write number sentences.

1. During Samson's scuba diving lesson, he descended 6 feet below the surface. He did this 5 more times. What is the total number of feet he descended? Write a number sentence to represent this situation.

2. Marilyn withdrew $20 from her bank account each week for 6 weeks. How much did Marilyn withdraw from her bank account? Write a number sentence to represent this situation.

3. Eduardo lost a total of 50 points playing a video game. He lost 5 points each time he missed a target. How many targets did Eduardo miss? Write a number sentence to represent this situation.

4. Laurie withdrew a total of $250 from her bank account over the past five weeks. If she withdrew the same amount each week from her bank account, how much did Laurie withdraw per week? Write a number sentence to represent this situation.

Unit 13 Mini-Lesson

Use Ratios and Equivalent Ratios

Standard

Proportionality

6.4B (RS) Apply qualitative and quantitative reasoning to solve prediction and comparison of real-world problems involving ratios and rates.

6.4C (SS) Give examples of ratios as multiplicative comparisons of two quantities describing the same attribute.

Model the Skill

Draw the following model on the board.

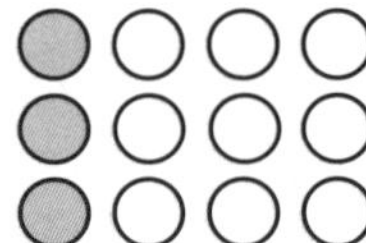

- **Say:** *Today we are going to be finding ratios and equivalent ratios. A ratio shows the relative sizes of two or more values. Ratios can be shown in different ways. A fraction is one way to show a ratio. Look at the circles in this array. Three of the twelve circles are shaded. Write a fraction that shows how many* ($\frac{3}{12}$).
- Explain to students that another way to express $\frac{3}{12}$ is 3:12 or 3 to 12. Then ask students to think of a way to simplify the expression by writing an equivalent ratio.

$$\frac{3}{12} = 3:12 = 3 \text{ to } 12$$

$$\frac{3}{12} = \frac{1}{4} = 1:4 = 1 \text{ to } 4$$

- Assign students the appropriate practice page(s) to support their understanding of the skill.

Assess the Skill

Use the following problems to pre-/post-assess students' understanding of the skill.

- Ask students to use the model below to find the following ratios:

□□□□
△△△△△
○○○○○○

□'s to △'s =
□'s to ○'s =
△'s to shapes =

○'s to shapes =
○'s to □'s + △'s =
□'s to ○'s + △'s =

When will you have a negative answer?

Name ______________________________ **Date** __________

Write ratios to describe the pictures.

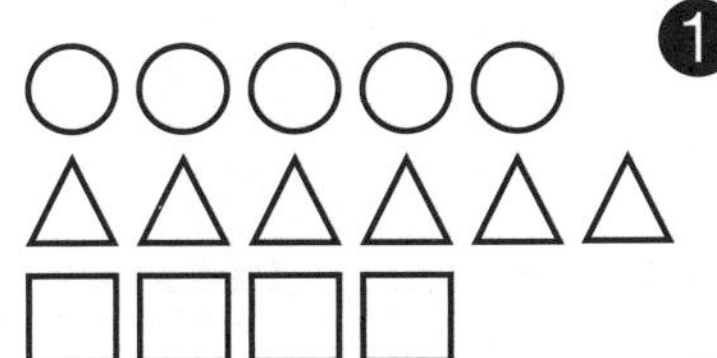

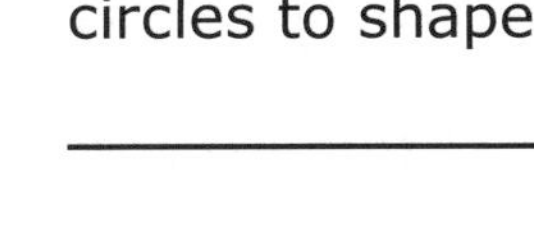

1. circles to shapes ____________

2. triangles to circles ____________

3. circles to squares ____________

4. squares to triangles ____________

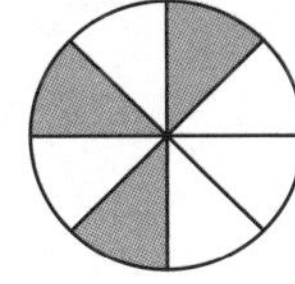

5. shaded parts to total parts ____________

6. shaded parts to white parts ____________

Write an equivalent ratio by multiplying by the given whole.

7. $\frac{5}{8} \times \frac{2}{2} =$ _____

8. $\frac{1}{2} \times \frac{6}{6} =$ _____

9. $\frac{2}{3} \times \frac{4}{4} =$ _____

10. $\frac{1}{6} \times \frac{3}{3} =$ _____

11. $\frac{5}{9} \times \frac{10}{10} =$ _____

12. $\frac{4}{5} \times \frac{2}{2} =$ _____

Write an equivalent ratio for each. Circle each ratio that is in simplified form.

13. $\frac{2}{6} =$ _____

14. $\frac{1}{5} =$ _____

15. $\frac{12}{24} =$ _____

16. $\frac{3}{4} =$ _____

17. $\frac{16}{18} =$ _____

18. $\frac{4}{6} =$ _____

19. $\frac{2}{10} =$ _____

20. $\frac{12}{16} =$ _____

Tell how you know that two ratios are equivalent.

Name ______________________________ **Date** __________

Use the information to write a ratio in simplest form.

1. The class has 14 boys, 12 girls, and 1 teacher.

   boys to girls ____ : ____

   girls to boys ____ : ____

   teachers to students ____ : ____

2. The recipe has 10 tomatoes, 6 cucumbers, and 3 peppers.

   tomatoes to peppers ____ : ____

   cucumbers to tomatoes ____ : ____

   peppers to cucumbers ____ : ____

3. The school has 550 students, 30 teachers, and 10 administrators.

   administrators to teachers ____ : ____

   teachers to students ____ : ____

   administrators to students ____ : ____

4. The math team has 11 boys, 10 girls, and 1 coach.

   boys to girls ____ : ____

   girls to boys ____ : ____

   coaches to students ____ : ____

Use the information to write a ratio in simplest form.

●	2	4			10
▲	10		30		

●			12	16
▲	6			24

7. $\frac{1}{3}$ = ____

8. $\frac{2}{10}$ = ____

9. $\frac{35}{40}$ = ____

10. $\frac{5}{10}$ = ____

11. $\frac{12}{18}$ = ____

12. $\frac{14}{28}$ = ____

13. $\frac{3}{9}$ = ____

14. $\frac{2}{3}$ = ____

15. $\frac{4}{5}$ = ____

16. $\frac{9}{12}$ = ____

17. $\frac{75}{100}$ = ____

18. $\frac{80}{84}$ = ____

Explain the steps you take to write the ratio 5:25 in simplest form.

Name ______________________________ Date __________

Solve.

1. A fruit salad recipe calls for 9 cups of berries and 6 cups of peaches. What is the ratio of peaches to berries?

2. The pancakes contain 1 cup of milk, 1 cup of flour, and 2 eggs. What is the ratio of milk to flour?

3. There are 25 students in the class. Ten students have sports practice after school. What is the ratio of students that do have practice to those that do not?

4. The baby nursery has 2 nurses for every 10 babies. What is the nurse-to-baby ratio?

5. The island has 600 bicycles and 900 people. What is the bicycle-to-person ratio?

6. The movie multiplex has four bathrooms and 16 theaters. What is the bathroom-to-theater ratio?

Circle the letter for the correct answer.

7. Emi buys 14 balloons. Three are red, four are white, and the rest are blue. What is the ratio of blue balloons to the total number of balloons?

   A 11:14

   B 2:1

   C $\frac{1}{2}$

   D $\frac{4}{14}$

8. The cafeteria sold 200 grilled cheese sandwiches, 100 tacos, and 150 grilled chicken salads. What is the ratio of grilled chicken salads sold to the total number of lunches sold?

   A 1:2

   B 2:1

   C 15:300

   D 1:3

Unit 14 Mini-Lesson

Use Rates

Standard

Proportionality

6.4B (RS) Apply qualitative and quantitative reasoning to solve prediction and comparison of real-world problems involving ratios and rates.

6.4C (SS) Give examples of ratios as multiplicative comparisons of two quantities describing the same attribute.

Model the Skill

Draw the following rates and model on the board.

rate	unit rate
\$33/11 lb.	\$3/1 lb.
60 mi/2 hr	30 mi/1 hr
6 triangles/3 circles	2 triangles/1 circle

- **Say:** *A rate is a ratio that compares two quantities of different increments, or units. For example, 33 dollars for 11 lbs of fruit is a rate. 60 miles per two hours is also a rate. A unit rate reduces the rate so that the denominator is 1. \$3 per pound is a unit rate. 30 miles per hour is a unit rate. 6 triangles per 3 circles can be reduced to a unit rate. What is the unit rate in this model?* (2 triangles per 1 circle, or $\frac{2}{1}$, or 2:1)
- Assign students the appropriate practice page(s) to support their understanding of the skill.

Assess the Skill

Use the following problems to pre-/post-assess students' understanding of the skill.

4 for \$32.00
rate: 4 : ____
unit rate: ____ : ____

rate: 30 km/hr
time: 5.5 hours
distance: ____

distance: 360 miles
rate: 15 mph
time: ________

Name ______________________________ **Date** __________

Complete the ratio tables. Write the unit rate.

1

km		50	150
h	1		6

unit rate ____ : ____

____ km per hour

2 6 for $36.00

unit rate __ for __

3 9:180

unit rate ____ : ____

4 5 for $46.00

unit rate __ for __

5 4:240

unit rate ____ : ____

6 35:70

unit rate ____ : ____

7 7:210

unit rate ____ : ____

8 8:64

unit rate ____ : ____

9 10 for $50.00

unit rate __ for __

10 3:180

unit rate ____ : ____

11 100 for $10.00

unit rate __ for __

12 12:72

unit rate ____ : ____

Use the formula *D* = *rt* to find the missing information.

13 rate: 50 miles/hr

time: 2 hours

Distance: ________

14 rate: 30 km/hr

time: 4 hours

Distance: ________

15 rate: 40 km/hr

time: 8 hours

Distance: ________

16 Distance: 400 miles

rate: 40 mph

time: ________

17 Distance: 10 km

rate: 10 kph

time: ________

18 Distance: 30 miles

rate: 15 mph

time: ________

19 Distance: 315 miles

time: 3 hours

rate: ________

20 Distance: 1,400 km

time: 70 hours

rate: ________

21 Distance: 100 m

time: 10 seconds

rate: ________

☆ **Tell the steps you take to find a unit rate.**

Name ______________________________ **Date** __________

Find the unit rate.

1. 24:6
   unit rate ____ : ____

2. 12:96
   unit rate ____ : ____

3. 80:40
   unit rate ____ : ____

4. $\frac{18}{3}$
   unit rate $\frac{\square}{\square}$

5. $\frac{44}{11}$
   unit rate $\frac{\square}{\square}$

6. $\frac{42}{6}$
   unit rate $\frac{\square}{\square}$

7. 12 for $136
   unit rate ____

8. 27 ft to 9 yd
   unit rate ____

9. 6 for $2.40
   unit rate ____

Use the formula *D* = *rt*.

10. rate: 55 mph
    time: 8 hours
    Distance: ________

11. rate: 20 mph
    time: 6 hours
    Distance: ________

12. rate: 30 kph
    time: 5 hours
    Distance: ________

13. Distance: 90 miles
    rate: 15 mph
    time: ________

14. Distance: 300 miles
    rate: 15 mph
    time: ________

15. Distance: 250 km
    rate: 50 kph
    time: ________

16. Distance: 350 miles
    time: 7 hours
    rate: ________

17. Distance: 40 km
    time: 8 hours
    rate: ________

18. Distance: 50 m
    time: 25 seconds
    rate: ________

19. Distance: 30 miles
    time: 30 minutes
    rate: ________

20. Distance: 85 km
    time: 5 minutes
    rate: ________

21. Distance: 200 m
    time: 5 minutes
    rate: ________

Explain how you used the formula *D* = *rt* to solve Problem 10.

Name ______________________________ Date ________

Solve.

1. Look at the sale prices. Which is the better buy? How much does one item cost?

SALE 5 for $1.00	**SALE** 12 for $3.00

2. Find and compare the unit prices. Which one is the better buy?

SALE 3 for $1.00	**SALE** 10 for $3.00

3. The diner sells bagels for $0.75 each. The bagel shop sells 1 dozen for $7.00. Which is the better buy?

4. The fisherman is selling salmon for $7.99/lb. The supermarket has 2-lb packages of salmon for $14.98. Which is a better buy?

5. Cheyenne drove 3,000 miles in 75 hours. At this rate, how long will it take her to drive 4,000 miles?

6. The factory makes 400 cars per day. If the workday is eight hours long, what is the hourly rate at which cars are produced?

Circle the letter for the correct answer.

7. A potter makes 6 bowls in 3 hours. How long would it take the potter to make 14 bowls?

   A 6 hours
   B 7 hours
   C 8 hours
   D 9 hours

8. The mechanic does 4 oil changes in 2 hours. How many oil changes can the mechanic do in 8 hours?

   A 2 oil changes
   B 4 oil changes
   C 10 oil changes
   D 16 oil changes

Unit 15 Mini-Lesson
Understand Percentages

Standard

Proportionality

6.4E (SS) Represent ratios and percents with concrete models, fractions, and decimals.

Model the Skill

Draw the following models on the board.

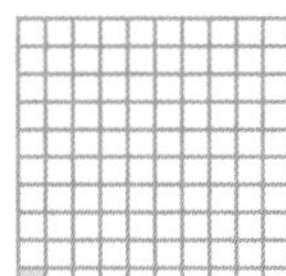 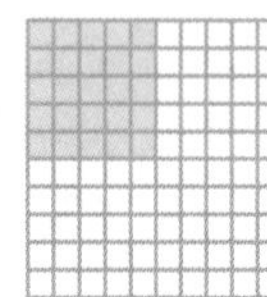 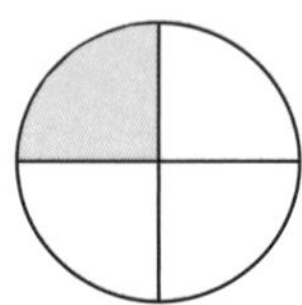 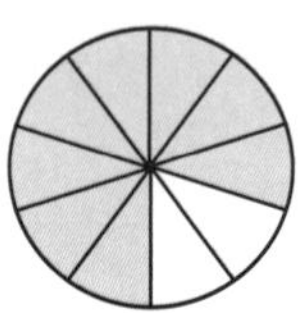

- **Say:** *Today we are going to be finding percentages. A percentage shows the rate per 100. For example, if 40 out of 100 people are wearing white socks, the portion of people wearing white socks would be $\frac{40}{100}$, or 40 per 100; therefore 40% of the people are wearing white socks.*
- **Say:** *Look at the models. What fraction does each model show? What percent does each model show?*
- Assign students the appropriate practice page(s) to support their understanding of the skill.

Assess the Skill

Use the following problems to pre-/post-assess students' understanding of the skill.

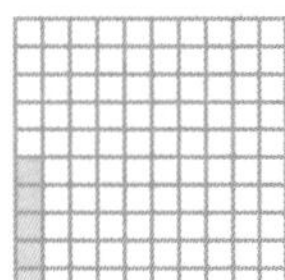 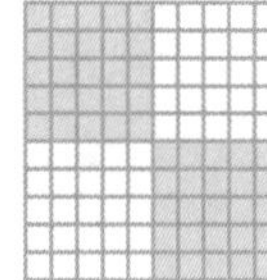 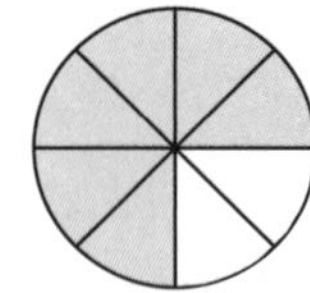 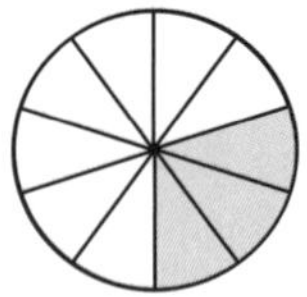

- Ask students to write percentages that describe each model.

Name ______________________________ Date __________

Write a percent to describe each shaded part.

 1

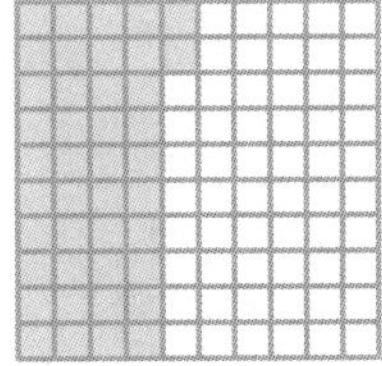

____

2

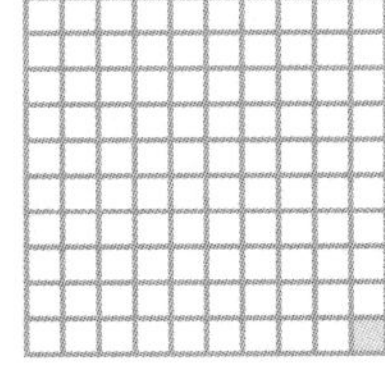

____

3

____

4

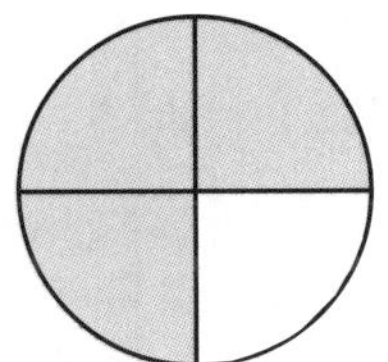

____

5

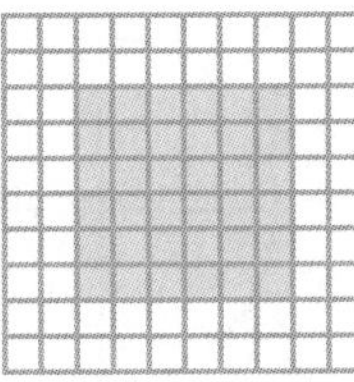

____

Remember: Percent is a ratio that compares a number to 100. Write an equivalent ratio $\frac{3}{10} = \frac{\square}{100}$

Write each ratio as a decimal and a percent.

6 $\frac{50}{100}$ ________ ________

 7 $\frac{65}{100}$ ________ ________

8 $\frac{3}{100}$ ________ ________

9 $\frac{8}{100}$ ________ ________

10 $\frac{1}{2}$ ________ ________

 11 $\frac{12}{100}$ ________ ________

12 $\frac{5}{100}$ ________ ________

13 $\frac{42}{100}$ ________ ________

14 $\frac{1}{100}$ ________ ________

 15 $\frac{7}{100}$ ________ ________

16 $\frac{58}{100}$ ________ ________

17 $\frac{23}{100}$ ________ ________

18 $\frac{9}{100}$ ________ ________

 19 $\frac{15}{100}$ ________ ________

 20 $\frac{4}{100}$ ________ ________

 21 $\frac{3}{4}$ ________ ________

☆ **Tell what 110% means. Draw a picture.**

Name ______________________________ Date __________

Write a decimal to describe each shaded part.

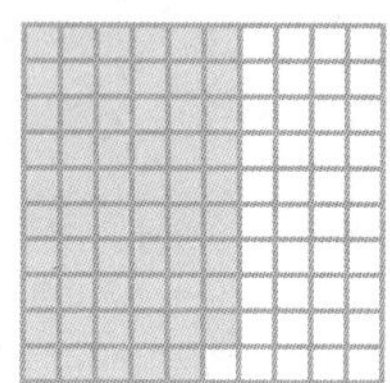

____

2

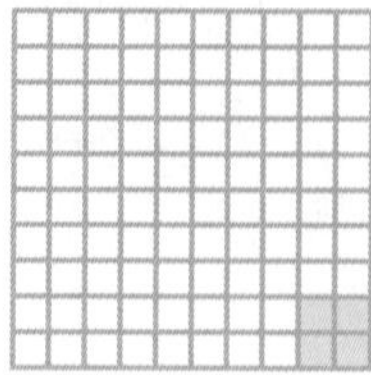

____

3

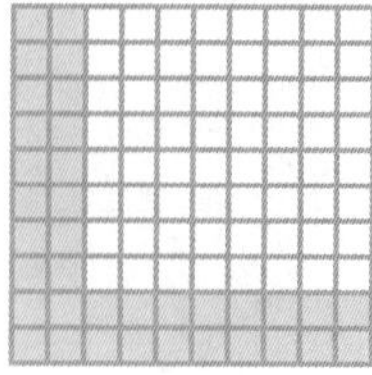

____

4

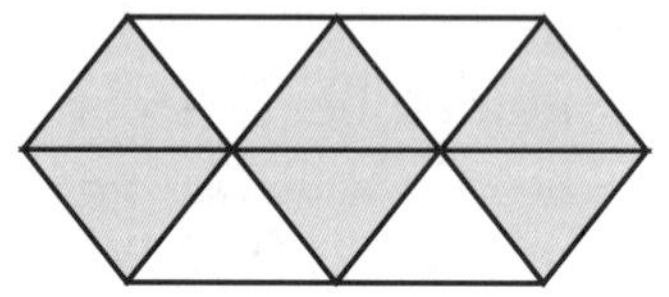

____

5

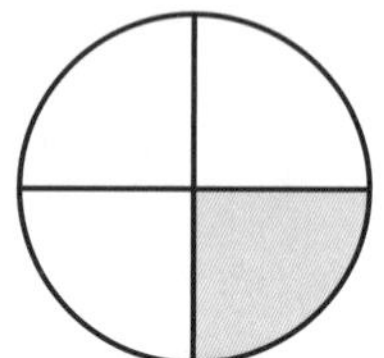

____

6

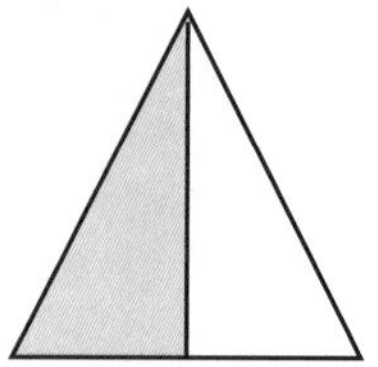

____

Complete. Write a ratio, decimal, and percent for each.

7 ratio $\frac{25}{100}$

decimal ________

percent ________

8 ratio $\frac{60}{100}$

decimal ________

percent ________

9 ratio $\frac{3}{10}$

decimal ________

percent ________

10 ratio $\frac{1}{2}$

decimal ________

percent ________

11 ratio ________

decimal 0.7

percent ________

12 ratio ________

decimal 0.2

percent ________

13 ratio ________

decimal 0.08

percent ________

14 ratio ________

decimal 0.65

percent ________

15 ratio ________

decimal ________

percent 50%

16 ratio ________

decimal ________

percent 90%

17 ratio ________

decimal ________

percent 2%

18 ratio ________

decimal ________

percent 100%

Look at Problem 11. In a class of boys and girls, 0.7 represents boys. What percentage represents girls? Explain how you found your answer.

Name ______________________________ **Date** __________

Solve.

1. Thirty-five girls out of 100 play a musical instrument. What percentage of the girls do not play a musical instrument?

2. Alice got 8 out of 10 questions correct on the quiz. What percentage of the quiz did she get correct?

3. Sean has 125 dollars saved. He pays 25 dollars for a ticket to the concert. What percentage of his savings did he spend on the ticket?

4. On Tuesday, 12 kittens at the shelter were adopted and 4 dogs also found new homes. What percentage of the newly adopted pets at the shelter were dogs?

5. Gabe read 10 books over the summer. 4 were nonfiction. The rest were fiction. What percentage were fiction?

6. Thirty out of fifty questions on the test were multiple choice. What percentage of the questions on the test were not multiple choice?

Circle the letter for the correct answer.

7. Which percent represents the part that is shaded?

B 4%

C 0.04%

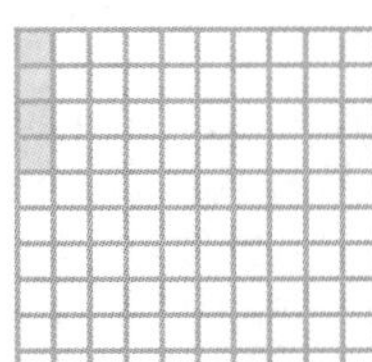

8. Which percent represents the shaded part?

B 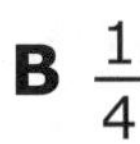

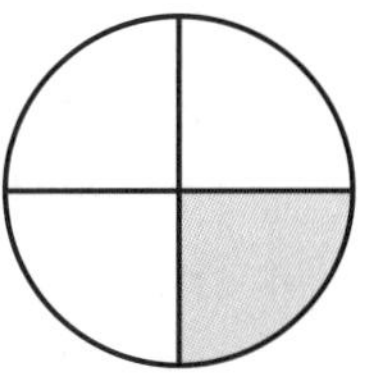

Unit 16 Mini-Lesson

Represent Relationships

Standard

Proportionality

6.1D (PS) Communicate mathematical ideas, reasoning, and their implications using multiple representations, including symbols, diagrams, graphs, and language as appropriate.

6.5A (SS) Represent mathematical and real-world problems involving ratios and rates using scale factors, tables, graphs, and proportions.

Model the Skill

Write the following vocabulary on the board.

variable, expression

- **Ask:** *What is a variable?* (a letter or other symbol that represents a number) Discuss student understandings. Create a word map on the board.
- **Ask:** *What is an expression?* (a combination of numbers and operation symbols) Show numerical expressions for each operation, then replace one number with a variable to show an algebraic expression, e.g., 2 x 4; 2*n*; 6 + (8 – 2); *x* + (8 – 2) Connect expression to the variable word map.
- **Say:** *We can write expressions to represent relationships.* Draw the table below on the board.

input (*x*)	5	10	15	20
output (*y*)	4	9	14	19

- **Ask:** *What pattern do you see? How can you describe the relationship of output to input?* (output is 1 less than input; subtract 1 from *x* to get *y*) Help students write an expression to find *y*. (*x* – 1)
- Assign students the appropriate practice page(s) to support their understanding of the skill.

Assess the Skill

Use the following problems to pre-/post-assess students' understanding of the skill.

Have students write an expression that could be used to find *n*.

Number of people	8	16	24	32	p
Number of tables	1	2	3	4	n

(p ÷ 8)

Number of boxes (*b*)	10	12	18	20
Number of crayons (*n*)	120	144	216	240

(12b)

Name ________________________________ **Date** __________

Write an expression to represent each statement.

1. 2 times more than *s* ____________________

2. 2 more than *s* ____________________

3. 2 less than *s* ____________________

4. half of *s* ____________________

5. a number *n* plus six ____________________

6. a number *n* divided by ten ____________________

Write a rule for each table in your own words. Then write an expression that can be used to find *y*.

7.

Input (x)	Output (y)
1	2
3	4
5	6
7	8

rule: __________

expression: __________

8.

Input (x)	Output (y)
1	2
3	6
5	10
7	14

rule: __________

expression: __________

9.

Club Dues	
Number of students	Number of dollars
4	$60
6	$90
10	$150
15	$225
s	y

rule: __________

expression: __________

10.

Height Converter	
Number of inches	Number of feet
144	12
120	10
72	6
48	4
n	y

rule: __________

expression: __________

 **Tell how you found the value of *n* and *y* in Problem 10.**

Name ______________________________ **Date** __________

Complete the table.

	Word Phrase	Variable	Expression
1	a number increased by 5		$a + 5$
2	eight times a number	n	
3			$v \times 7$
4	a number divided by 2		
5			$(y + 1) \times 4$
6	a number decreased by 3		
7			$(n + 10) \div 6$
8	a number squared plus 1		

Write a rule for each table in your own words. Then write an expression that can be used to find *y*.

9

Input (x)	Output (y)
42	14
27	9
12	4
6	2

rule: ____________

expression: ____________

Input (x)	Output (y)
1	2
3	10
5	26
7	50

rule: ____________

expression: ____________

Train Fare	
Number of rides	Number of dollars
6	\$15
12	\$30
24	\$60
48	\$120
r	y

rule: ____________

expression: ____________

Measurement Converter	
Number of quarts	Number of gallons
72	18
56	14
40	10
24	6
n	y

rule: ____________

expression: ____________

What is an algebraic expression? Explain.

Name ______________________________ **Date** ________

Solve.

1 Use the expression $a - 2$ to complete the table.

a	3	5	9	10
b	1			

2 The formula for the perimeter of a rectangle is $P = 2l + 2w$. The perimeter of a rectangular yard is 190 feet. If the width of the yard is 35 feet, what is the length of the yard?

The formula for the area of a square is $A = s^2$. The perimeter of a square parking lot is 184 yards. What is the area of the parking lot in square yards?

What is the area of the parking lot in square feet?

Write an expression that shows how to find the perimeter of the lot in feet.

If someone wanted to fence in a lawn that was 17 yards wide and 9 yards long, how many feet of fence would they need to buy?

Circle the letter for the correct answer.

The table below shows how Maya's income changes depending on the number of dogs she walks.

Dog-Walking Income	
Number of dogs	**Income (dollars)**
5	65
7	91
9	117
10	130
d	n

7 Which expression could be used to find n, the income Maya would earn if she walked d dogs?

A $13d$

B $n + 130$

C $65d$

D $n + 26$

Unit 17 Mini-Lesson

Generate Formulas

Standard

Expressions, Equations, and Relationships

6.6B (SS) Write an equation that represents the relationship between independent and dependent quantities from a table.

6.6C (RS) Represent a given situation using verbal descriptions, tables, graphs, and equations in the form $y = kx$ or $y = x + b$.

Model the Skill

Write $P = 4s$ on the board next to a square with each side labeled 5 cm.

- **Say:** *A formula is an equation that shows a mathematical relationship. The formula for the perimeter of a square is* ***P*** *= 4****s****.*
- **Ask:** *What does the variable* ***P*** *stand for?* (perimeter) *What does the variable* ***s*** *stand for?* (side) *How can you use the formula to find the perimeter of the square on the board?* (multiply 5 cm x 4 cm = 20 cm)
- **Ask:** *How does the formula help you find the perimeter of any square?* Help students understand that the formula gives them a rule and that they can substitute the length of one side of any square for *s* to find *P*.
- Draw the table below to illustrate the formula. Have students use the table to write a formula for finding the side length, given the perimeter. ($s = P \div 4$) Discuss the relationship.

Side length (cm)	3	4	5	6	*s*
Perimeter	12	16	20	24	*P*

- Assign students the appropriate practice page(s) to support their understanding of the skill.

Assess the Skill

Use the following problems to pre-/post-assess students' understanding of the skill.

Ask students to use the data to write formulas.

x	5	7	11	14
y	8	10	14	17

$y =$ ______________________ $(x + 3)$

$x =$ ______________________ $(y - 3)$

Name ______________________________ **Date** __________

Choose an equation for each problem.

1

x	5	8	11	15
y	12	15	18	22

$y =$ ____________

$x =$ ____________

2

x	41	30	25	22
y	37	26	21	18

$y =$ ____________

$x =$ ____________

3

x	10	20	30	40
y	2	4	6	8

$y =$ ____________

$x =$ ____________

Formulas
$y = x - 4$
$y = \frac{x}{5}$
$y = x + 7$
$x = y - 7$
$x = 5y$
$x = y + 4$

Use the data in each table.

4 Write a formula that expresses the relationship between the dependent variable *w*, the weight of water, and the independent variable *g*, the number of gallons.

$w =$ ____________

$g =$ ____________

Water

number of gallons	weight (pounds)
2	16
4	32
5	40
10	80
g	*w*

5 Write a formula that expresses the relationship between the independent variable *s*, the length of a side in a regular hexagon, and the dependent variable *p*, its perimeter.

$s =$ ____________

$p =$ ____________

Regular Hexagon

length of side (in.)	perimeter
4	24
7	42
9	54
12	72
s	*p*

 **For Problem 4, tell how you used the table to write a formula.**

Name ______________________________ **Date** __________

Write formulas to represent relationships shown in each table.

1. y = ______________

Which is the independent variable? ______

Which is the dependent variable? ______

x = ______________

Which is the independent variable? ______

Which is the dependent variable? ______

x	3	5	7	9
y	18	20	22	24

2. ______________

____

a	9	18	27	36
b	4	13	22	31

3. ______________

____

r	21	35	63	84
s	3	5	9	12

4. This table shows the relationship between the area of a square and the length of one side of the square. Define the relationships.

A = ______________

s = ______________

Area of a Square

side length (cm)	area (sq cm)
4	16
5	25
6	36
7	49
s	*A*

5. A rescue group provides food in emergency situations. The table shows how much rice (r) is needed to feed people (p). What formula can the group use to plan how much rice it needs for 1,750 people?

____

____

rice (in pounds)	number of people
30	120
50	200
100	400
125	500
r	*p*

 **For Problem 4, tell how you used the table to write a formula.**

Name ______________________________ Date __________

Solve.

1 Using the table, write a formula that expresses the relationship between s, the length of each side of an equilateral triangle, and P, its perimeter.

____

Equilateral Triangle

Perimeter	Side Length
27	9
45	15
54	18
72	24
P	s

2 What formula can you use, if you know the perimeter of an equilateral triangle, to find the length of its side?

____

3 This table shows the number of cups of milk (m) to add to pancake mix (p). Write a formula that explains the relationship of cups of milk to cups of mix.

____

____

pancake mix (in cups)	milk (in cups)
2	$1\frac{1}{2}$
3	$2\frac{1}{4}$
4	3
5	$3\frac{3}{4}$
p	m

Circle the letter for the correct answer.

4 This table shows the ages of two brothers at different times.

Mike's age (m)	13	21	25	42
Dan's age (d)	9	17	21	38

Which formula shows the relationship between their ages?

A $m = 4d$

B $m = 2d - 5$

C $d = m + 4$

D $d = m - 4$

5 This table shows the perimeter and area of different squares.

Perimeter (P)	16	36	40	44
Area (A)	16	81	100	121

Which formula shows how you can use the perimeter to find the area of each square?

A $P = 4s$

B $P = A \div 4$

C $A = (P \div 4)^2$

D $A = (P + s^2)$

Unit 18 Mini-Lesson

Write Equations

Standard

Expressions, Equations, and Relationships

6.6B (SS) Write an equation that represents the relationship between independent and dependent quantities from a table.

6.6C (RS) Represent a given situation using verbal descriptions, tables, graphs, and equations in the form $y = kx$ or $y = x + b$.

Model the Skill

Write the following equations on the board:

$y = 4x$ $a + 3 = d$ $d \div 5 = 3$ $27 = d - 12$

- **Say:** *An equation is a mathematical sentence with an equal symbol. It states that the expressions on either side of the equal symbol have the same value. We can write an equation to represent a problem situation.*
- **Ask:** *Which equation on the board could represent this situation: I have some doughnuts. You have 3 more doughnuts than me. How many doughnuts do you have?* Guide students' interpretation of the various equations and the selection of $a + 3 = d$.
- **Ask:** *What might a problem situation be for $d \div 5 = 3$?* Discuss that d is divided by 5 and the result is 3. It could represent the number of doughnuts shared by 5 people. Devise contexts for the other equations on the board.
- Write the following problem on the board: Owen ran 24 miles in 5 days. He ran 6 miles each day for the first 3 days. He ran y miles the next day. How many miles did he run the last day, m? Remind students of the order of operations. Guide them to writing the equation $m = 24 - (6 \bullet 3) - y$ (dot for multiplication).
- Assign students the appropriate practice page(s) to support their understanding of the skill.

Assess the Skill

Use the following problems to pre-/post-assess students' understanding of the skill.

Ask students to write an equation for each of the following.

- A number, n, is five times more than b.
- A number, y, is 4 more than x.
- Six less than the number of cookies, c, is 31.

Name ______________________________ **Date** __________

Write an equation to represent each statement.

1. A number, n, divided by 3 is 6. ______________________________

2. Two more than a number, n, is 16. ______________________________

3. A number, y, is two times more than x. ______________________________

4. An amount, a, is half of c. ______________________________

5. A number, n, plus 8 is 32. ______________________________

6. A number, n, is 4 less than b. ______________________________

Choose the equation that represents each problem.

7. Kwame scored 3 more points than Leo. Kwame has 31 points. How many points does Leo have? Let p represent the number of points. ______________________________

8. Jen bought 8 pounds of apples for $14.00. What was the price, p, per pound?

____

9. What is y?

input	3	6	8	10	x
output	5	8	10	12	y

____

10. How much money can Paul earn in y hours?

hours	2	4	6	8	x
wages	14	28	42	56	y

____

Which is the dependent variable, hours or wages?

Equations
$p + 3 = 31$
$3p = 31$
$31 - p = 3$
$p + 83 = 14$
$p = 14 - 8$
$8p = 14$
$y = x + 2$
$y = 2x$
$x = 2y$
$x = 56 - y$
$y = 7x$
$yx = 7 + x$

Tell how an equation is different from an expression.

Name ______________________________ Date __________

Write an equation to represent each statement or problem situation.

1. A number, n, divided by 7 is 3. ______________________

2. A number, y, is 5 more than x. ______________________

3. A number, s, is half of t. ______________________

4. 8 more than a, multiplied by 2, is equal to b. ______________________

5. A number, g, multiplied by 2 is 10. ______________________

6. A number, y, is equal to x squared and then increased by 2. ______________________

7. Adele is five inches shorter than her sister. Adele is 47 inches tall. How tall is her sister? Use s to represent her sister's height.

   ____

8. Will bought 8 pounds of figs for $17.60. Write the formula that shows how to calculate the price (p) per pound. ______________________

   What was the price, p, per pound? ______________________

9. What is y?

input	3	6	8	14	x
output	7	10	12	18	y

   ____

10. This table shows how many hours Toro works (h) to earn different amounts of wages (w). Write the formula that shows how to calculate Toro's hourly wage.

hours	2	4	6	8	h
wages	42	84	126	168	w

______________________ Which is the independent variable, hours or wages?

For Problem 7, tell how the equation you wrote describes the situation.

Name ______________________________ Date __________

Write an equation for each problem.

1 Erika is thinking of a number. She says her mystery number is 2 more than a number, *n*, divided by 3. What is Erika's mystery number? Use *m* to represent Erika's mystery number.

____

2 The number *c* is 4 times greater than the number *b*.

3 Graydon is building a skate ramp. He wants to make sure that he has enough boards. For every foot of height (*h*), he needs 2 pieces of particle board (*b*). What formula can he use to calculate his materials (*m*)?

4 Kristen has 9 days of school before the science fair. She has to convert a number of tables (*t*) of lab results into graphs for the fair. Write an equation that shows how many graphs (*g*) she will have to do each day if she wants to finish in time.

5 Yen is training for a marathon. This chart shows his training plan for how many miles he will run each week leading up to the big race. Write a formula that shows the relationship between week (*w*) and miles run (*m*).

Week # (*w*)	Miles (*m*)
2	8
4	14
6	20
8	26

Circle the letter for the correct answer.

6 Dylan read 210 pages of a book in 5 days. He read 37 pages each day for the first 3 days. He read *y* pages the fourth day. Which equation can be used to find *p*, the number of pages Dylan read on the fifth day?

A $p = 210 - 37\ (3 \bullet y)$

B $p = 210 - (37 \bullet 3) - y$

C $p = 210 - 3\ (37 + y)$

D $p = 210 - (y \bullet 3) - 37$

7 Suri is making costumes for the school show. For every costume (*c*) she needs 2 yards of cloth at $12 per yard, 3 yards of trim at $7 per yard, and 1 yard of ribbon at $5 per yard. Which equation can Suri use to calculate the costume budget (*b*) for the show.

A $b = c \bullet 36$

B $c = b \bullet (c \times 24 + 21 + 5)$

C $b = c \times 50$

D $c = b \times 48$

Unit 19 Mini-Lesson

Classify Triangles

Standard

Expressions, Equations, and Relationships

6.8A (SS) Extend previous knowledge of triangles and their properties to include the sum of angles of a triangle, the relationship between the lengths of sides and measures of angles in a triangle, and determining when three lengths form a triangle.

Model the Skill

Draw and label the following triangles on the board.

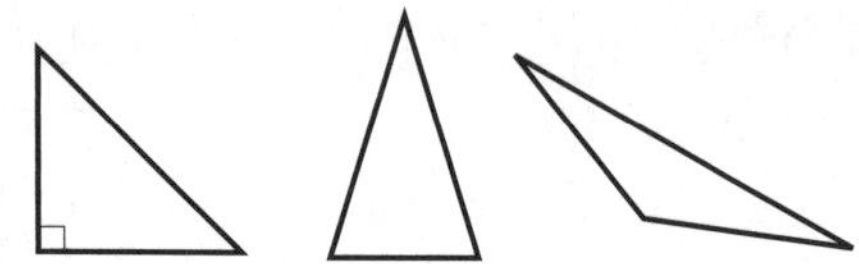

- **Say:** *Some triangles are named by the size of their angles. A right triangle has 1 right angle.* Point to the right angle. *A right angle measures 90 degrees. The rays that form the right angle are perpendicular.*
- **Ask:** *What can you tell me about the angles in the acute triangle?* (3 angles, no right angles) *Are the sizes of the angles greater or less than 90º?* (less) Have students use the corner of a page to compare a right angle with the angles in the acute triangle. Point out that all 3 angles are acute in an acute triangle.
- **Ask:** *What can you tell me about the angles in the obtuse triangle?* (3 angles, no right angles) *Are the sizes of the angles greater or less than 90º?* (1 angle is greater and 2 are less) Allow students to compare the angles to a right angle. Note that an obtuse triangle has 1 obtuse angle.
- **Say:** *In any triangle the sum of the angle measures is 180 degrees.* Write 90º and 45º on the right triangle. *If we know the measure of two angles, we can find the measure of the third angle.* Help students find the missing angle measure and determine if the angle is acute or obtuse.
- Assign students the appropriate practice page(s) to support their understanding of the skill.

Assess the Skill

Use the following problems to pre-/post-assess students' understanding of the skill.

Have students classify each triangle as right, obtuse, or acute.

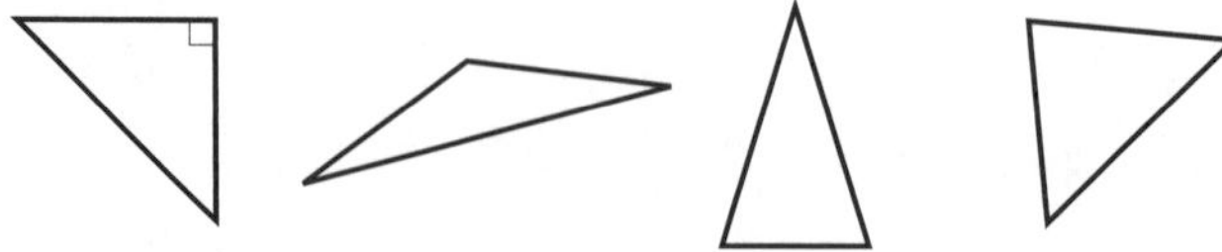

Name ______________________________ **Date** __________

Classify each triangle as acute, obtuse, or right.

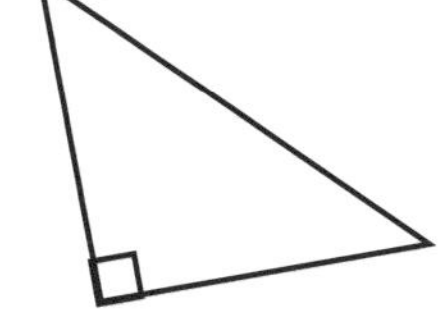

____

2

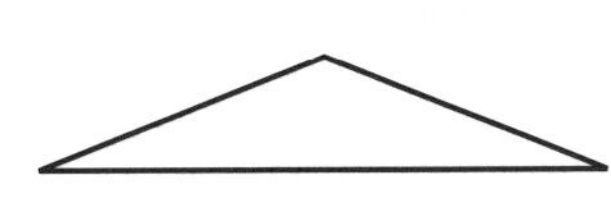

____

3

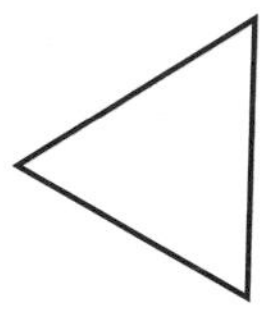

____

4

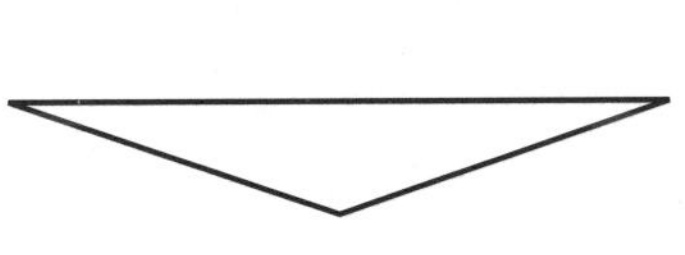

____

5

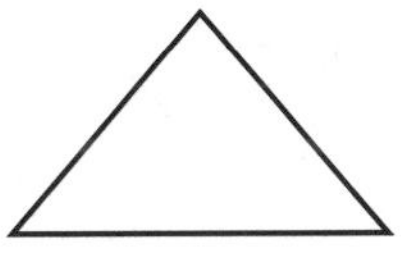

____

6

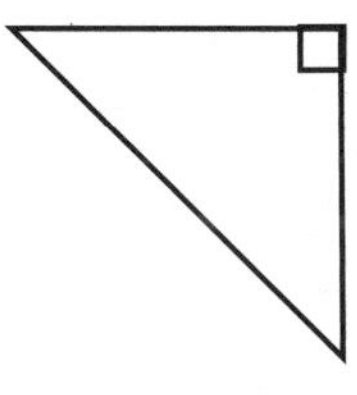

____

7

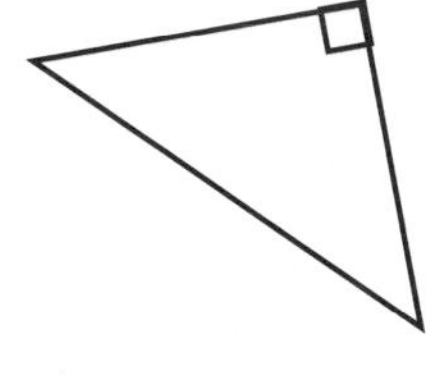

____

8

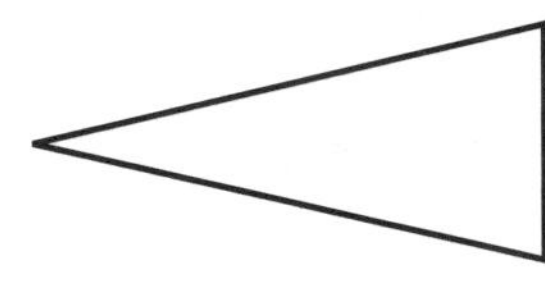

____

9

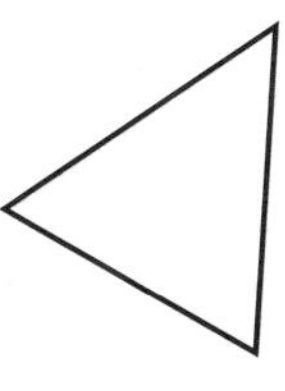

____

Solve.

10 If two angles of a triangle are each 45°, what kind of triangle is it? ______________

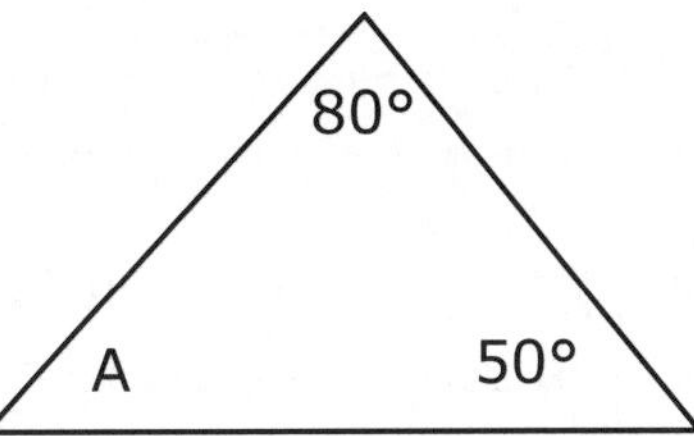

11 What is the measure of angle ∠ A? ______________

 **Tell how you know if a triangle is an acute triangle.**

Name ______________________________ **Date** __________

Classify each triangle as acute, obtuse, or right.

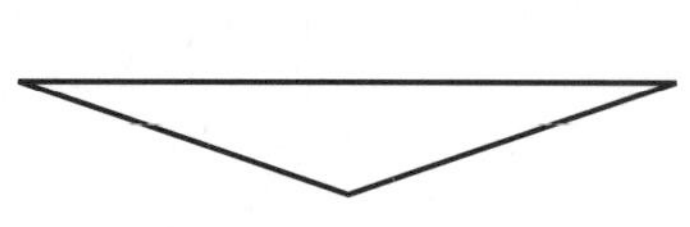

____

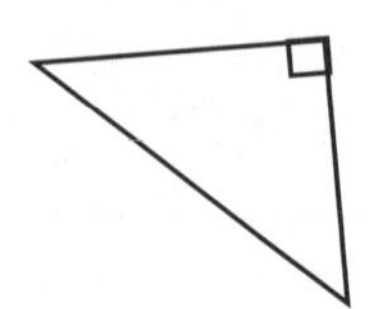

____

3

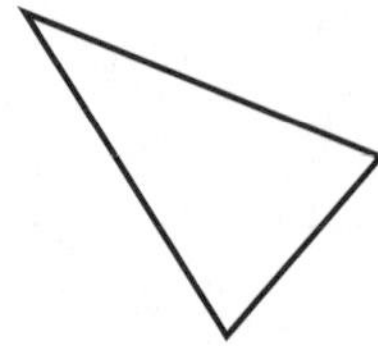

____

4

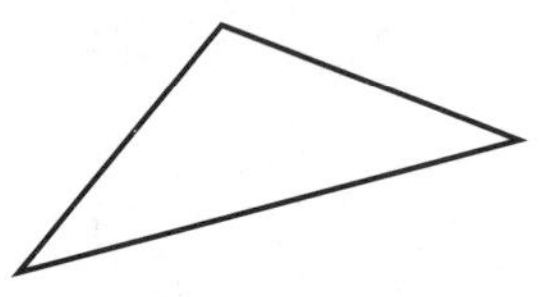

____

5

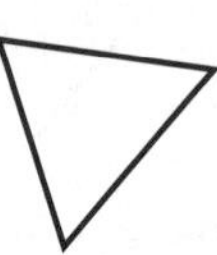

____

6

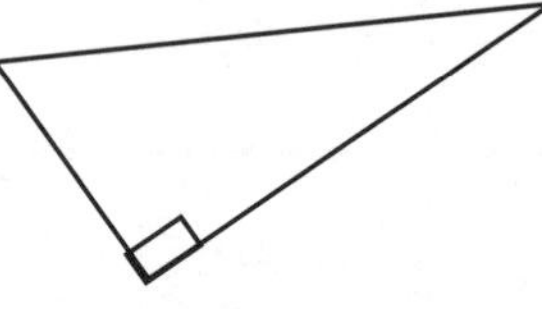

____

Solve.

7 All triangles have 3 angles. What is the sum of their measures?

____

8 What is the measure of all three angles in an equilateral triangle?

9 What is the measure of angle ∠ B?

____

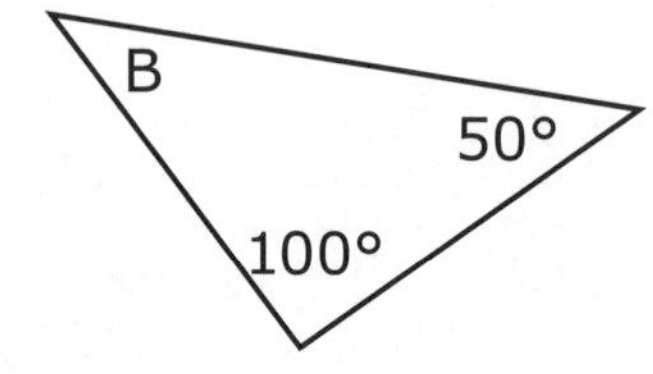

10 What is the measure of angle ∠ G?

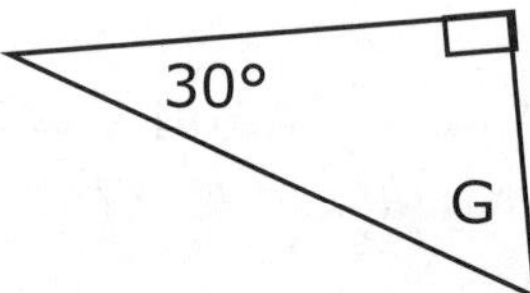

11 In a right triangle, the right angle is always equal to the sum of the other angles. True or false?

____

12 In an obtuse triangle, the hypotenuse is always opposite the triangle's ______________ angle.

Tell how you found the missing measure of an angle in Problem 10.

Name ______________________________ **Date** __________

Solve.

1 Which triangle is an acute triangle? Tell how you know.

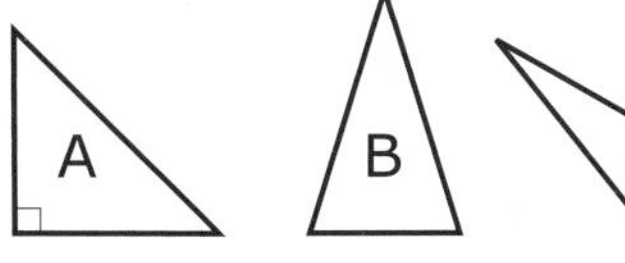

____
____

2 Which triangle has no obtuse angles? Tell how you know.

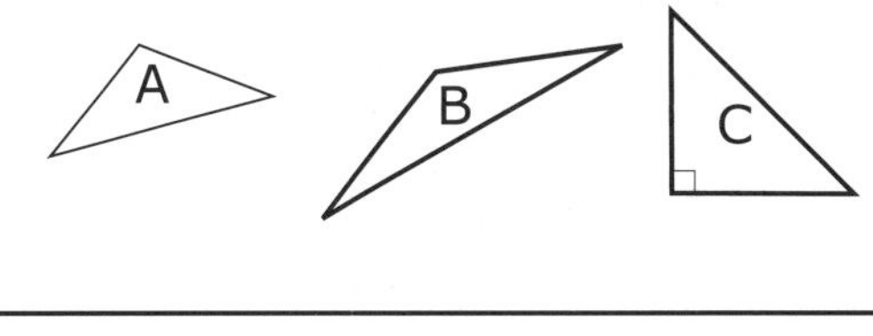

____
____

3 If two angles of a triangle are each 35°, what is the measure of the third angle?

4 If one angle of a right triangle is 65°, what is the measure of the third angle?

5 What is the measure of angle C?

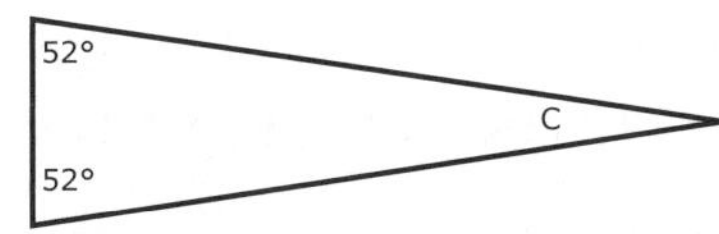

6 If angle N is 40°, what is the measure of angle M?

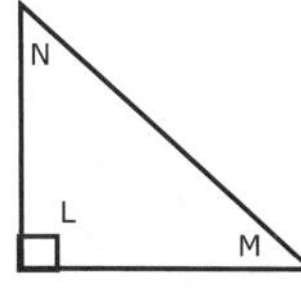

Circle the letter for the correct answer.

7 Which statement about triangles is NOT true?

A If all the angles of a triangle are congruent, then the measure of each angle is 60°

B If a triangle has a right angle, then both of the other angles are acute.

C If a triangle has an obtuse angle, then both of the other angles are acute.

D If a triangle has an acute angle, then one of the other angles must be right or obtuse.

8 If angle Q is ten degrees less than angle R, what is the measure of angle S?

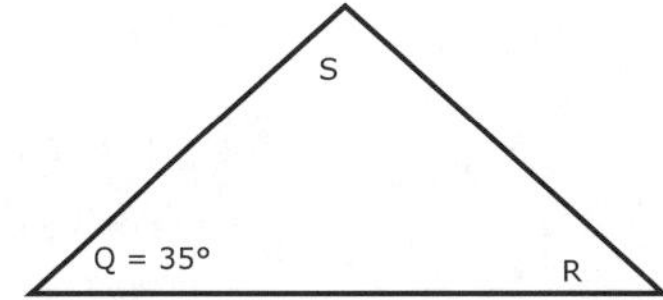

A 100°

B 90°

C 80°

D 55°

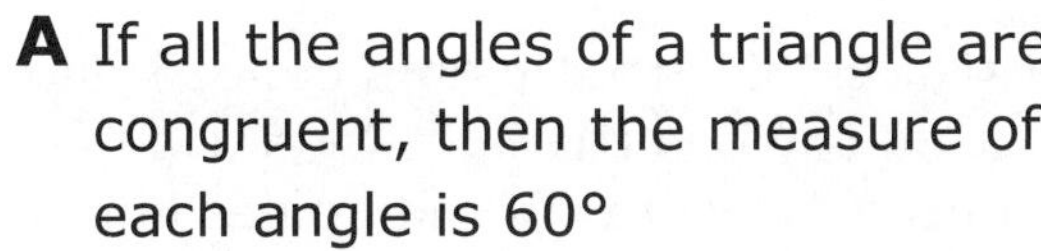

Unit 20 Mini-Lesson

Quadrilaterals

Standard

Mathematical Process Standards

6.1F (PS) Analyze mathematical relationships to connect and communicate mathematical ideas.

Model the Skill

Draw and label the following quadrilaterals on the board.

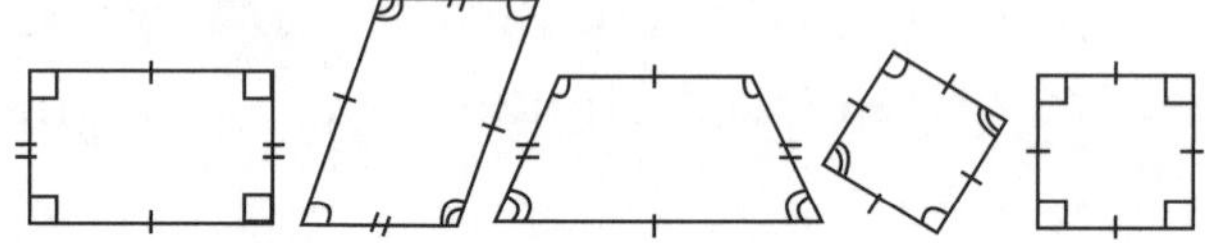

- **Say:** *We learned about polygons with 3 sides and 3 angles—triangles.* ("tri" meaning 3) *Today we are going to learn about polygons with 4 sides and 4 angles—quadrilaterals.* ("quad" meaning 4) *Look at the quadrilaterals on the board.*

- **Ask:** *What can you tell me about the first one?* (rectangle; opposite sides congruent and parallel; 4 right angles) Write properties under the shape as they are discussed. Continue in the same fashion for all the quadrilaterals:

  - Parallelogram (opposite sides congruent and parallel; opposite angles are congruent) Ask: *Is a rectangle a parallelogram?* (yes)
  - Trapezoid (exactly one pair of parallel sides)
  - Rhombus (a parallelogram; opposite angles congruent; 4 congruent sides)
  - Square (a rectangle; 4 right angles with 4 congruent sides)

- **Ask:** *What do you think the sum of the angle measures of a rectangle is?* (360°)

- *Is that true for all quadrilaterals?* (yes) Guide students to see that every quadrilateral can be divided into exactly two triangles by drawing a diagonal. Remind students that the sum of the measures of the angles in a triangle is 180° ($180 \times 2 = 360$)

- Assign students the appropriate practice page(s) to support their understanding of the skill.

Assess the Skill

Use the following problems to pre-/post-assess students' understanding of the skill.

Have students identify angle relationships for each figure and name the quadrilateral.

Name ______________________________ **Date** __________

Match each quadrilateral to its properties.

1. ____________

2. ____________

3. ____________

4. ____________

A. Opposite angles are congruent and parallel.

B. Has exactly one pair of parallel sides.

C. Has 4 right angles and opposite sides are congruent and parallel.

D. Has 4 right angles and 4 congruent sides.

E. Opposite angles are congruent and opposite sides are parallel; all sides are congruent.

Find the missing angle measure.

5. n 90°

The measure of $\angle n$ is __________

6. 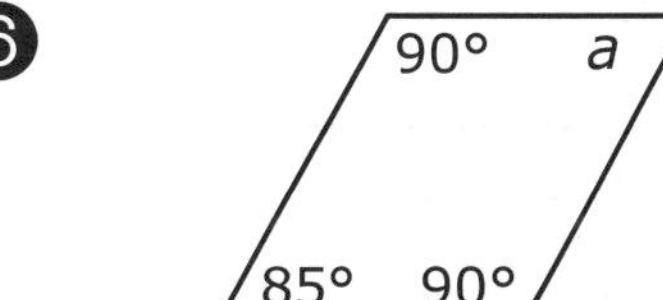

The measure of $\angle a$ is __________

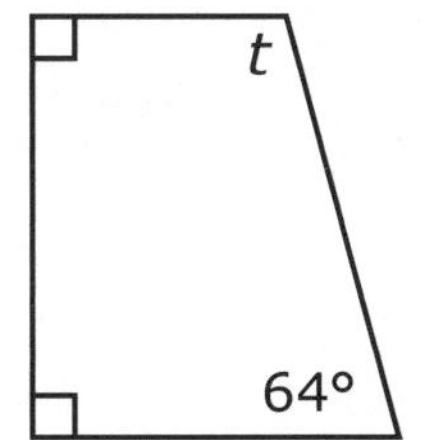

The measure of $\angle t$ is __________

8. 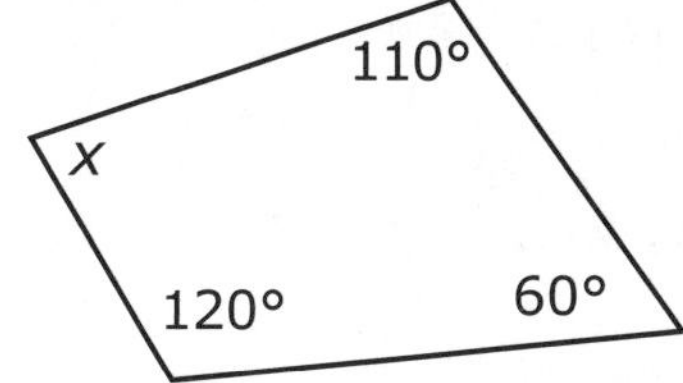

The measure of $\angle x$ is __________

Tell how you know if a triangle is an acute triangle.

Name ______________________________ **Date** __________

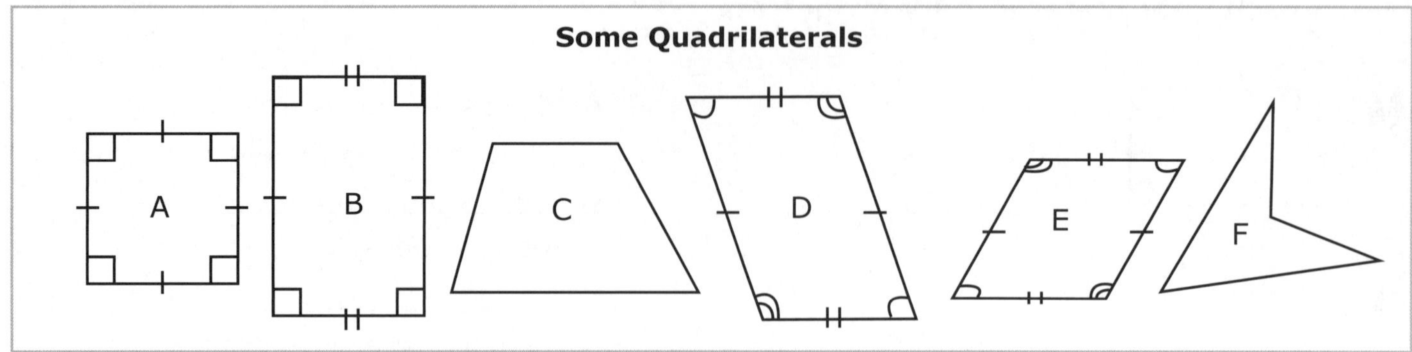

Write the name that best describes each quadrilateral.

1. A: ____________________
2. B: ____________________
3. C: ____________________
4. D: ____________________
5. E: ____________________
6. F: ____________________

List all of the quadrilaterals above that have the following properties:

7. 4 congruent sides ____________________
8. 2 pairs of parallel sides ____________________
9. congruent opposite angles ____________________
10. 4 right angles ____________________

Find the missing angle measure.

11.

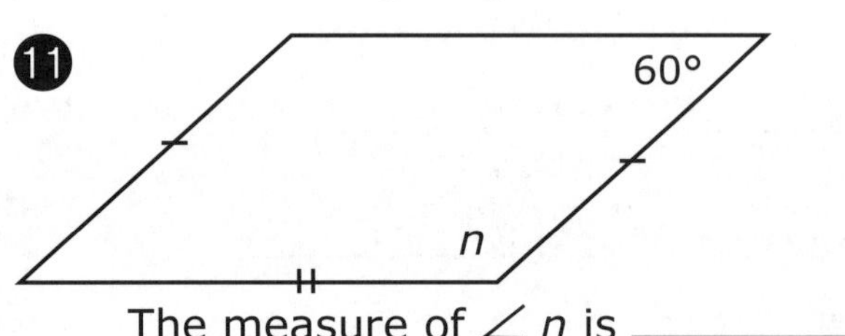

The measure of $\angle n$ is __________

12.

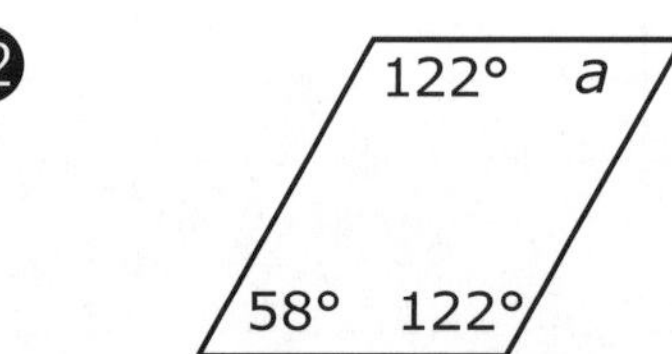

The measure of $\angle a$ is __________

13.

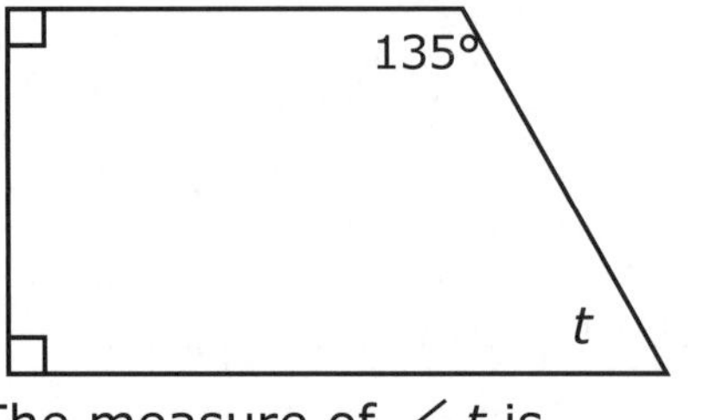

The measure of $\angle t$ is __________

14.

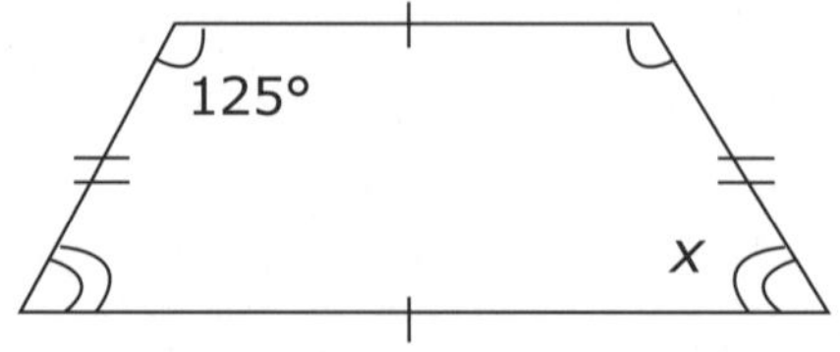

The measure of $\angle x$ is __________

Tell which quadrilaterals can be classified as parallelograms.

Name ______________________________ **Date** __________

Solve.

1. Which quadrilaterals must have perpendicular sides? Explain.

2. Which quadrilaterals must have at least one set of parallel sides? Explain.

3. Which quadrilaterals have two sets of congruent sides?

4. Which quadrilaterals have 4 congruent sides?

5. What is the measure of angle J?

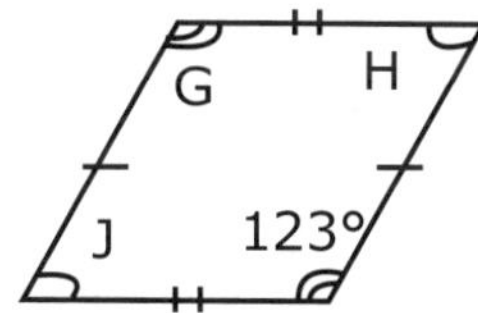

6. What is the measure of angle C?

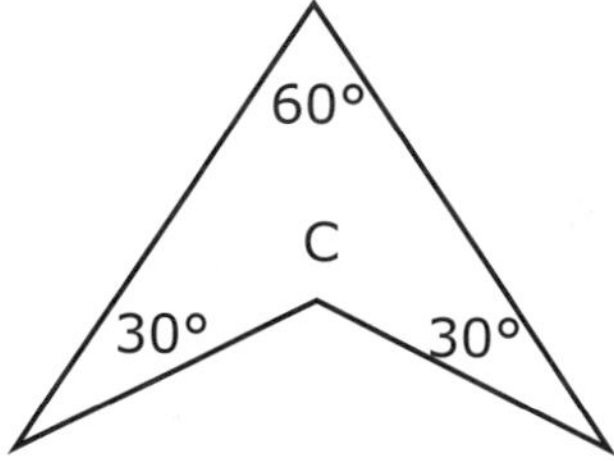

Circle the letter for the correct answer.

7. Which statement about quadrilaterals is NOT true?

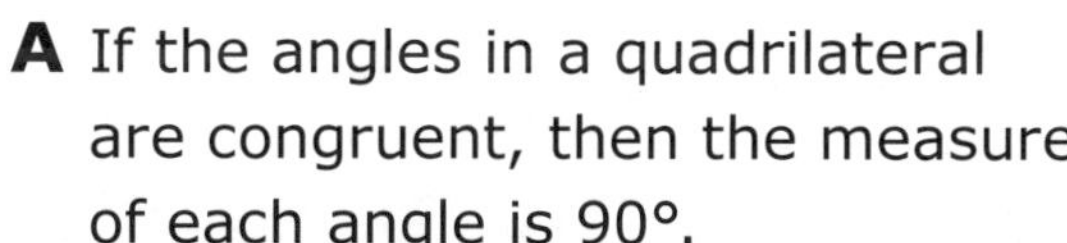

A If the angles in a quadrilateral are congruent, then the measure of each angle is 90°.

B If a quadrilateral has exactly 2 obtuse angles, then each of the other angles is a right angle.

C If a figure is a parallelogram, then its opposite angles are congruent.

D If a figure is a rhombus, then its parallel sides are congruent.

8. Which polygon is a trapezoid?

A 

B 

C 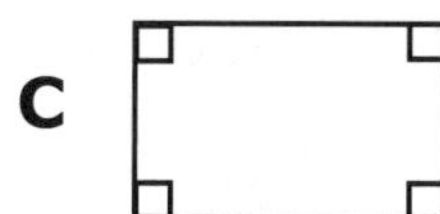

D 

Unit 21 Mini-Lesson

Locate Points on the Coordinate Plane

Standard

Measurement and Data

6.11A (RS) Graph points in all four quadrants using ordered pairs of rational numbers.

Model the Skill

Draw the coordinate plane on the board and list the following coordinates in written and table form.

A (−3, 2) B (−1, 3) C (7, 7) D (9, 8)

x	*y*
−3	2
−1	3
7	7
9	8

- **Say:** *We can use ordered pairs, or coordinates, to plot points. The first number in the ordered pair (x) tells how far to move along the x-axis. The second number (y) tells how far to move along the y-axis.* Point A is at (3, 5). Have students plot points A–D and connect the points to form a line.
- Assign students the appropriate practice page(s) to support their understanding of the skill.

Assess the Skill

Use the following problems to pre-/post-assess students' understanding of the skill.

- Have students graph the following coordinates on the coordinate plane.

A (3, 5)
B (5, 3)
C (8, 5)
D (6, 7)

x	*y*
1	2
2	4
3	6
4	8

x	*y*
3	2
5	4
7	6
9	8

Name ______________________________ **Date** __________

Graph and label the following points using the (*x*, *y*) coordinates.

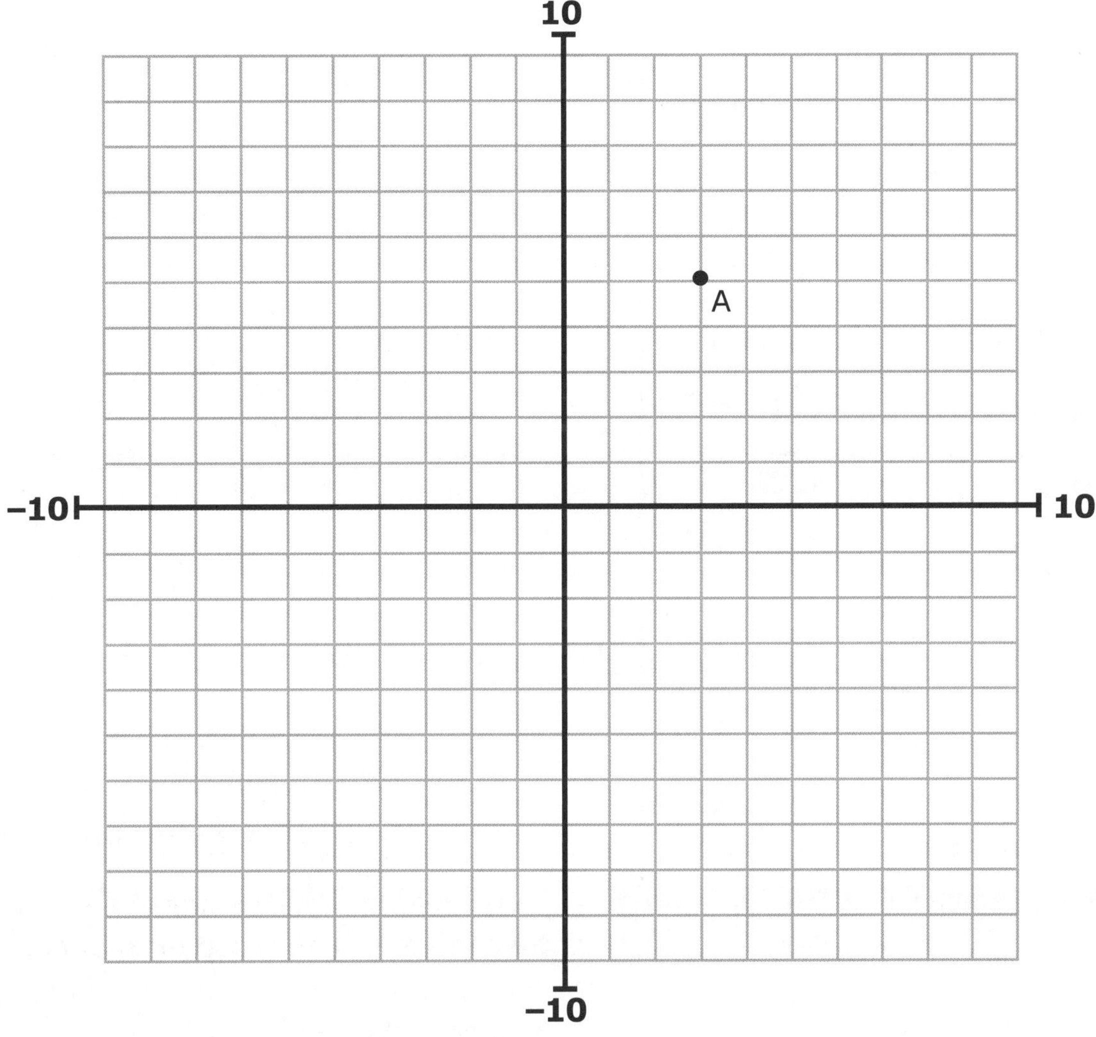

1 Point A: (3, 5)

2 Point B: (–4, –1)

3 Point C: (–2, 5)

4 Point D: (8, –6)

5 Point E: (–2, –3)

6 Point F: (8, 1)

7

hours (*x*)	3	4	5	6
dollars (*y*)	5	6	7	8

8

x	*y*
–4	4
–6	6
–8	8
–10	10

 **Tell how you use an ordered pair to graph a point.**

Name ______________________________ **Date** __________

Graph each point.

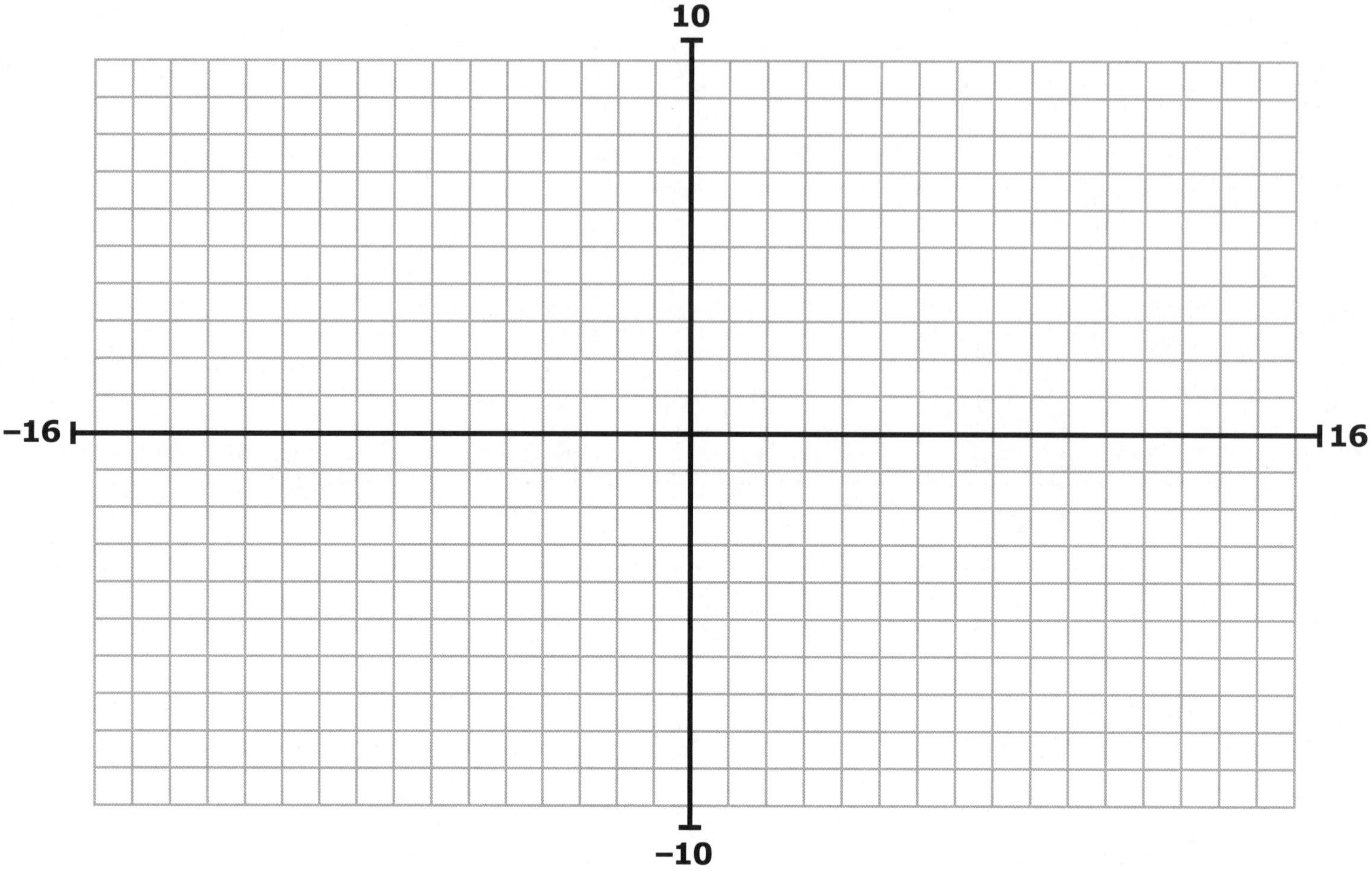

10

−16 16

−10

1. Point J: (1, 7)
2. Point K: (−2, −9)
3. Point L: (4, 9)
4. Point M: (5, −7)
5. Point N: (−4, 5)
6. Point O: (2, −5)

7.

quarts (x)	−4	−8	−12	−16
gallons (y)	1	2	3	4

8.

pints (x)	2	4	6	8
quarts (y)	1	2	3	4

9.

x	y
11	9
11	8
11	7
11	6

Explain why K is a point, KL is a line segment, and y = 9 is a line.

Name ______________________________ **Date** __________

Solve.

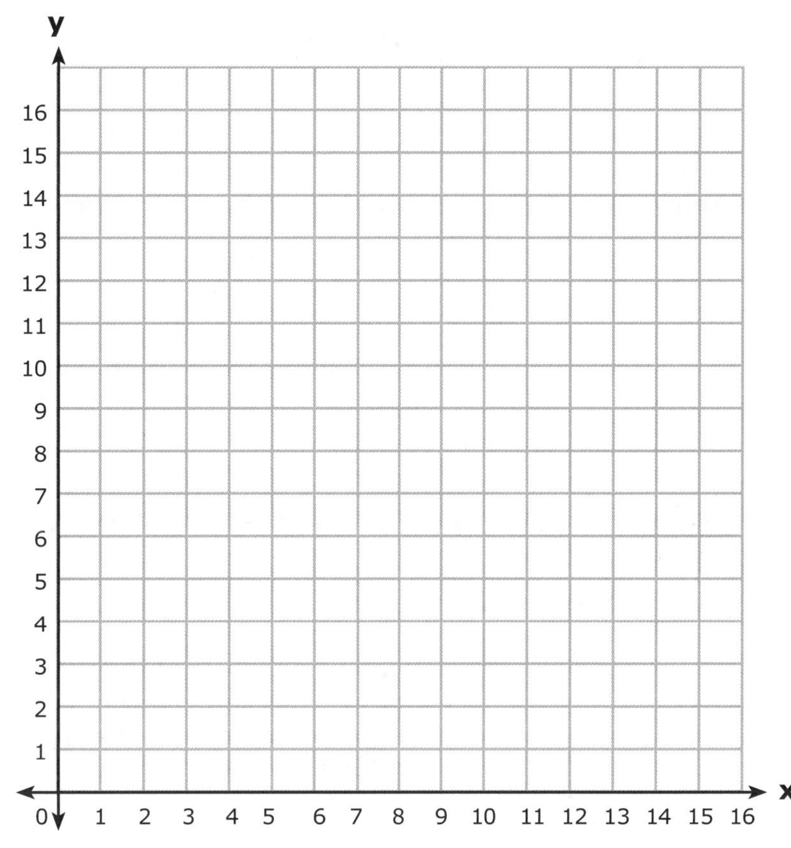

1. Use the ordered pair in the table to graph point A on the coordinate plane.

x	*y*
1	7

2. Graph triangle DEF using the following coordinates: (4, 2), (8, 2), and (8, 4)

3. Graph the line $x = y + 1$ using the coordinates in the table.

x	2	3	4	5
y	1	2	3	4

4. In 1 hour, factory workers can make 4 cars. In 2 hours, they can make 8 cars. In 4 hours, they can make 16 cars. Complete the table. Then graph the points in the table.

input	output
x	*y*
1	4
2	
3	
4	

Circle the letter for the correct answer.

5. How many cars can the factory workers make in 10 hours?

A 10
B 40
C 48
D 56

6. Which of the following points is on the line $y = 4x$?

A (8, 2)
B (4, 12)
C (5, 20)
D (20, 5)

Unit 22 Mini-Lesson
Measure Angles

Standard

Mathematical Process Standards

6.1C (PS) Select tools, including real objects, manipulatives, paper and pencil, and technology as appropriate, and techniques, including mental math, estimation, and number sense as appropriate, to solve problems.

Model the Skill

Draw a right angle on the board.

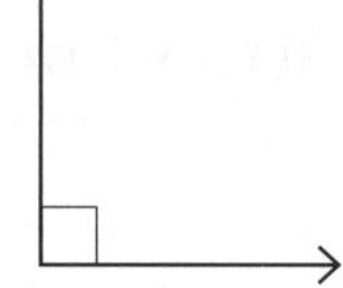

- **Say:** *We are going to find some right angles in our classroom. A right angle looks like the corner of this page.* Remind students that an angle is formed by two rays with the same vertex and that perpendicular lines form right angles.
- **Ask:** *What right angles can you see in our room?* (corners of windows, doors, books, etc.) Draw a circle on the board with perpendicular lines through the center to create four right angles. Relate angle measures to turns. **Say:** *We measure angles in degrees. A right angle measures 90 degrees. A right angle is a quarter turn.*
- Demonstrate how to use the corner to determine which angle is greater than, less than, or equal to 90º. Point out that angles are named by their relationship to a right angle.
- Assign students the appropriate practice page(s) to support their understanding of the skill.

Assess the Skill

Use the following problems to pre-/post-assess students' understanding of the skill.

- Ask students to draw examples of right, acute, and obtuse angles.
- Then have them use a protractor to measure and describe the following angles.

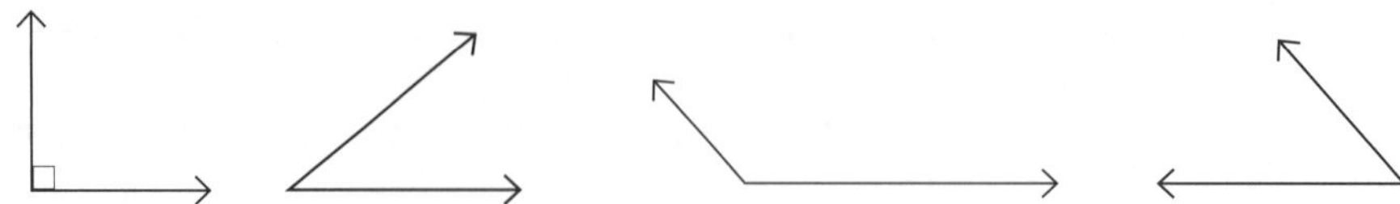

Name ________________________________ Date __________

Use a protractor. Measure each angle.

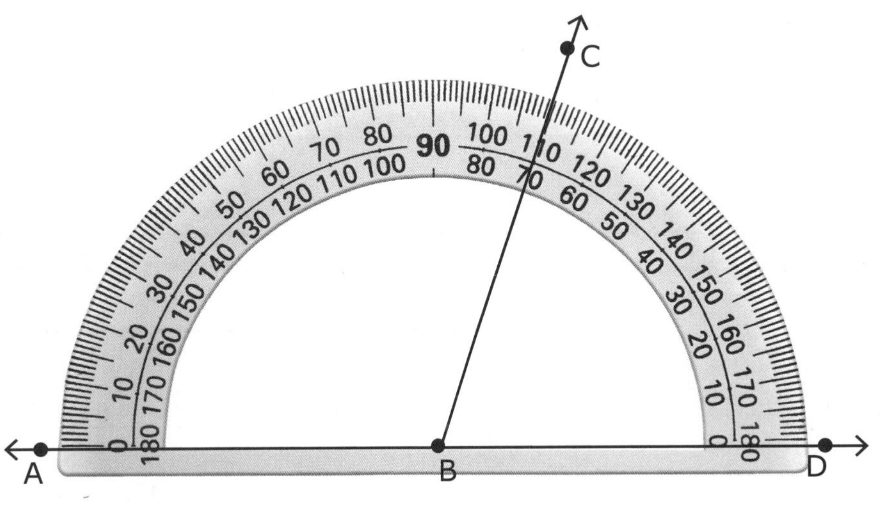

1 Angle ∠ CBD measures

__________ degrees.

2 Angle ∠ ABC measures

__________ degrees.

3 Angle ∠ ABD measures

__________ degrees.

4 ∠ EFG measures __________.

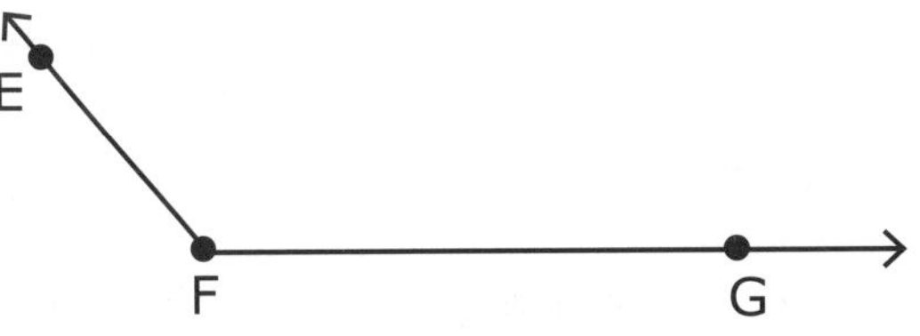

5 ∠ HIJ measures __________.

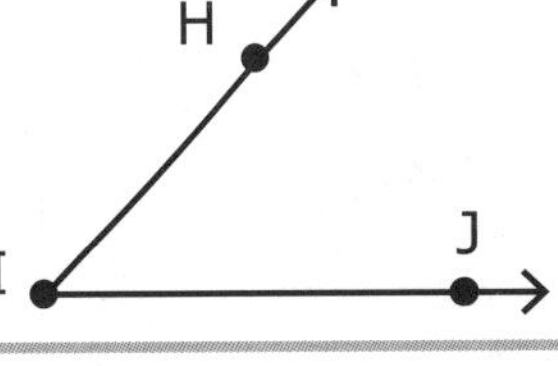

6 ∠ KLM measures __________.

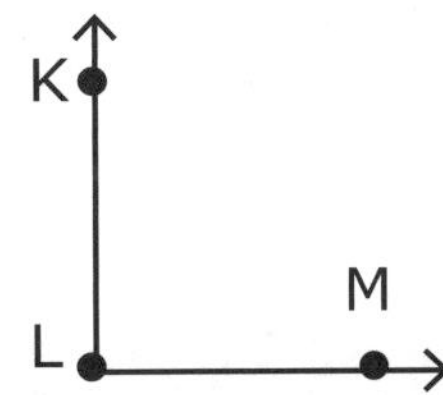

7 ∠ NOP measures __________.

8 ∠ XYZ measures __________.

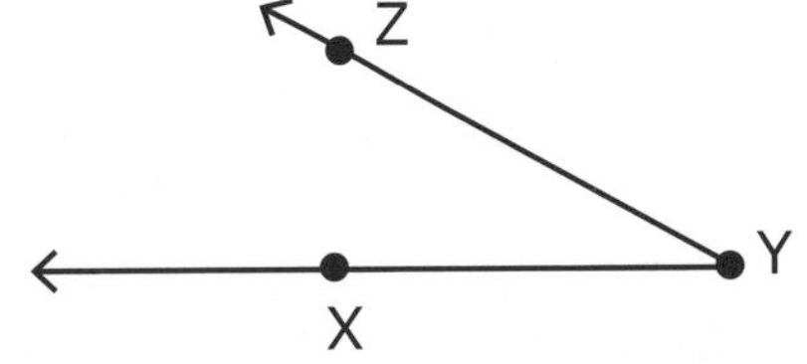

 **Tell how you use a protractor.**

Name ______________________________ **Date** __________

Use a straight edge. Draw an angle for each problem. Use the diagram to help.

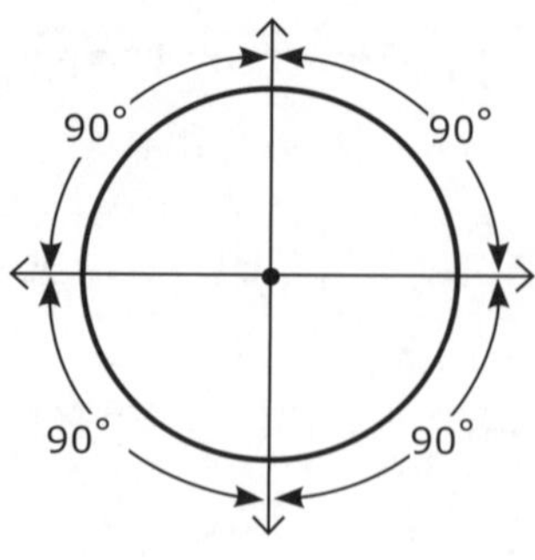

1. Sketch an angle that measures about 90º.

2. Sketch an angle that measures less than 90º.

3. Sketch an angle that measures about 45º.

4. Sketch an angle that measures about 140º.

5. Sketch an angle that measures about 180º.

6. Sketch an angle that measures about 225º.

In Problem 6, tell how you know the angle is about 225º.

Name ______________________________ **Date** __________

Solve.

1. Which angle is greater than 90°?

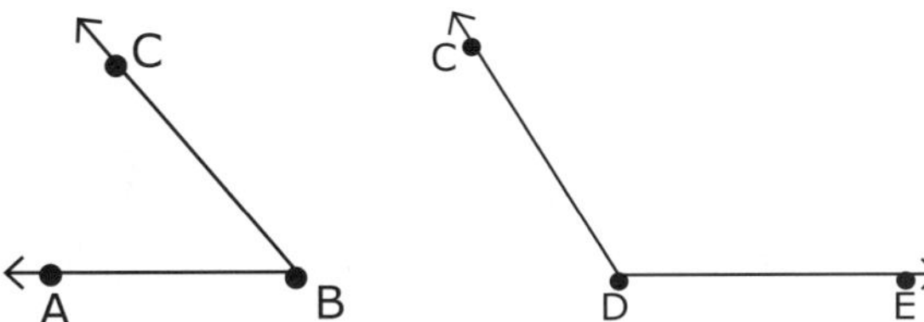

2. Sketch a right angle.

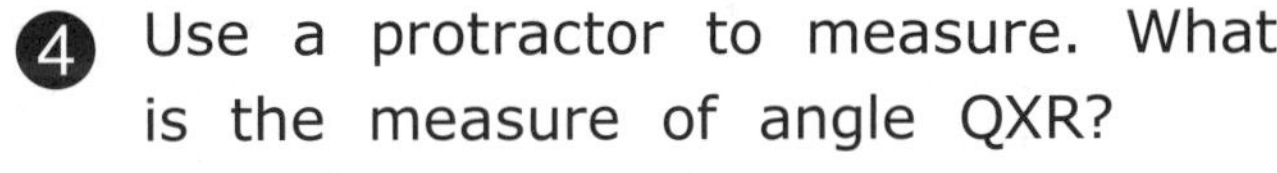

3. If you divide this half-circle into six equal angles, what will be the measure of each angle?

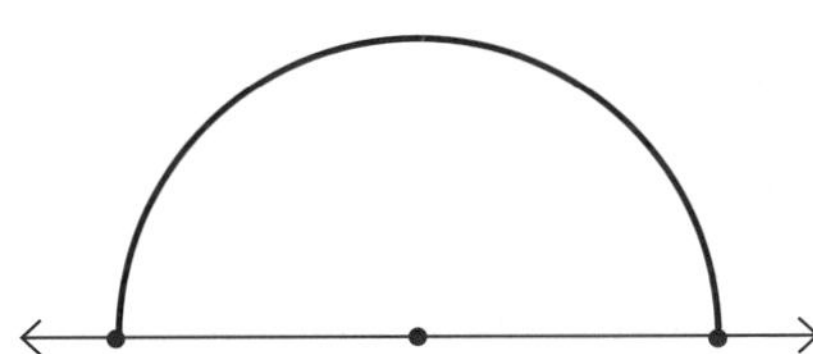

4. Use a protractor to measure. What is the measure of angle QXR?

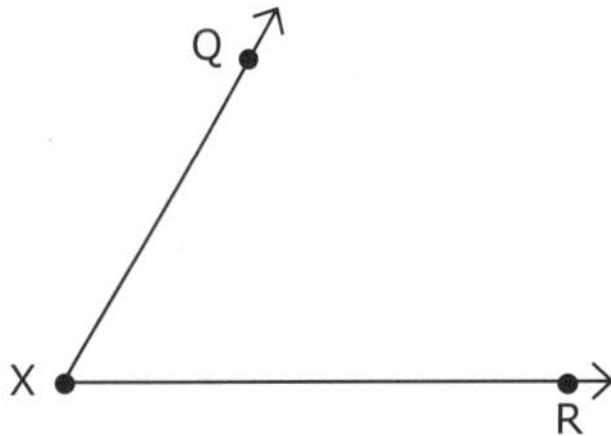

Circle the letter for the correct answer.

5. The ∠ XYZ measures 100°. What is the measure of ∠ WYZ?

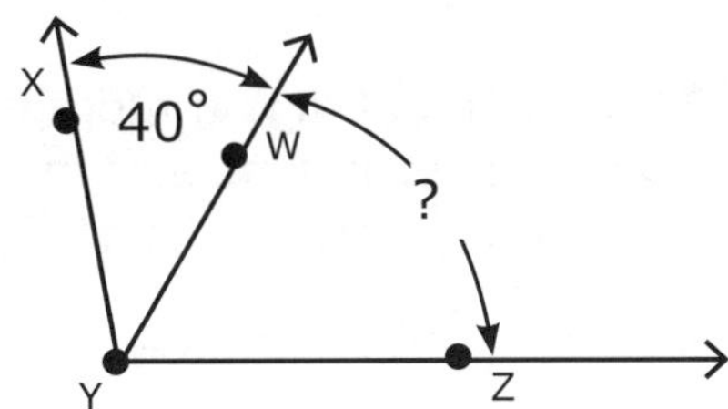

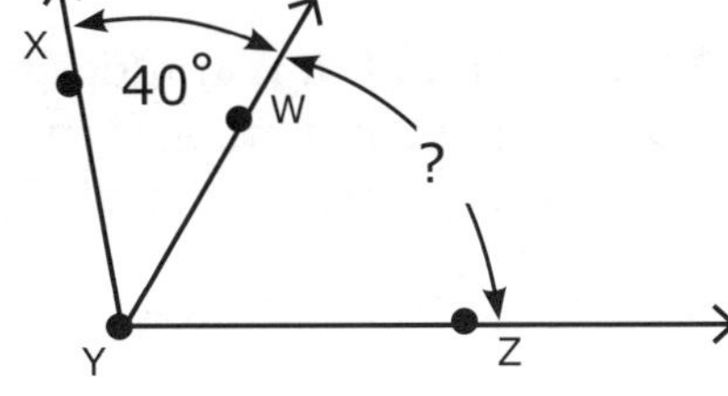

A 40°

B 60°

C 80°

D 140°

6. What is the measure of ∠ KMN?

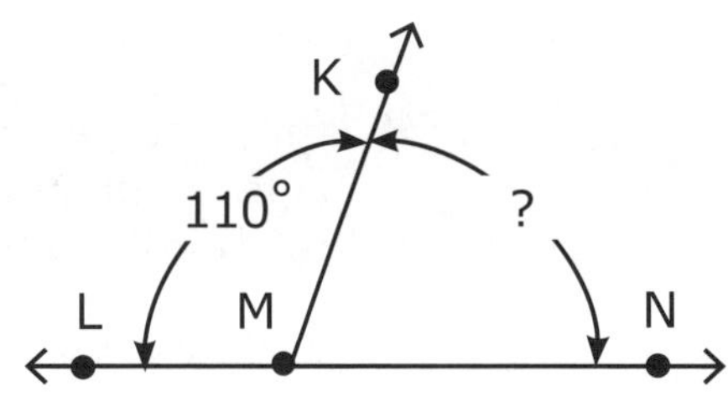

A 250°

B 140°

C 90°

D 70°

Unit 23 Mini-Lesson

Convert Measures

Standard

Proportionality

6.1B (PS) Use a problem-solving model that incorporates analyzing given information, formulating a plan or strategy, determining a solution, justifying the solution, and evaluating the problem-solving process and the reasonableness of the solution.

6.4H (RS) Convert units within a measurement system, including the use of proportions and unit rates.

Model the Skill

- Post or write on the board both metric and customary equivalent units for length, weight/mass, and capacity. Have students copy them into a notebook for reference and use.
- **Ask:** *If I have a board 100 centimeters long, how many meters long is it?* (1 meter) *What if the board is 3 feet long? How many yards long is it?* (1 yard) *How do you know the answer to these questions?* (we can convert among units within the same system)
- **Say:** *In the metric system, which is used in most of the world, the conversions are based on the decimal system, so, for example, 1,000 grams is equivalent to 1 kilogram, and 500 grams is equal to 0.5 kilogram.* Using metric equivalents, have students make up and solve conversion problems.
- **Say:** *Converting customary measures is not so easy. We need to remember how many cups are in a quart* (4) *and how many ounces are in a pound.* (16) **Ask:** *How would you solve this problem?*

  We need $8\frac{1}{2}$ feet of tape to mark a starting line for a race. We have $1\frac{1}{3}$ yards of tape on one roll and 45 inches of tape on another roll. If we need more tape, how much more do we need? (9 in. or $\frac{3}{4}$ ft)
- Guide students to develop a plan, determine how to find a common unit, and decide how to express the answer. If students are not sure of the relationships between units, allow them to use their reference chart.
- Assign students the appropriate practice page(s) to support their understanding of the skill.

Assess the Skill

Use the following problems to pre-/post-assess students' understanding of the skill.

365 cm = __________ m   2.5 L = __________ mL   3,000 g = __________ kg

78 in. = __________ ft   5 gal = __________ qt   3 lbs. = __________ oz

Name ______________________________ **Date** __________

Convert metric units.

1. 5 m = ________ cm
   5 x ______ = ______

2. 800 cm = ________ m
   800 ÷ ______ = ______

3. 350 cm = ________ m
   350 ÷ ______ = ______

4. 6 km = ________ m
   6 x ______ = ______

5. 1,750 g = ________ kg
   1,750 ÷ ______ = ______

6. 4.3 kg = ________ g
   4.3 x ______ = ______

7. 2.25 L = ________ mL
   2.25 x ______ = ______

8. 5,000 mL = ________ L
   5,000 ÷ ______ = ______

Metric Units
Length
1 centimeter (cm) = 10 mm
1 meter (m) = 100 cm
1 kilometer (km) = 1,000 m
Mass
1 gram (g) = 1,000 mg
1 kilogram (kg) = 1,000 g
Capacity
1 liter (L) = 1,000 mL

Convert customary units.

9. 15 ft = ________ yd
   15 ÷ ______ = ______

10. 5 ft = ________ in.
    5 x ______ = ______

11. 2 mi = ________ yd
    2 x ______ = ______

12. 64 oz = ________ lbs.
    64 ÷ ______ = ______

13. 3 t = ________ lbs.
    3 x ______ = ______

14. 5 pt = ________ c
    5 x ______ = ______

15. 10 qt = ________ gal
    10 ÷ ______ = ______

16. 3 qt = ________ c
    3 x ______ = ______

Customary Units
Length
1 foot (ft) = 12 inches (in.)
1 yard (yd) = 3 ft
1 mile (mi) = 1,760 yd
Weight
1 pound (lb) = 16 ounces (oz)
1 ton (t) = 2,000 lbs.
Capacity
1 cup (c) = 8 fluid ounces
1 pint (pt) = 2 c
1 quart (qt) = 2 pt
1 gallon (gal) = 4 qt

 **Tell the operation you use to convert from a larger unit to a smaller unit.**

Name ______________________________ **Date** __________

Complete.

1. 60 m = ________ cm
2. 72 km = ________ m
3. 4.5 cm = ________ mm
4. 250 g = ________ mg
5. 5.8 km = ________ m
6. 750 mL = ________ L
7. 87 L = ________ mL
8. 4,008 m = ________ cm
9. 18,900 m = ________ km
10. 98 c = ________ gal
11. 7 mi = ________ yd
12. 8,400 lbs. = ________ t
13. 48 lbs. = ________ oz
14. 195 ft = ________ yd
15. 15 yd = ________ in
16. 753 ft = ________ yd
17. 84 qt = ________ gal
18. 16 gal = ________ pt

---

19. Elena buys 3,500 grams of grapes. How many kilograms is that?

20. Andy runs 5 miles. How many yards is that?

Tell the operation you use to convert from a smaller unit to a larger unit.

Name ______________________________ Date __________

Solve.

1. Robyn bought 32 ounces of orange juice. How many quarts of juice is that?

2. If Hector ran 35.5 kilometers last week and 22.5 kilometers this week, how many meters did he run over the last two weeks?

3. The boat weighs 6,628 pounds. The tow hitch can safely pull a maximum of 3 tons. Can the tow hitch safely tow the boat?

4. The salt factory has 2 tons of table salt ready to be packaged. If the salt is packaged in 16-ounce containers, how many containers can be filled?

5. The dresser is 78 inches long. The length of the bedroom wall between the two closets is 7 feet. If the dresser is centered on the wall between the two closets, how many inches will separate the dresser and the closet on either side?

6. For her science project, Flora has to dilute 100 mL of solvent into every 2 liters of water. How many liters of solvent would she need to dilute into 10 liters of water?

Circle the letter for the correct answer.

7. Jake is making broth for his famous Thanksgiving soup. The recipe calls for 1 bouillon cube for every quart of soup. If he ends up making 16 pints of soup, how many cubes will he have used?

   A 4 cubes

   B 16 cubes

   C 8 cubes

   D 32 cubes

8. The town half-marathon is 13.1 miles long. If the town has to place 2 cones every 2 yards along the course, how many cones will the town need to complete the course?

   A 13,100 cones

   B 23,056 cones

   C 11,528 cones

   D 5,764 cones

Unit 24 Mini-Lesson

Solve Problems Involving Measurements

Standard

Expressions, Equations, and Relationships

6.1C (PS) Select tools, including real objects, manipulatives, paper and pencil, and technology as appropriate, and techniques, including mental math, estimation, and number sense as appropriate, to solve problems.

6.8C (SS) Write equations that represent problems related to the area of rectangles, parallelograms, trapezoids, and triangles and volume of right rectangular prisms where dimensions are positive rational numbers.

6.8D (RS) Determine solutions for problems involving the area of rectangles, parallelograms, trapezoids, and triangles and volume of right rectangular prisms where dimensions are positive rational numbers.

Model the Skill

Display measuring tools such as rulers, scales, clocks, and thermometers. Review how to use them.

- **Say:** *Today, we are going to solve problems involving length, weight, time, and temperature. Some problems may require measurement with an appropriate tool. Others may require converting units of measure.*
- Write this problem on the board: *I have two sections of fence. One section is $3\frac{1}{2}$ ft long. The other is 57 inches long. I need to fence one side of my garden that is 10 feet long.*
- **Ask:** *What is the total length of the fence sections?* (99 in. or $8\frac{1}{4}$ ft) *How much more fencing will I need?* ($1\frac{3}{4}$ ft or 21 in.) Discuss how to add and subtract measurements. Note that they must be like measures and students will need to convert units.
- **Say:** *It is 10:03 AM now and the temperature is 68 degrees Fahrenheit.* (Use actual time and temperature) **Ask:** *What time will it be in 3 hours and 25 minutes?* (1:28 PM) *If the temperature rises 17 degrees in that time, how hot will it be?* (85°F)
- Have students use measuring tools to create and solve other similar problems.
- Assign students the appropriate practice page(s) to support their understanding of the skill.

Assess the Skill

Use the following problems to pre-/post-assess students' understanding of the skill.

358 cm + 2.5 m = __________ m   5 h 45 min – $1\frac{1}{2}$ h = _____ h _____ min

650 g x 4 = _______ kg   32°C – 17°C = _______ °C

Name ______________________________ **Date** __________

Solve.

1. 2.5 h – 1 h 48 min = ________ min

2. 412 g x 10 = ________ kg

3. 5 lb ÷ 4 = ________ oz

4. 3 lb 7 oz + 12 oz = ____ lb ____ oz

5. 6 ft ÷ 8 = ________ in

6. 23°C – 15°C = ________ °C

7. Mr. Foster is a teacher. He drives past the library going to and from school. How many km does he drive round trip?

____

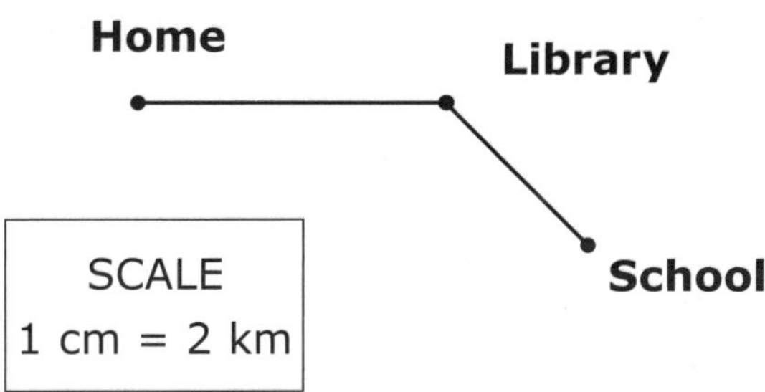

8. The kitchen clock loses 1 minute every 12 hours. How many days will it take for the clock to be 10 minutes slow?

____

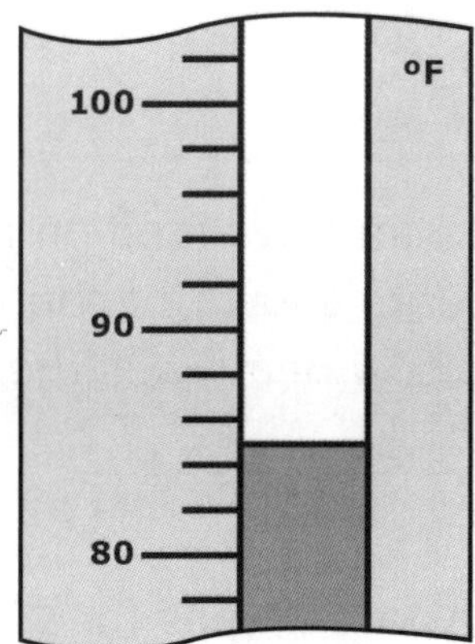

9. Temperatures today are forecast to reach 102°F. It is 85°F now. How many degrees will the temperature increase if the forecast is accurate?

____

10. If the temperature on the thermometer falls 9 degrees from the current temperature, what will the temperature be?

____

☆ **Tell how you solved Problem 7. How do you know your answer is reasonable?**

Name ______________________________ **Date** __________

Solve.

1. 7.25 h – 4 h 15 min = ________ min

2. 50 mi – 5,000 yd = ________ yd

3. 1,700 lb x 5 = ________ t

4. 6 lb 8 oz – 20 oz = ____ lb ____ oz

5. 20 yd ÷ 16 = ________ in.

6. 67°C – 39°C = ________ °C

7. What is the length of the trail in meters?

____

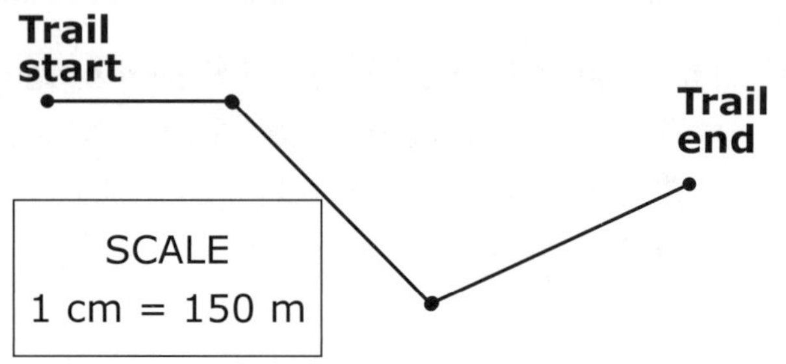

8. The diagram shows the distance between Corpus Christi and San Antonio. Driving at an average of 50 miles per hour, how many hours would it take to get from one city to the other? Use the ruler to measure.

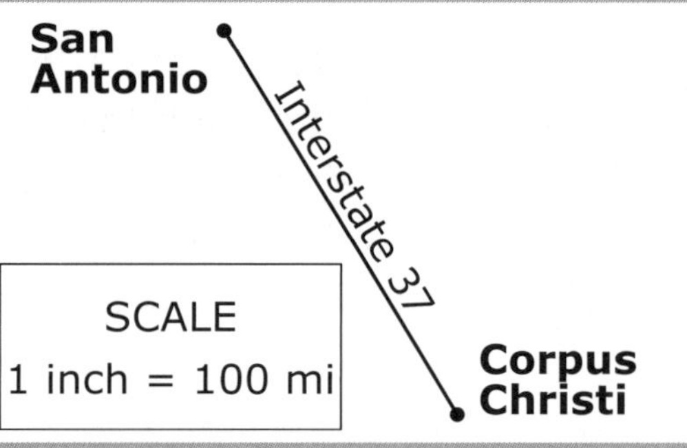

9. Mrs. Kim buys food on her shopping list in the amounts shown. If she places everything in one bag, how heavy will the bag be in ounces?

____

10. Beans are 3 cans for $2.00. If Mrs. Kim buys $4.00 worth of beans, how many pounds of beans does she buy?

____

Shopping List
apples - 3.3 lbs.
cherries - 18 oz
eggplant - 1.5 lbs.
beans (can) - 15 oz
garlic - 6 oz

 **Tell how you solved Problem 9. How do you know your answer is reasonable?**

Name ______________________________ **Date** ________

Solve.

1 Sara gets to school at 8:35 A.M. She leaves school at 2:40 P.M. and then spends $1\frac{1}{2}$ hours at the library. What time is it when she leaves the library? How many hours did Sara spend at school and library together?

2 Adrian's house has a 30-gallon water heater. He has 3 children. If each of his children takes a bath using 20 quarts of hot water, how many gallons of hot water are left for his shower?

3 The driving distance from Amarillo to Abilene is 280 miles. Driving at an average of 45 miles per hour, how many hours would it take to get from one city to the other?

4 The couch is 3 meters long. The length of the living room wall between the two windows is 4 meters. If the couch is centered on the wall between the two windows, how many centimeters of empty wall space will be on either side?

5 The current temperature is 65°F. The forecast says the high temperature for the day will be 82°F. How many degrees will the temperature increase if the forecast is accurate?

6 Rafi bought $1\frac{1}{2}$ pounds of apples, 16 ounces of blueberries, 8 ounces of raspberries, 14 ounces of blackberries, 10 ounces of kiwi, $\frac{1}{2}$ pound of grapes, and 2 pounds of watermelon to make a fruit salad. How many pounds of fruit did he buy?

Circle the letter for the correct answer.

7 On average, the human eye blinks once every 5 seconds. About how many times does the eye blink in 1 hour?

A 12
B 72
C 300
D 720

8 The tea factory has 3 tons of dried tea leaves ready to be packaged. If each box of tea contains 8 ounces of tea leaves, how many boxes can be filled?

A 12,000
B 1,200
C 2,400
D 24,000

Unit 25 Mini-Lesson

Estimate Perimeter and Circumference

Standard

Mathematical Process Standards

6.1C (PS) Select tools, including real objects, manipulatives, paper and pencil, and technology as appropriate, and techniques, including mental math, estimation, and number sense as appropriate, to solve problems.

Model the Skill

Draw the following figures on the board.

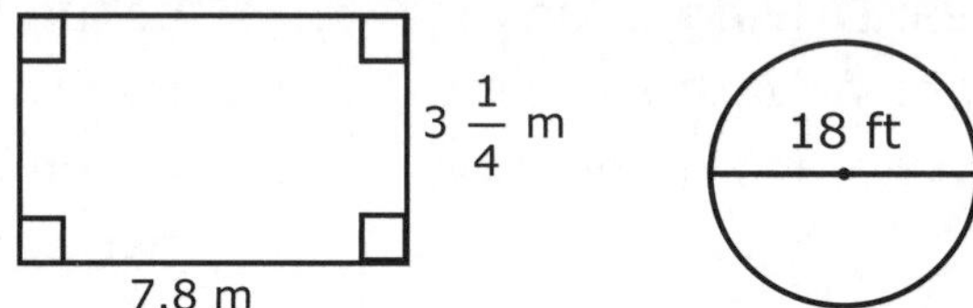

- **Say:** ***Perimeter*** *is the distance around the outside of a figure with vertices.* ***Circumference*** *is the distance around a circle. We can estimate the perimeter of a figure by rounding the measurements and applying an appropriate formula.*
- **Ask:** *What is 7.8 rounded to the nearest whole number?* (8) *What is* $3\frac{1}{4}$ *rounded to the nearest whole number?* (3) Write the formula $P = 2l + 2w$ on the board and guide students in estimating the perimeter with the rounded numbers. (P is about 22 m)
- **Say:** *To estimate the distance around a circle, we use the relationship of the diameter to the circumference*. Review circle relationships in Unit 20 if necessary, reminding students that the circumference is about 3 times the length of the diameter.
- **Ask:** *What is 18 rounded to the nearest ten?* (20) *What should I do next to estimate the circumference?* (multiply by 3) *About how long is the circumference?* (about 60 ft)
- Assign students the appropriate practice page(s) to support their understanding of the skill.

Assess the Skill

Use the following problems to pre-/post-assess students' understanding of the skill.

Perimeter is about ________

$2\frac{3}{4}$ m

$2\frac{3}{4}$ m

Circumference is about ________

31 cm

Name ______________________________ **Date** __________

Complete the chart.

	Figure	Round numbers	Formula	Estimate
1	56 cm, 56 cm	56 → (rounds to) ☐	$P = 4s$ $P = 4 \times$ ___	*P is about* ___
2	4.5 m, 6 m, 3.2 m	4.5 → ☐ 3.2 → ☐ 6 → ☐	$P = s + s + s$	*P is about* ___
3	19 ft, $12\frac{1}{3}$ ft	$12\frac{1}{3}$ → ☐ 19 → ☐	$P = 2l + 2w$	*P is about* ___

Estimate each circumference.

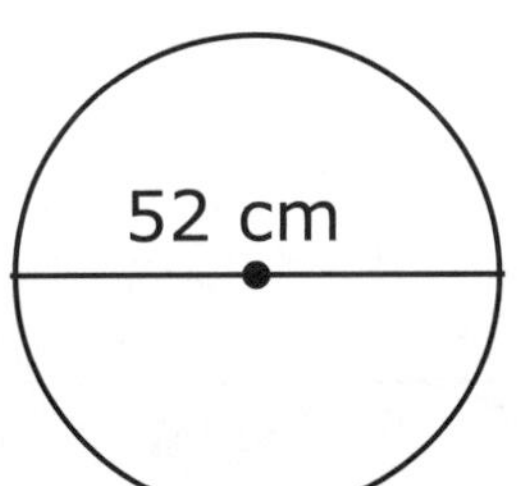

52 rounds to → ☐

___ x 3 = ___

Circumference is about ___

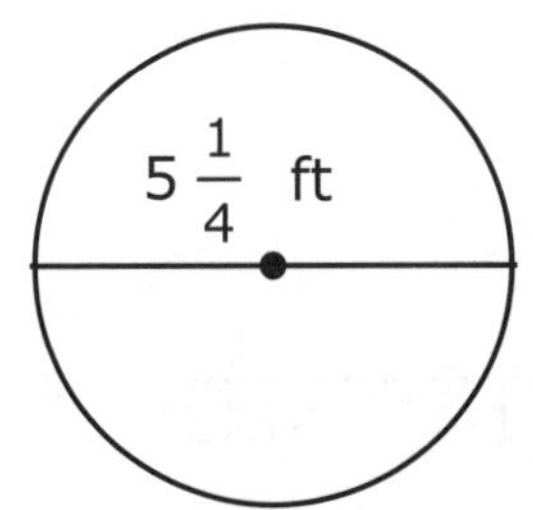

$5\frac{1}{4}$ → ☐

___ x 3 = ___

Circumference is about ___

Tell why we use rounded numbers to estimate.

Name ______________________________ **Date** __________

Estimate each perimeter or circumference. Show your work.

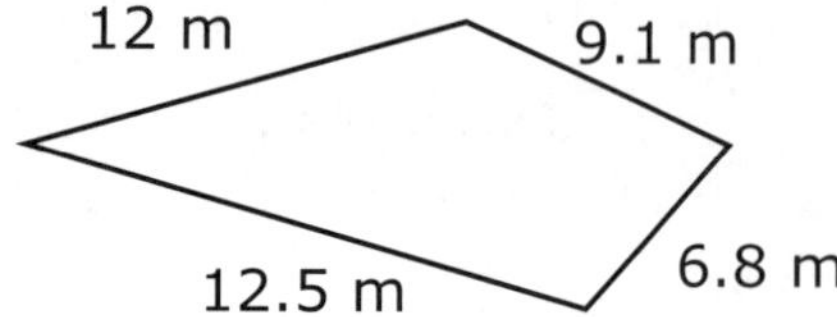

12.5 rounds to → ________
6.8 → ________
9.1 → ________
12 → ________
Perimeter is about ________

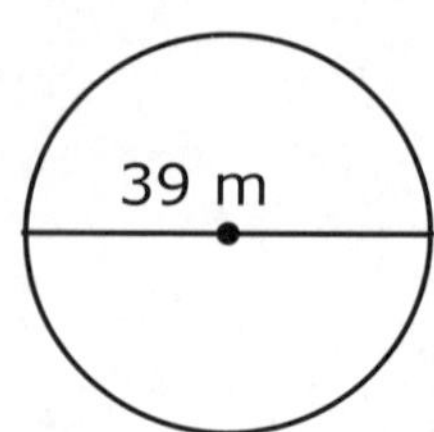

39 rounds to → ________
_____ x 3 = _____
Circumference is about _____

3

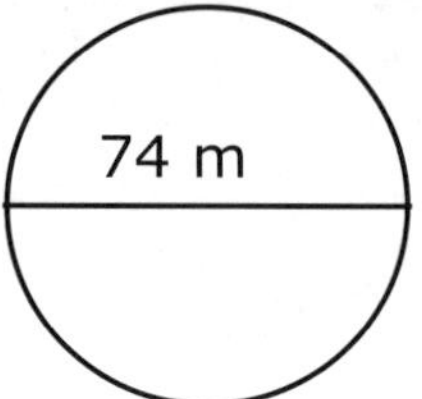

Circumference is about _____

4

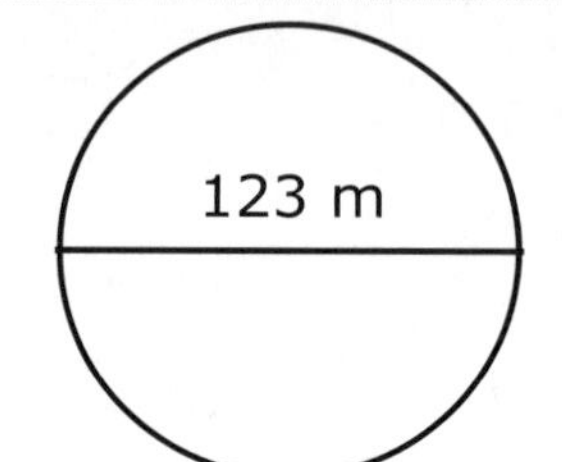

Circumference is about _____

5

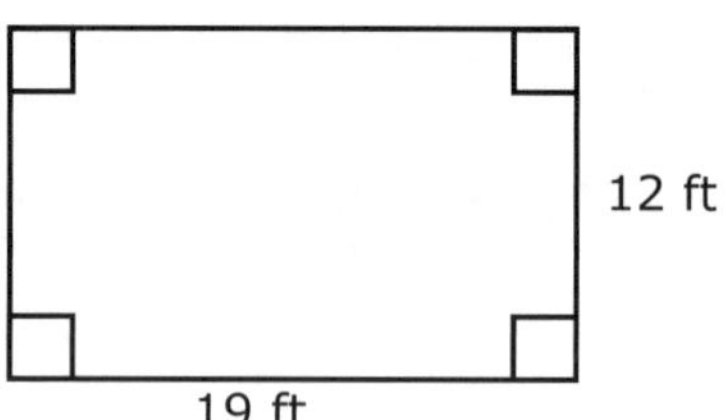

Perimeter is about _____

6

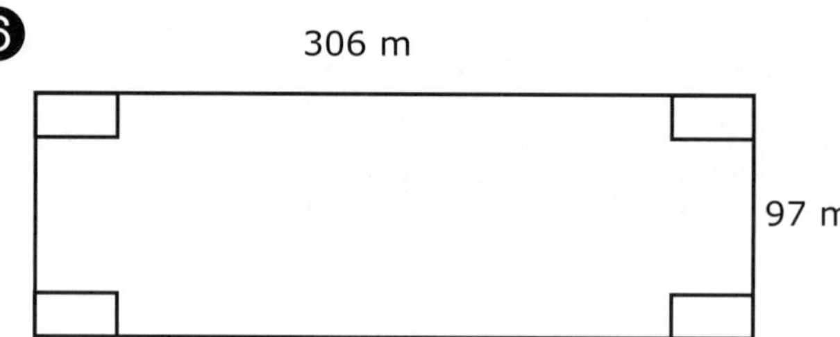

Perimeter is about _____

7

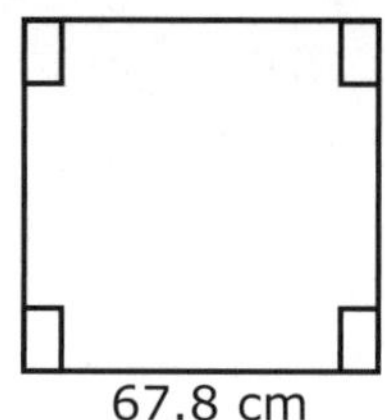

Perimeter is about _____

8

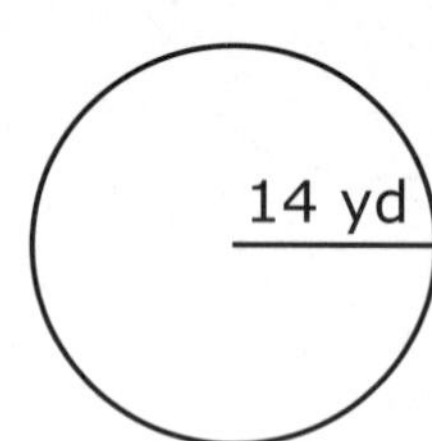

Perimeter is about _____

 **Tell why we multiply the diameter by 3 to estimate circumference.**

Name ______________________________ **Date** __________

Solve.

1. The perimeter of a square room is about 52 feet. About how long is one side of the room?

2. The circumference of a circular mirror is about 1 meter. About how long is the diameter of the mirror in centimeters?

3. Use a ruler to measure the figure to the nearest $\frac{1}{2}$ inch. Then estimate the perimeter.

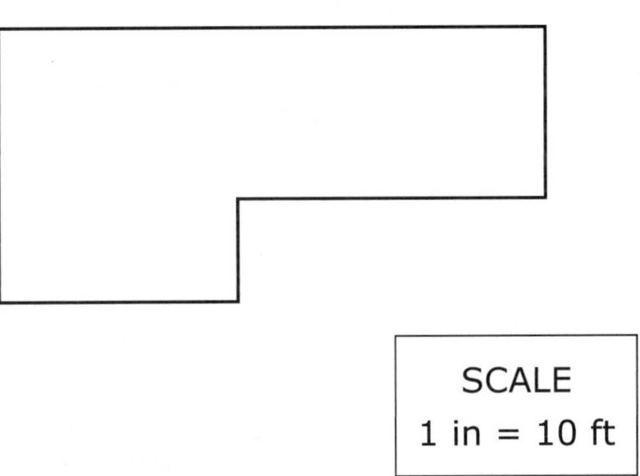

SCALE
1 in = 10 ft

Circle the letter for the correct answer.

4. Which is the best estimate for the circumference of the circle below?

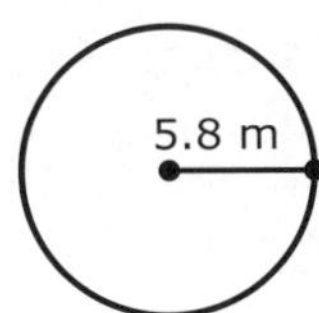

A about 12 m
B about 15 m
C about 18 m
D about 36 m

5. Which is the best estimate for the perimeter of the figure below?

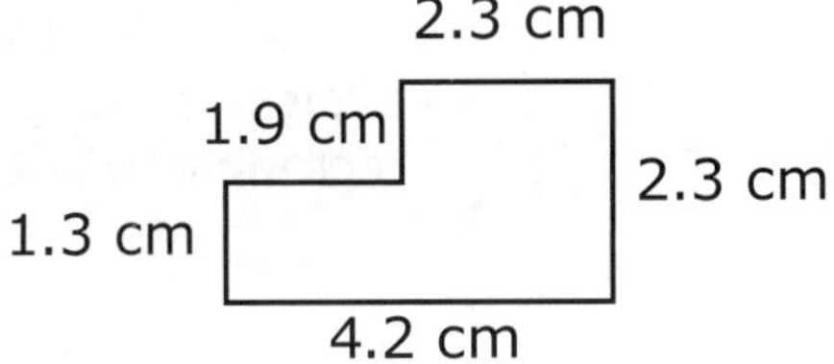

A about 12 cm
B about 9 cm
C about 18 cm
D about 15 cm

Unit 26 Mini-Lesson
Estimate and Find Area

Standard

Expressions, Equations, and Relationships

6.8B (SS) Model area formulas for parallelograms, trapezoids, and triangles by decomposing and rearranging parts of these shapes.

6.8C (SS) Write equations that represent problems related to the area of rectangles, parallelograms, trapezoids, and triangles and volume of right rectangular prisms where dimensions are positive rational numbers.

6.8D (SS) Determine solutions for problems involving the area of rectangles, parallelograms, trapezoids, and triangles and volume of right rectangular prisms where dimensions are positive rational numbers.

Model the Skill

Draw the following figures on the board.

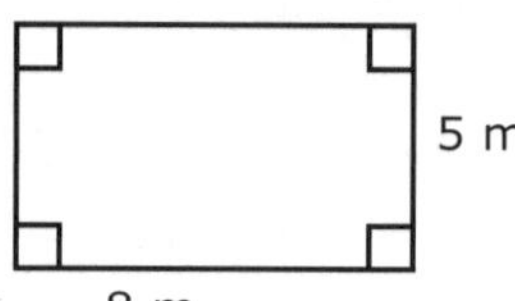

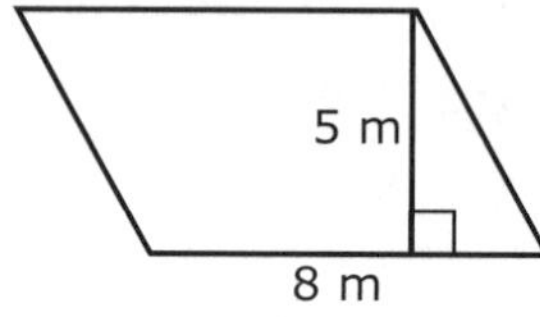

- **Ask:** *What is area?* (The number of square units in a region) *How do we find the area of a rectangle?* (multiply length times width) Write the formula, $A = l \times w$, below the rectangle and have a volunteer find the area of the rectangle. Then draw a diagonal on the rectangle, forming 2 triangles.
- **Ask:** *How can you describe the area of this triangle?* (half the area of the rectangle) Point out that the formula for the area of a triangle shows just that. Draw a triangle and label base and height. Write the formula $A = \frac{1}{2} b \times h$.
- **Say:** *Look at the parallelogram. We can find its area by multiplying the base times height just as we can do for the rectangle. Why?* Guide students to understand that length and width in a rectangle represents the same relationship as base and height in a parallelogram. Write the formula $A = b \times h$ below the rectangle and the parallelogram. Allow students to explore cutting a triangle from a parallelogram and moving it to create a rectangle with the same area.

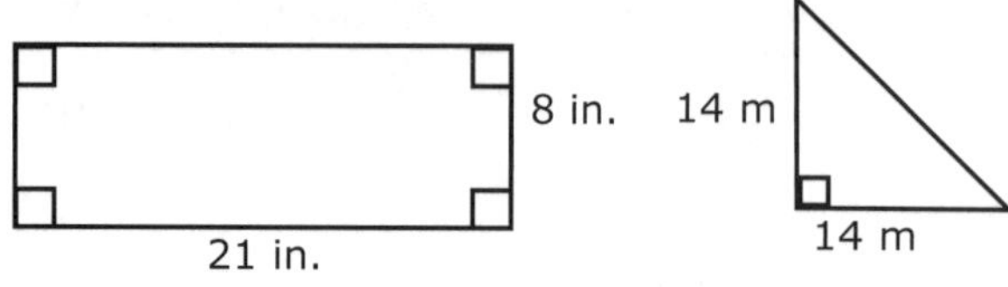

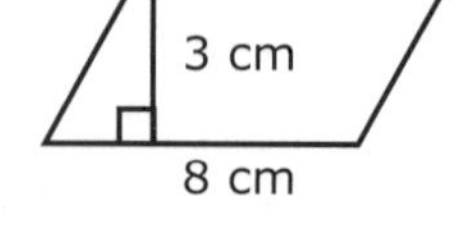

- Assign students the appropriate practice page(s) to support their understanding of the skill.

Assess the Skill

Use the following problems to pre-/post-assess students' understanding of the skill.

8 in.

21 in.

Area = ____

14 m

14 m

Area = ____

3 cm

8 cm

Area = ____

Name ______________________________ **Date** __________

Complete the chart.

	Figure	Formula	Estimate
1	34 ft; $16\frac{1}{2}$ ft	$A = l \bullet w$ or $A = b \bullet h$	$A =$ ________ ft^2
2	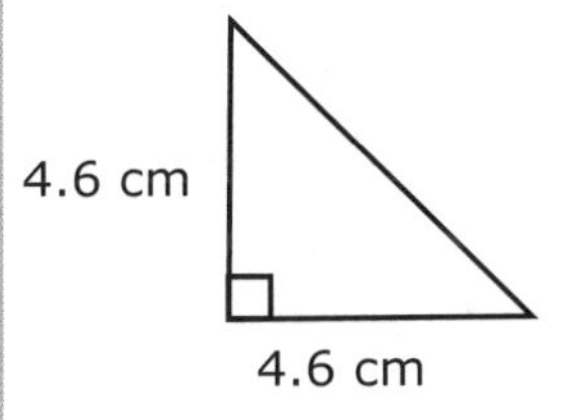 4.6 cm; 4.6 cm	$A = \frac{1}{2} b \bullet h$ $A = \frac{b \bullet h}{2}$	$A =$ ________ cm^2
3	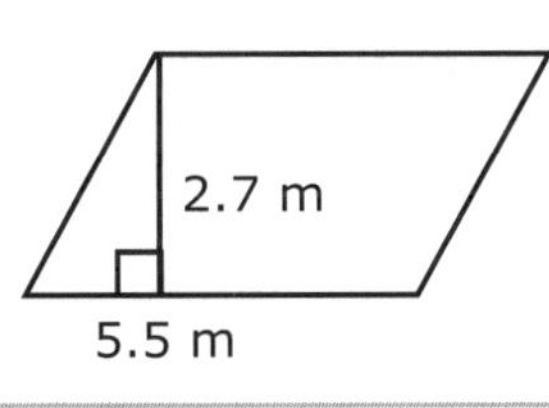 2.7 m; 5.5 m	$A = b \bullet h$	$A =$ ________
4	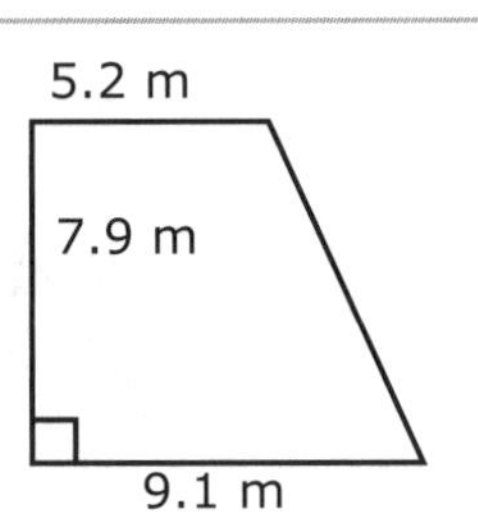 5.2 m; 7.9 m; 9.1 m	$A = \frac{1}{2}(b_1 + b_2)$	$A =$ ________

Estimate the area of each figure. Round measurements to the nearest whole number.

5

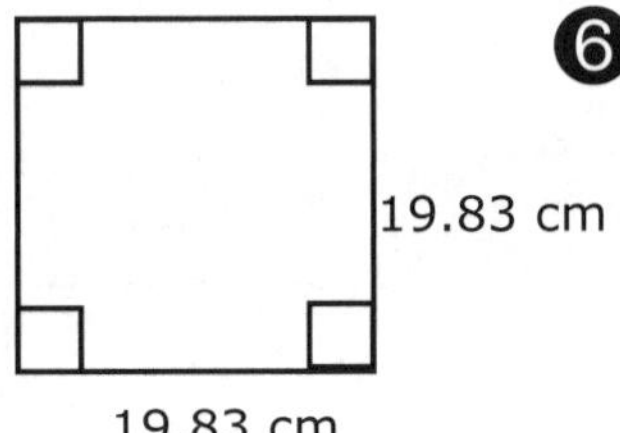

19.83 → ________

$A =$ ________________

6

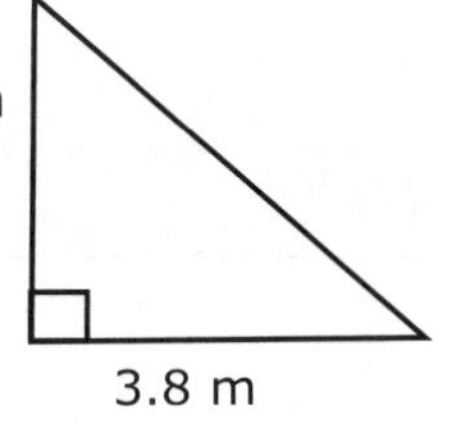

3.4 → ________

3.8 → ________

$A =$ ________________

7

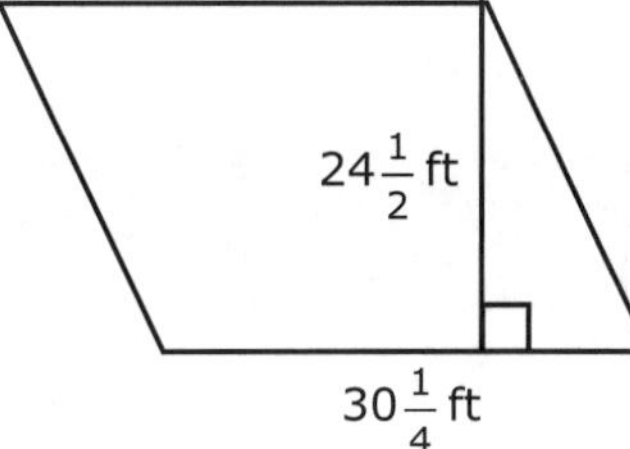

$24\frac{1}{2}$ → ________

$30\frac{1}{4}$ → ________

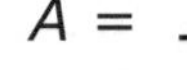

$A =$ 

Tell what the base and height of a rectangle mean.

Name ______________________________ **Date** __________

Choose the best estimate for the area of each figure.

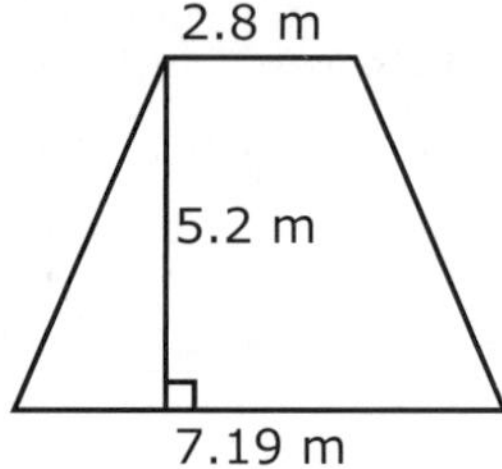

Area is about

____

2

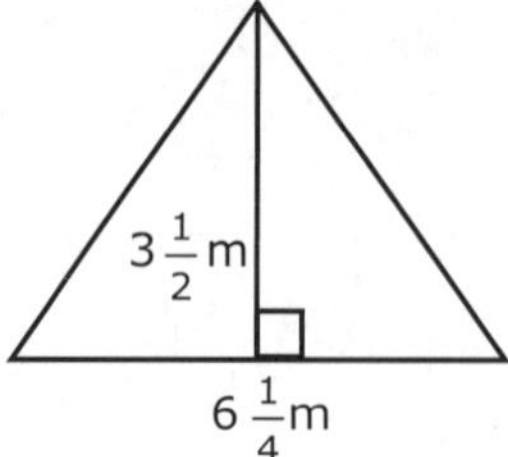

Area is about

____

Estimates
21 m^2
18 m^2
28 m^2
25 m^2
12 m^2

3

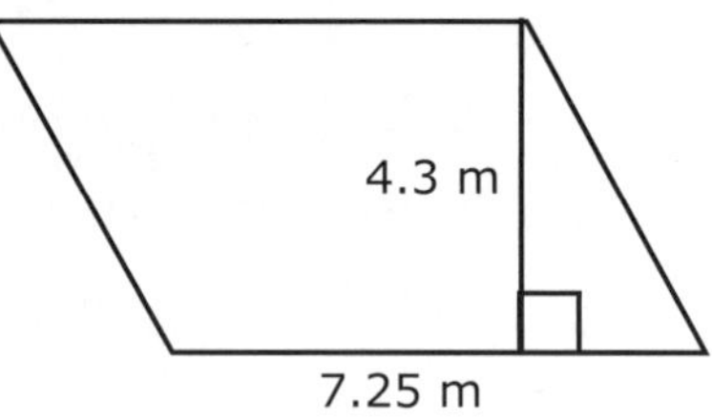

Area is about

____

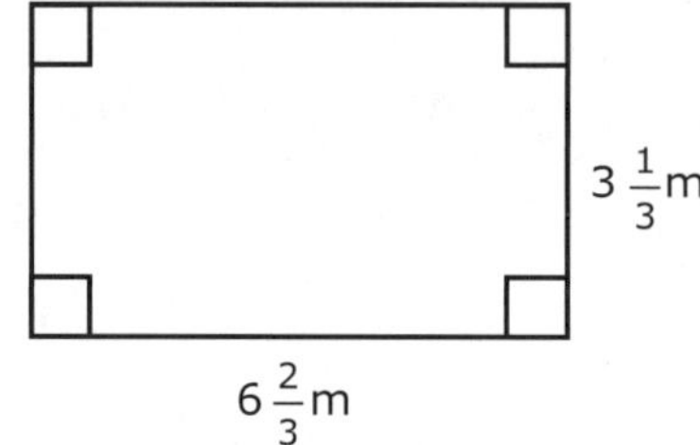

Area is about

____

Estimate the area of each figure.

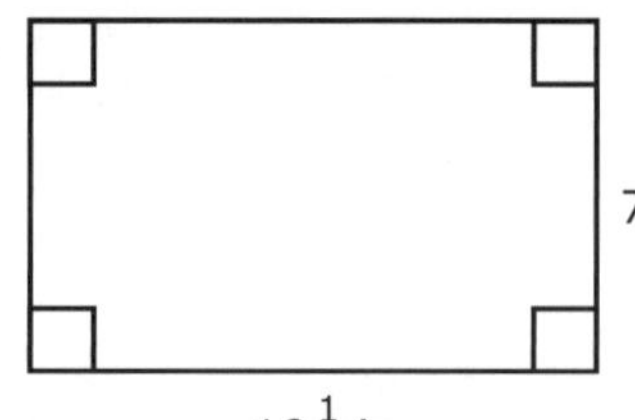

Area = __________

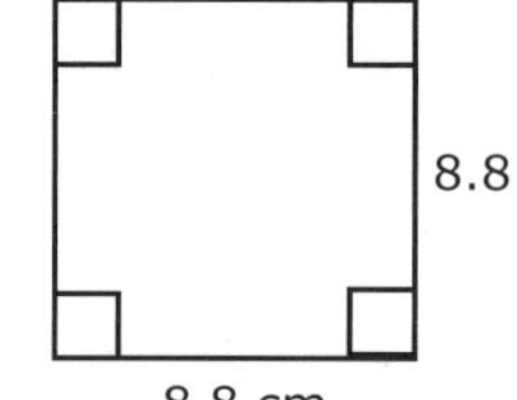

Area = __________

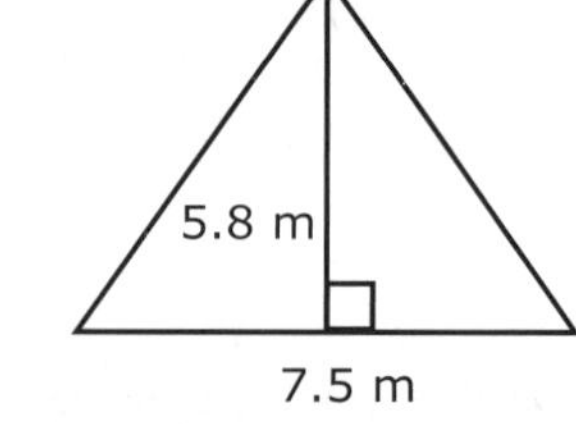

Area = __________

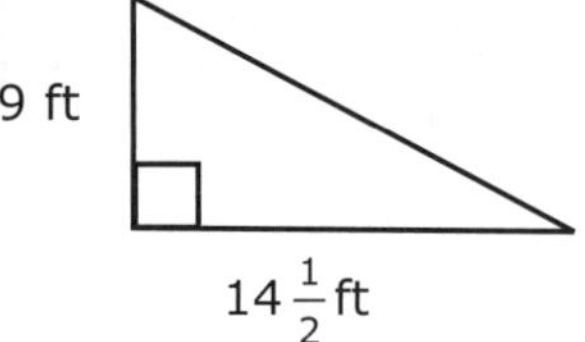

Area = __________

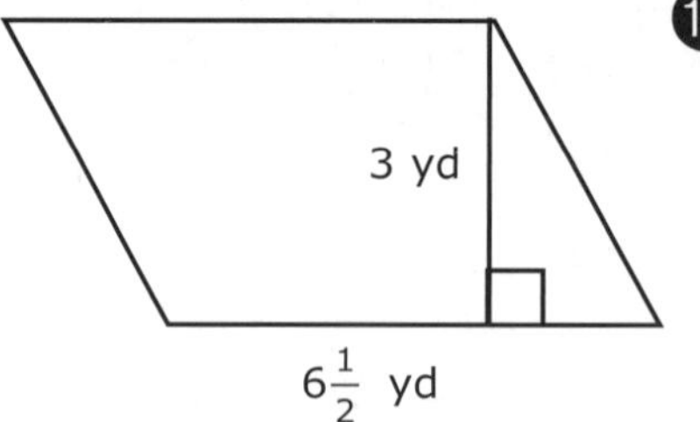

Area = __________

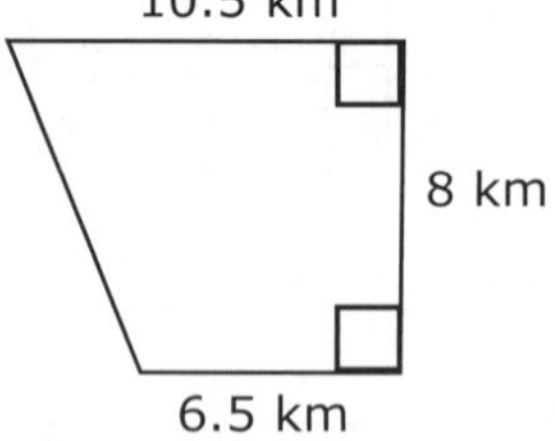

Area = __________

☆ **Tell why the area of a triangle is $\frac{1}{2}$ the area of a parallelogram.**

Name ______________________ **Date** __________

Solve.

1. Mrs. Orlando wants to carpet the floor of a rectangular room that is 14 feet long and 12 feet wide. How many square feet of carpet does she need to cover the floor?

2. Felix bought a new sail for his sailboat. The sail is a right triangle that has a height of 25 feet and base of 12 feet. About how many square yards of sailcloth were used to make the sail?

3. Find the area of the triangle below.

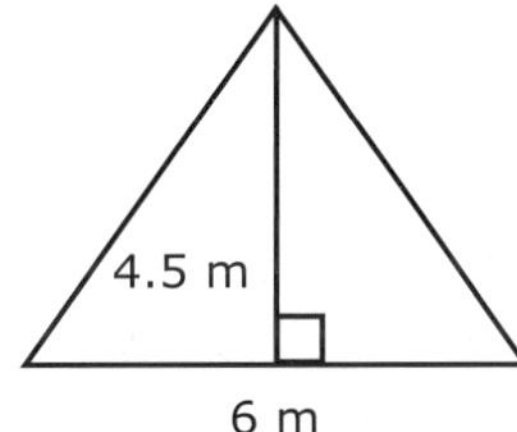

4. Estimate the area of the parallelogram below.

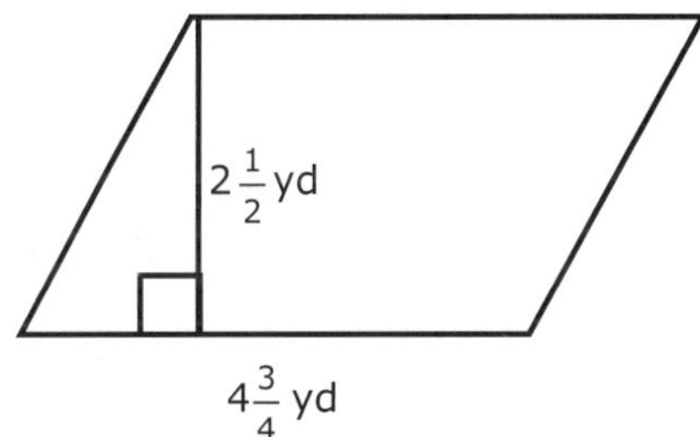

5. Estimate the area of a window that has a height of 64 inches and a width of 48 inches.

6. Find the area of a scalene triangle that has a height of 35 cm and a base of 72 cm.

Circle the letter for the correct answer.

7. Which is the best estimate for the area of the triangle?

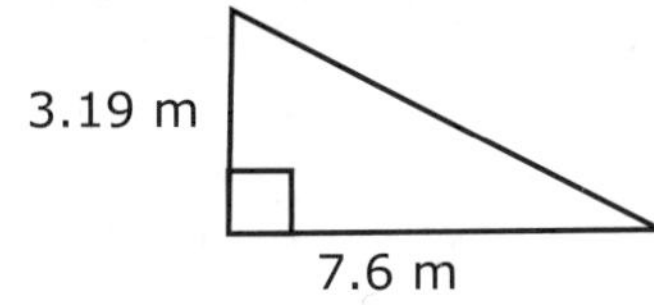

A 12 m^2
B 21 m^2
C 24 m^2
D 28 m^2

8. Which is the best estimate for the area of the quadrilateral?

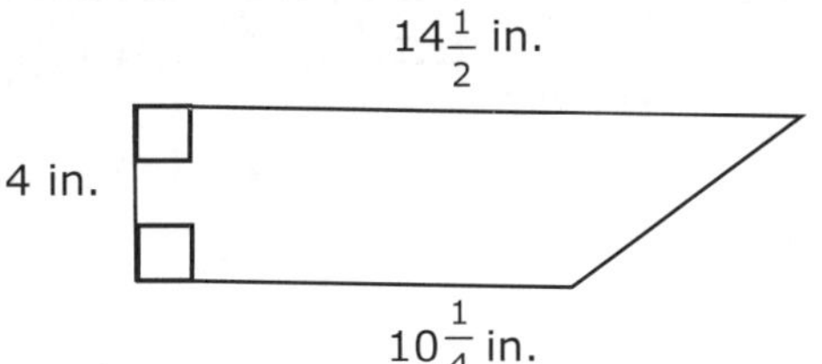

A 60 in.^{2}
B 40 in.^{2}
C 30 in.^{2}
D 50 in.^{2}

Unit 27 Mini-Lesson

Estimate and Find Volume

Standard

Expressions, Equations, and Relationships

6.8C (SS) Write equations that represent problems related to the area of rectangles, parallelograms, trapezoids, and triangles and volume of right rectangular prisms where dimensions are positive rational numbers.

6.8D (SS) Determine solutions for problems involving the area of rectangles, parallelograms, trapezoids, and triangles and volume of right rectangular prisms where dimensions are positive rational numbers.

Model the Skill

- **Say:** *We can find the volume of different solid or three-dimensional shapes in different ways. Today we are going to use formulas to find the volume of cubes and other rectangular prisms.*

$$V = l \times w \times h$$
or
$$V = \text{Area of base} \times h$$

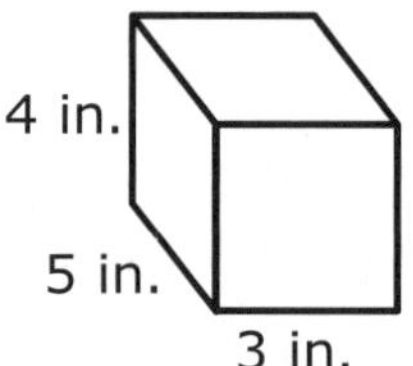

- **Say:** *Use the formula to find the volume of this rectangular prism. Remember, when we multiply to find the area, we multiply the unit x unit* (unit^2), *so we show our answer in square units. When we multiply to find volume, we multiply unit x unit x unit* (unit^3) *so therefore we show our answer in cubic units. What is the volume?* (60 cubic inches)

- Assign students the appropriate practice page(s) to support their understanding of the skill.

Assess the Skill

Use the following problems to pre-/post-assess students' understanding of the skill.

- Ask students to calculate the volume of these figures.

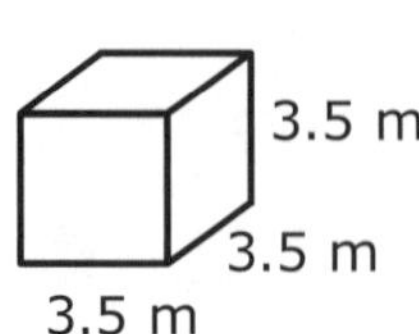

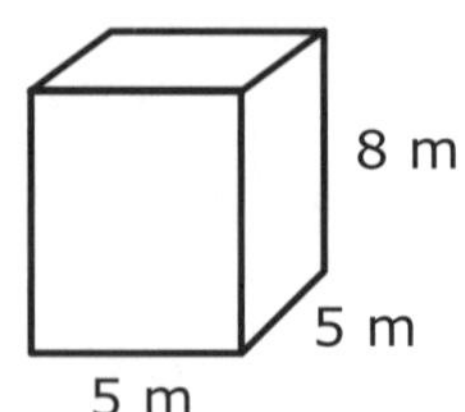

Name ______________________________ **Date** __________

Use the formula *V* = *bh* or *V* = *l* x *w* x *h* to find the volume of each.

1

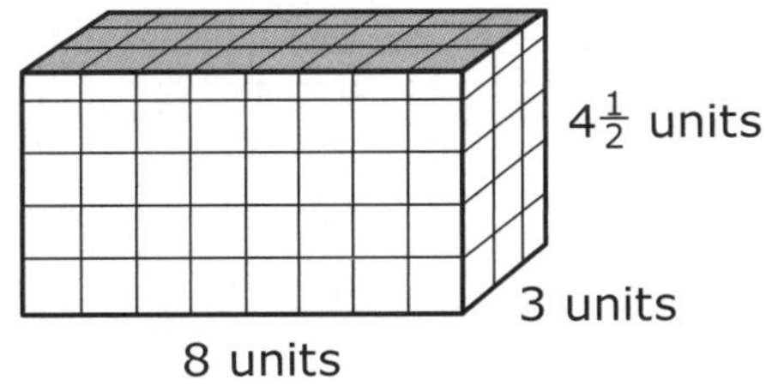

Area of base: 8 x 3 = _____ square units

Height: $4\frac{1}{2}$ units

$V = bh$

V = _____ x _____

V = _____ cubic units

2

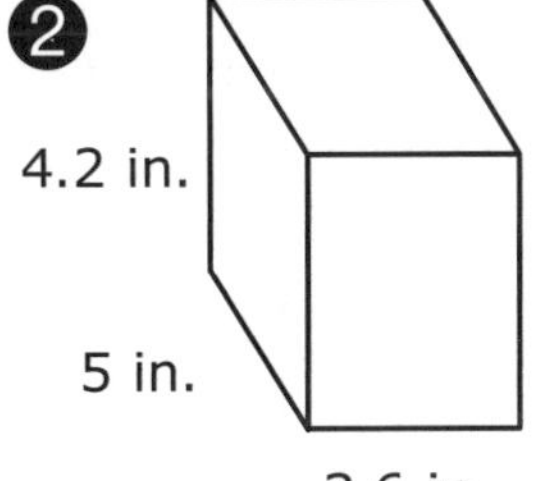

$V = l \times w \times h$

$V = bh$

V = _____ x _____ x _____

V = _____ cubic inches

3

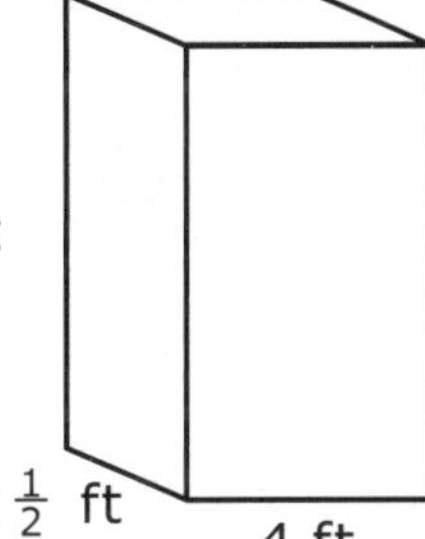

V = ______________

4

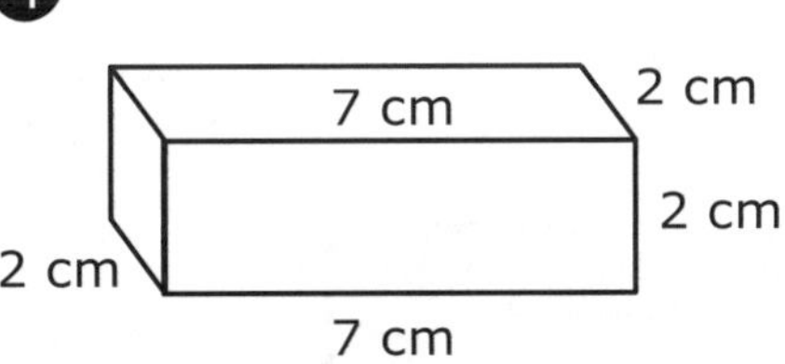

V = ______________

5

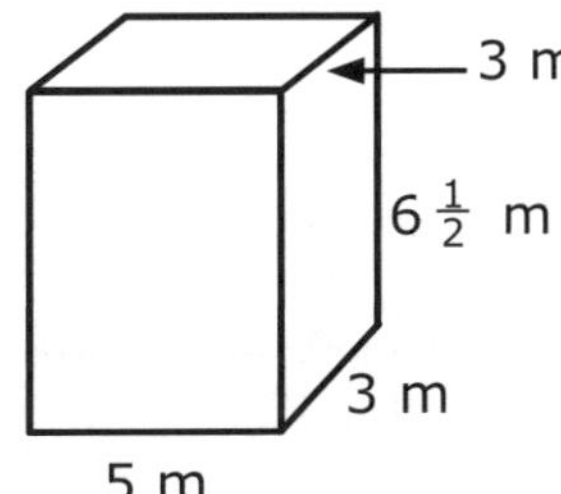

V = ______________

6

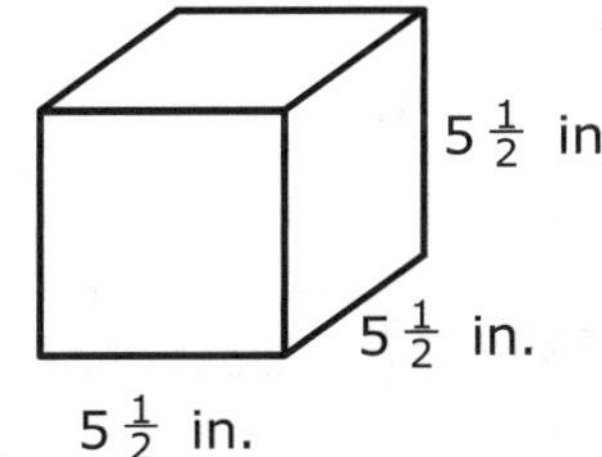

V = ______________

 A rectangular box 9.7 feet long, 6 feet wide, and 4 feet high

V = _____ cubic feet

 A cube $7\frac{1}{2}$ inches long

V = _____ cubic inches

 A rectangular box 11 feet long, 3 feet wide, and $5\frac{1}{2}$ feet high

V = _____ cubic feet

 **Tell which formula for finding volume you prefer to use. Tell why.**

Name ______________________________ **Date** __________

Use the formula $V = bh$ or $V = l \times w \times h$ to find the volume of each.

1. 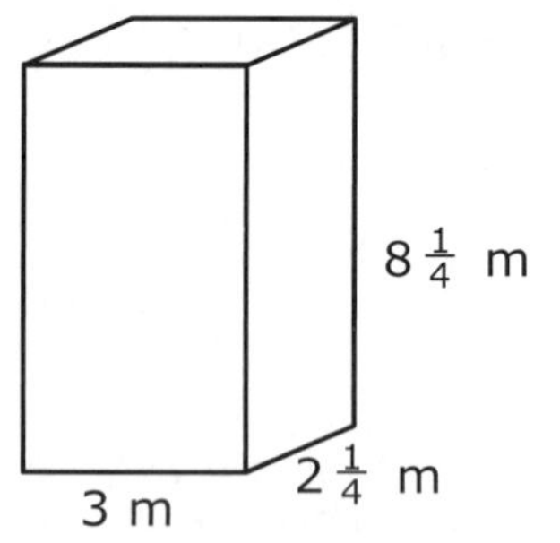

$V =$ ______________

2. 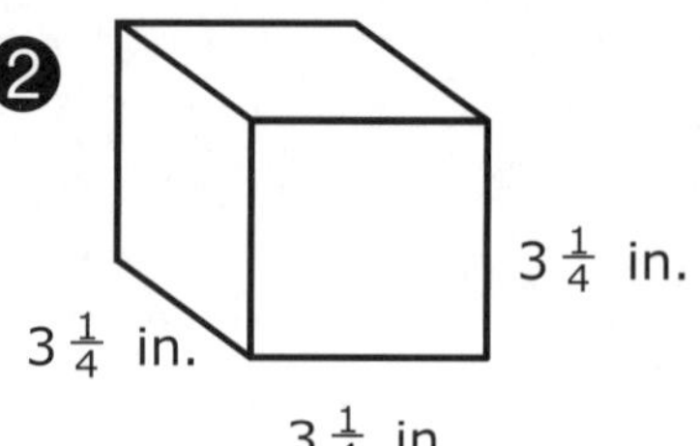

$V =$ ______________

3. 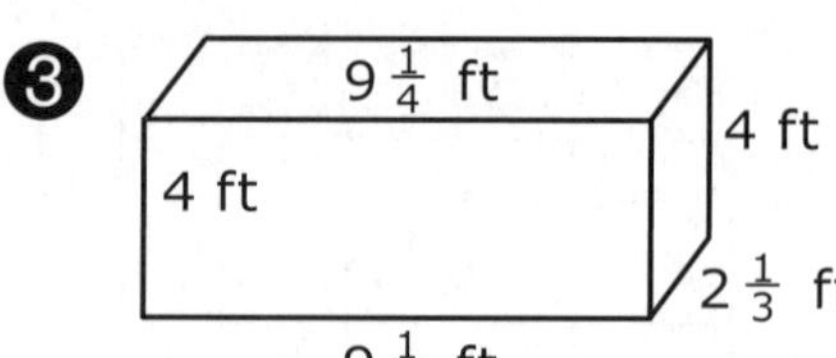

$V =$ ______________

4. 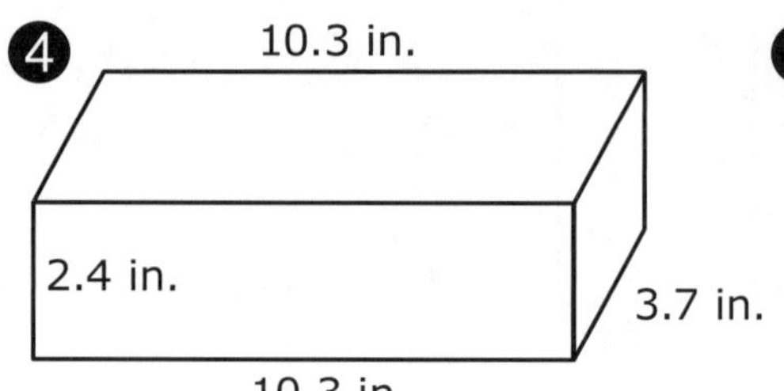

$V =$ ______________

5. 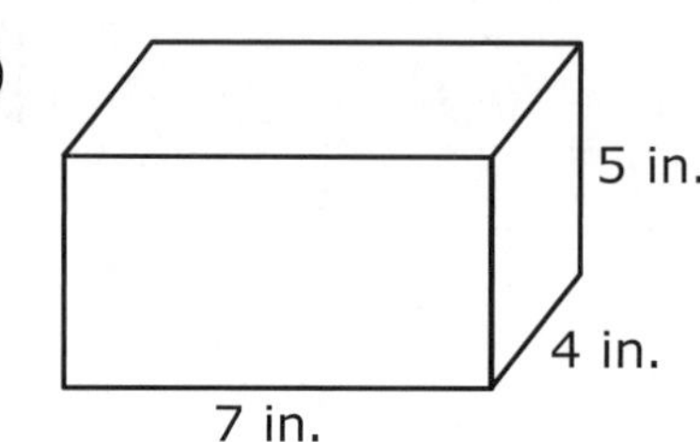

$V =$ ______________

6. 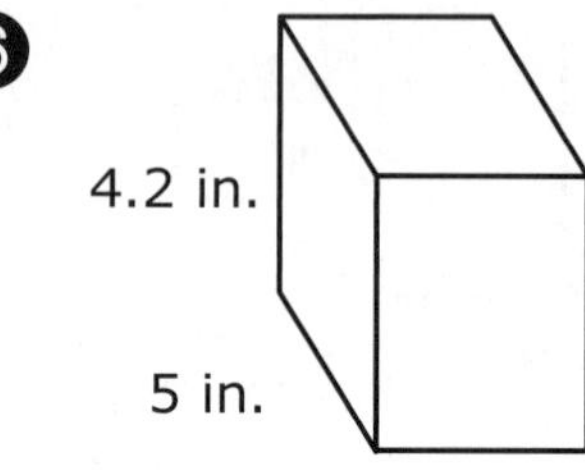

$V =$ ______________

7. 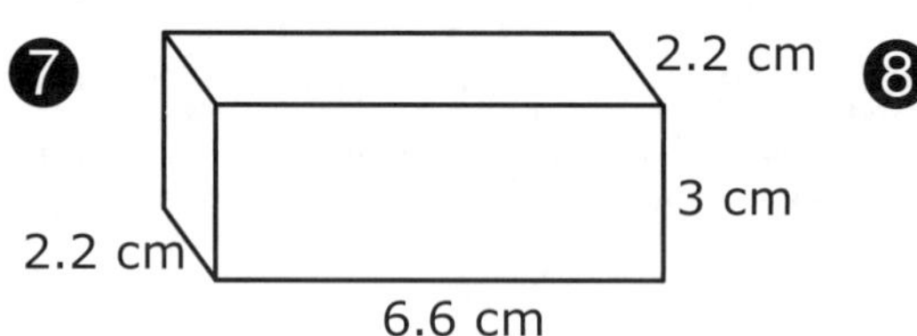

$V =$ ______________

8. 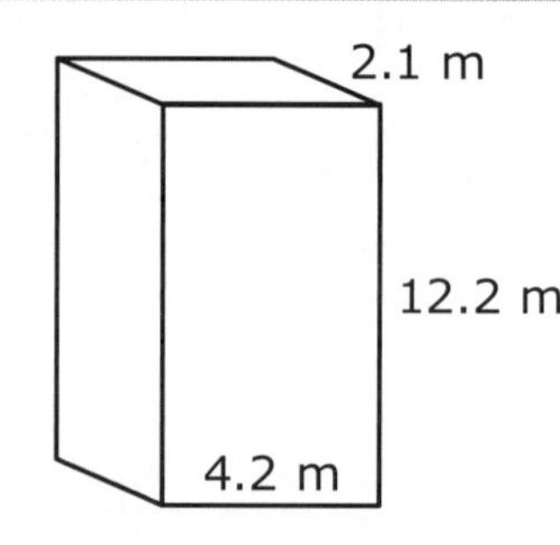

$V =$ ______________

9. 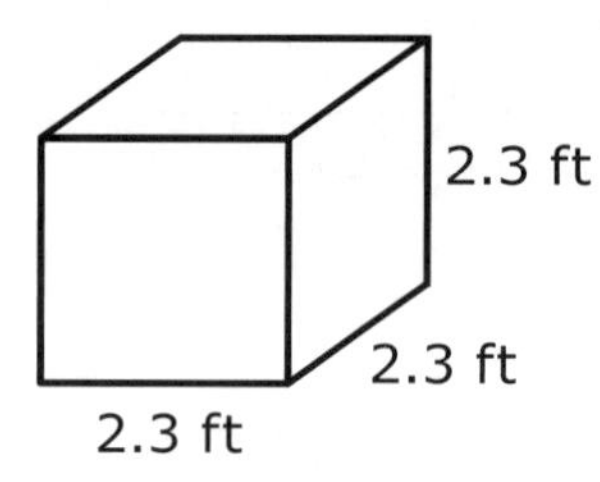

$V =$ ______________

10. A rectangular box 12.7 cm long, 7.1 cm wide, and 3 cm high

$V =$ _____ cubic cm

11. A cube $11\frac{1}{4}$ inches long

$V =$ _____ cubic inches

12. A rectangular box 9.8 feet long, 4 feet wide, and $2\frac{1}{2}$ feet high

$V =$ _____ cubic feet

Look at Problem 5. How would you change the dimensions of the box to double the volume? Explain.

Name ______________________________ **Date** __________

Solve.

1. A locker is 1 foot long, 1 foot wide, and $4\frac{1}{4}$ feet high. What is the volume of the locker?

2. The refrigerator came in a box that was 6 feet high, 3 feet wide, and $3\frac{1}{2}$ feet deep. What was the volume of the box?

3. A pizza box is 2 inches high, $16\frac{3}{4}$ inches wide, and $16\frac{3}{4}$ inches long. What is the volume of the pizza box?

4. The feeding trough is 4 meters long, 0.5 meters wide, and 0.25 meters high. What is the volume of the trough?

5. The fish tank is 40 centimeters wide, 100 centimeters long, and 60 centimeters deep. If 1 cubic centimeter is equal to 1 milliliter, how many milliliters of water will we need to fill the tank?

6. The reflection pool is 1 meter deep, 10 meters wide, and 20.5 meters long. What is the volume of the pool?

Circle the letter for the best answer.

7. A moving company sells boxes for packing. What is the volume of the box below?

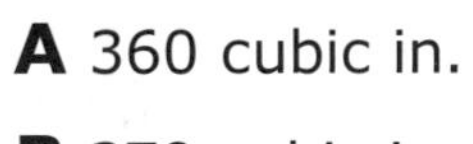

A 360 cubic in.

B 370 cubic in.

C 380 cubic in.

D 3,600 cubic in.

8. The suitcase is 50 centimeters long, 35 centimeters wide, and 20 centimeters deep. What is the volume of the suitcase?

A 350 cubic cm

B 3,500 cubic cm

C 35,000 cubic cm

D 350,000 cubic cm

Unit 28 Mini-Lesson
Use Lists and Tree Diagrams

Standard

Measurement and Data

6.12A (SS) Represent numeric data graphically, including dot plots, stem-and-leaf plots, histograms, and box plots.

6.13A (RS) Interpret numeric data summarized in dot plots, stem-and-leaf plots, histograms, and box plots.

Model the Skill

Draw two spinners on the board.

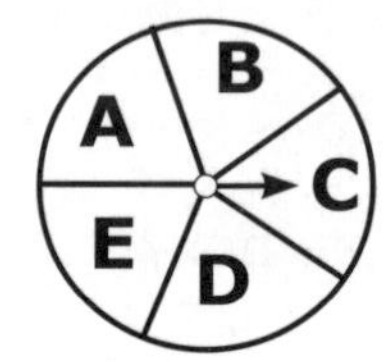

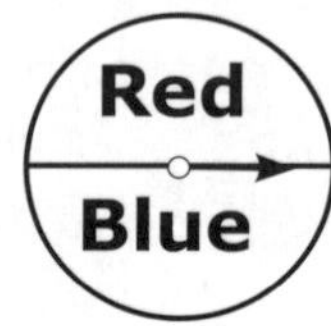

- **Ask:** *What are all the possible outcomes of spinning the first spinner one time?* (ABCDE) *How many possible outcomes is that?* (5) List the outcomes on the board. *What are all the possible outcomes of spinning the second spinner one time?* (red, blue) *How many possible outcomes is that?* (2)
- **Ask:** *What if we spin the first spinner and then the second spinner? How can we can show the outcomes from two different experiments?* Discuss how to write an organized list: red A, red B, . . . blue A, blue B, . . .
- **Say:** *Another way to show the outcomes from two different experiments, or* ***compound event****, is to make a tree diagram*. Construct a tree diagram on the board.
- **Ask:** *How many possible outcomes does the tree diagram show?* (10) Guide students to see that the number of possible outcomes listed for each spinner, when multiplied together, gives the number of possible outcomes shown by the tree diagram.
- Assign students the appropriate practice page(s) to support their understanding of the skill.

Assess the Skill

Use the following problems to pre-/post-assess students' understanding of the skill.

Have students list all the possible outcomes of each experiment, then make a tree diagram to show the outcomes for doing both experiments one time.

Tossing a number cube,
each face labeled 1, 2, 3, 4, 5, 6

Tossing a coin

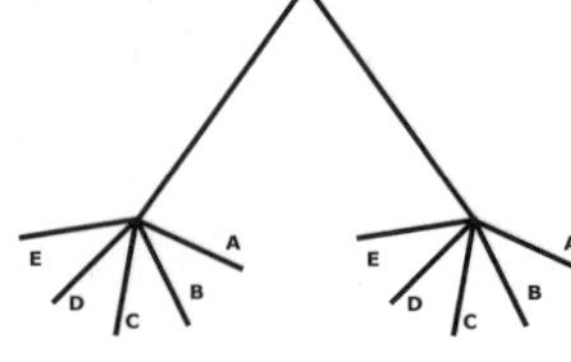

Name ______________________________ **Date** __________

Make a list for each.

1. What are the possible outcomes of spinning spinner I once?

   ____

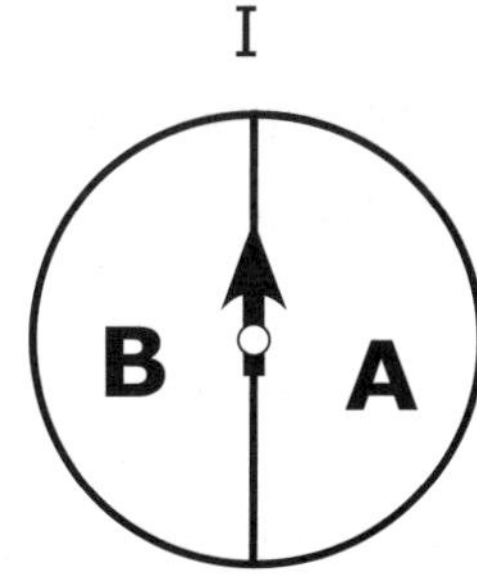

2. What are the possible outcomes of spinning spinner II once?

   ____

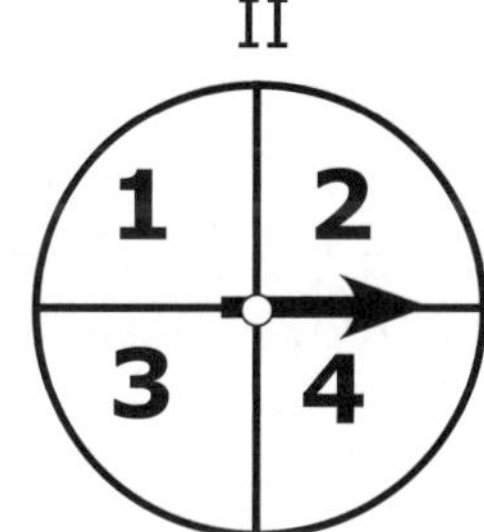

3. What are all the possible outcomes of spinning spinner I and spinner II one time?

   A1, A2, ____, ____, B1, ____, ____, ____

Complete the tree diagram for each compound event.

4. Spinning Spinner I and Spinner II once.

   What is the number of total outcomes?

   ____

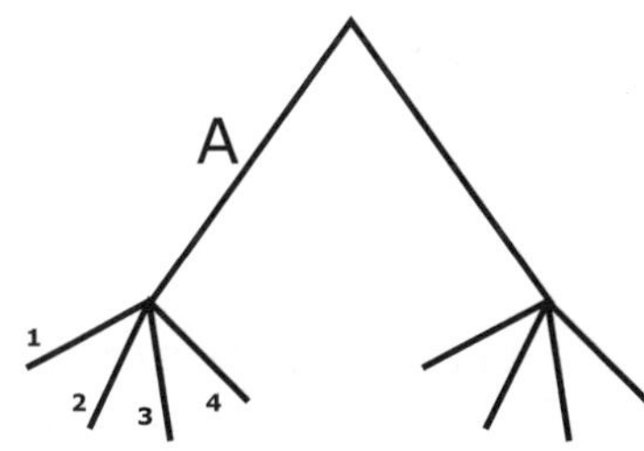

5. Tossing a coin twice.

   What is the number of total possible outcomes?

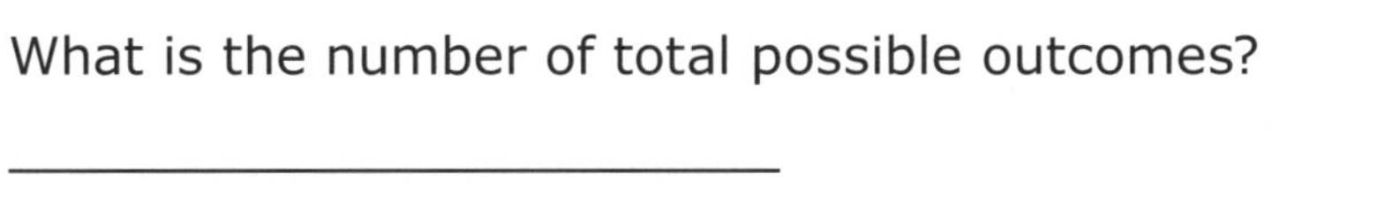

   ____

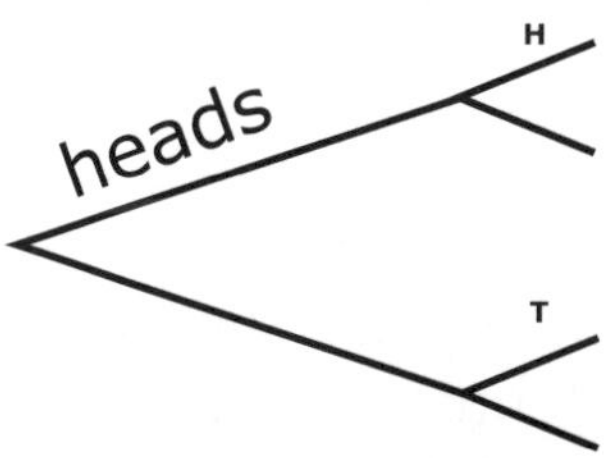

6. Showing the results of choosing at random among 3 sandwiches (tuna, egg, or cheese), and 2 fruits (apple or pear).

   What is the number of total possible outcomes?

   ____

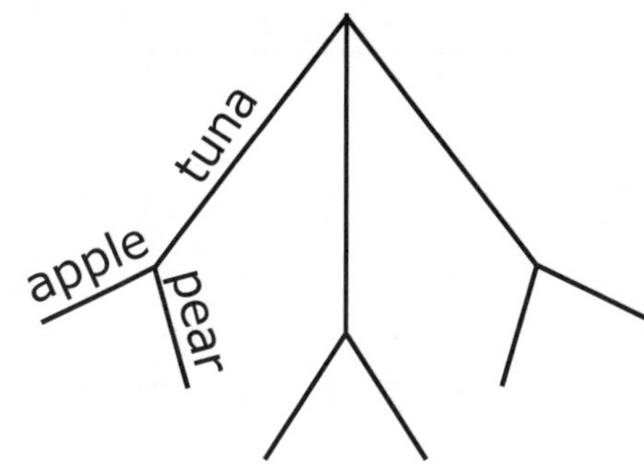

 **Tell what a compound event is.**

Name ______________________________ **Date** __________

Make a list for each.

❶ A number cube has the numbers 1–6 on its faces. What are the potential outcomes of tossing the number cube once?

____

❷ What are the outcomes of spinning the spinner once?

____

❸ What are all the possible outcomes of tossing the number cube and spinning the spinner one time?

____

❹ Without making a list, how can you tell how many outcomes are possible if the number cube is tossed twice?

____

Make a tree diagram for each compound event.

❺ Rolling a number cube numbered 1–6 twice. What is the number of total outcomes?

____

❻ Spinning a spinner twice on a color wheel with the primary colors red, blue, and yellow. What is the number of total possible outcomes?

____

❼ Showing the results of a person choosing at random among 4 breakfasts: pancakes, waffles, french toast, or cereal, and two juices: orange or apple. What is the number of total possible outcomes?

____

Tell the ways you can find the number of total possible outcomes for a compound event.

Name ______________________________ **Date** __________

Solve.

1. A bag of bows for gift wrapping has large and small bows in gold, silver, red, white, and blue. Make a tree diagram to show all possible outcomes of picking one bow at random.

2. A triangular pyramid with sides numbered 1–4 is tossed 3 times. Make a tree diagram to show all possible outcomes.

Circle the letter for the correct answer.

3. Which tree diagram shows the possible outcomes of a coin being tossed twice? Show the possible outcomes

A heads (H, H); heads (T, H)

B heads (H, T); tails (H, T)

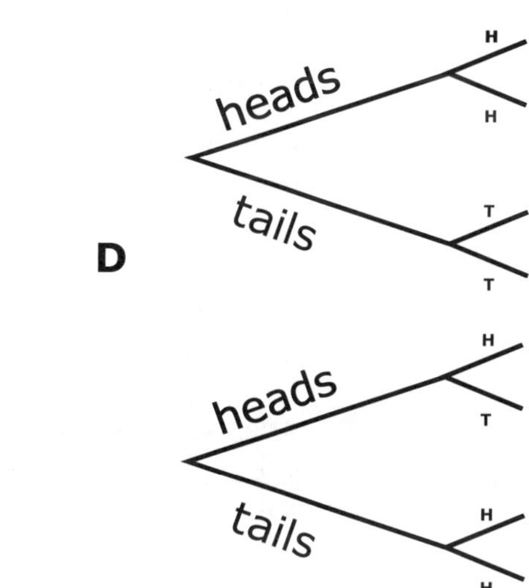

4. Which is NOT a possible outcome if you spin the spinners below one time?

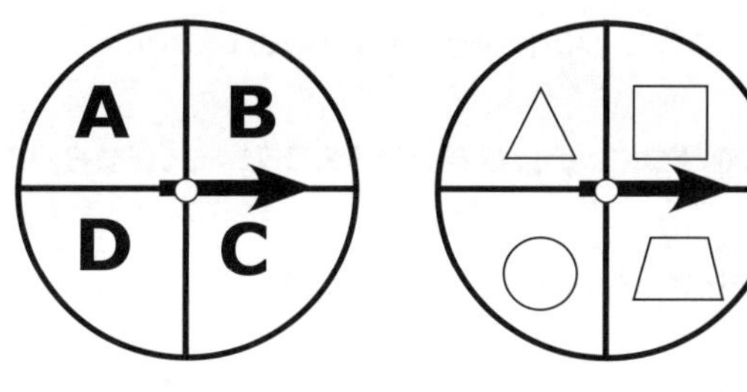

A A ○
B ○ □
C D △
D D ⏢

Unit 29 Mini-Lesson
Find Probability

Standard

Measurement and Data

6.12A (SS) Represent numeric data graphically, including dot plots, stem-and-leaf plots, histograms, and box plots.

6.13A (RS) Interpret numeric data summarized in dot plots, stem-and-leaf plots, histograms, and box plots.

Model the Skill

Draw this spinner on the board.

- **Say:** *We find the probability of an event by writing a ratio. Remember how we listed all the outcomes of an experiment?* Write *P* (*E*) = the number of favorable outcomes/number of possible outcomes on the board.
- **Ask:** *What are the possible outcomes of the spinner on the board?* (QRST) *How many possible outcomes are there?* (4)
- **Ask:** *So if Q is the outcome we want, or the favorable outcome, what is the probability of the spinner stopping on Q?* (1:4) As you write P (Q) = $\frac{1}{4}$, read the equation, the probability of Q is 1 out of 4, or one-fourth.
- **Ask:** *What is the probability of the spinner stopping on Q, R, S, or T?* ($\frac{4}{4}$ or 1)
- *What is the probability of the spinner NOT landing on Q?* ($\frac{3}{4}$) Discuss the idea that the probability of an event occurring falls between 0, impossible to happen, and 1, certain to happen. So if *P* (*Q*) = $\frac{1}{4}$, then *P* (not *Q*) = $\frac{3}{4}$. Think 1 – $\frac{1}{4}$.
- Assign students the appropriate practice page(s) to support their understanding of the skill.

Assess the Skill

Use the following problems to pre-/post-assess students' understanding of the skill.

Have students find the probability for each event.

P (4) = __________ *P* (not 4) __________

P (*H*) = __________ *P* (not *H*) __________

Name ______________________________ **Date** __________

Solve.

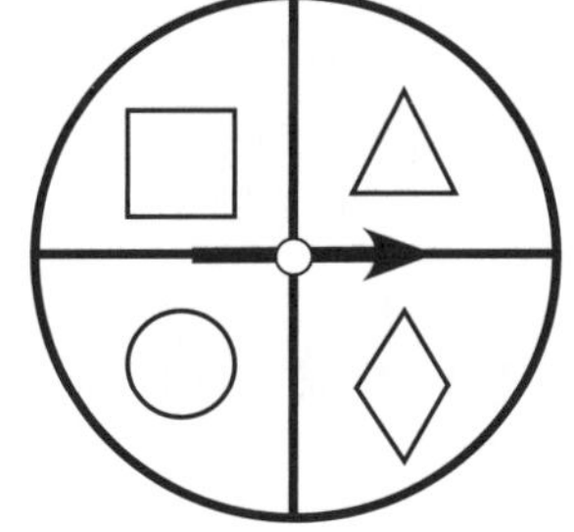

1. What are the outcomes of spinning the spinner once?

   ____

2. How many possible outcome are there?

   ____

3. What is the probability of the spinner stopping on △?

   P (△) = ________

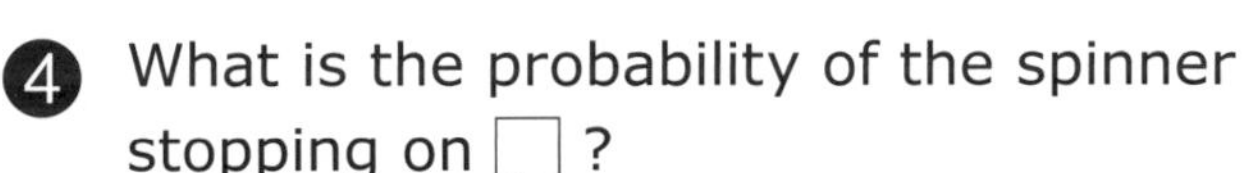

4. What is the probability of the spinner stopping on □ ?

   P (□) = ________

5. What is the probability of the spinner NOT stopping on □ ?

   P (not □) = ________

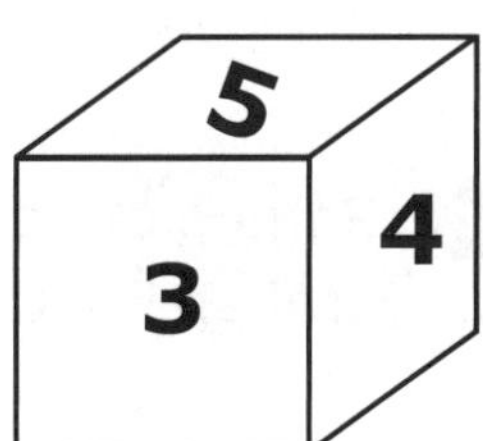

A number cube has the numbers 1–6 on its faces.
If the number cube is tossed once, what is the probability of:

6. tossing 1?

   P (1) = ________

7. tossing 4?

   P (4) = ________

8. NOT tossing 5?

   P (not 5) = ________

9. tossing an odd number?

   P (odd number) = ________

10. tossing an even number?

    P (even number) = ________

11. tossing a number less than 3?

    P (number less than 3) = ________

 **Tell what number represents a certain event. Explain.**

Name ______________________________ **Date** __________

Use the spinner to find the probability for each event.

1. P (9) ________
2. P (even number) ________
3. P (composite number) ________
4. P (divisible by 3) ________
5. P (2-digit number) ________
6. P (factor of 10) ________
7. P (1-digit number) ________
8. P (not divisible by 6) ________

Solve.

9. A bag is filled with 20 doughnuts. If a doughnut is selected at random, the probability of choosing a jelly doughnut is $\frac{7}{20}$. How many doughnuts in the bag are jelly doughnuts? How many are not jelly doughnuts? ____________

10. Sofia picks a card on the right without looking. What is the probability that she will pick the star? ________

11. What is the probability that Sofia will pick a fruit? ________

12. Riley has 4 books to read this vacation. One is a realistic fiction novel, one is a historical novel, one is a sci-fi adventure, and one is a nonfiction book about space exploration. If he reads them in any order, what is the probability that he will read a nonfiction book first?

13. What is the probability that he will read a fiction book first?

If the probability of rain is $\frac{2}{3}$, tell what the probability is of no rain. Why?

Name ______________________________ **Date** __________

Solve. Use the spinner for Problems 1–4.

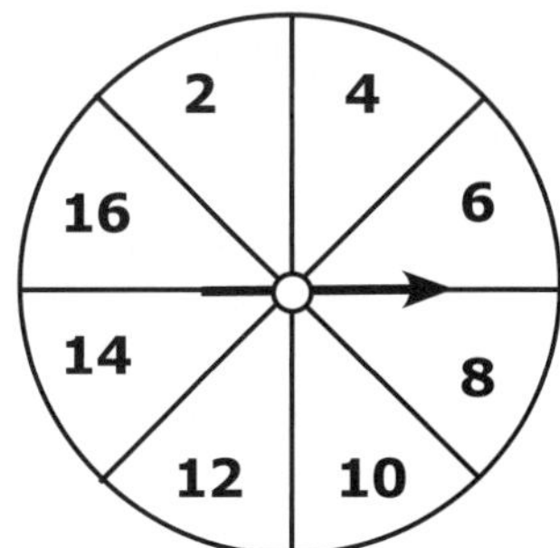

1. What is the probability that the spinner will stop on an even number?

2. What is the probability that the spinner will stop on a prime number?

3. What is the probability that the spinner will stop on a 1-digit number?

4. What is the probability that the spinner will stop on a 2-digit number twice in a row?

Circle the letter for the correct answer.

5. Dan downloads 15 songs on his phone. Seven songs are country music and the rest are hip-hop. If Dan plays a song at random, which expression represents the probability that the song he plays will be hip-hop?

   A $1 + \frac{7}{15}$

   B $1 + \frac{8}{15}$

   C $1 - \frac{8}{15}$

   D $1 - \frac{7}{15}$

6. If Dan's phone plays music in a random shuffle and never plays the same song twice in a row, which expression represents the probability that the phone will play 2 different country songs in a row?

   A $\frac{7}{15} + \frac{6}{15}$

   B $\frac{7}{15} \times \frac{6}{15}$

   C $\frac{8}{15} - \frac{7}{15}$

   D $\frac{7}{15} \div \frac{6}{15}$

Unit 30 Mini-Lesson

Find Mean, Median, and Mode

Standard

Measurement and Data

6.12C (RS) Summarize numeric data with numerical summaries, including the mean and median (measures of center) and the range and interquartile range (IQR) (measures of spread), and use these summaries to describe the center, spread, and shape of the data distribution.

6.12D (RS) Summarize categorical data with numerical and graphical summaries, including the mode, the percent of values in each category (relative frequency table), and the percent bar graph, and use these summaries to describe the data distribution.

Model the Skill

Write the following definitions on the board, followed by the data set below.

Mean: the average; the sum of all the data divided by the number of data

Median: the middle number in an ordered set of data

Mode: the number that occurs most often in a set of data (there can be more than one mode or no mode)

- **Say:** *Today we are going to be finding the mean, median, and mode for different data sets. What is the mean?* (The mean is the sum of all the data, divided by the number of data.)
- Assign students the appropriate practice page(s) to support their understanding of the skill. Remind students to check and recheck their work.

Assess the Skill

Use the following problems to pre-/post-assess students' understanding of the skill.

- Ask students to find the mean, mode, and median for the following data sets:

$50, $35, $50, $25, $30   **130, 142, 134, 140, 134, 133, 135**

Name ______________________________ **Date** __________

Mean (average): the sum of all the data divided by the number of the data
Median: the middle number in a set of data when the data are arranged in order
Mode: the number that occurs most often in a set of data (there can be more than one mode or no mode)

Find the mean, median, or mode for each data set.

1 Weekly earnings of 5 dog walkers:
$48, $35, $50, $27, $25

(____ + ____ + ____ + ____ + ____) ÷ ____

Mean = $________

$25, _____, _____, _____, _____

Median = $________

Think: Order the data to find the middle number.

2 Monthly rainfall (in inches):
1, 0, 3, 0.5, 0.5, 1

Mean = ________

Median = ________

Remember: When there are two middle numbers, the median is the average of the two.

3 Annual snowfall (in inches):
20, 16, 20, 17.5, 19.5, 18, 23

Mean = ________ Median = ________

4 Foreign-language class sizes (students):
21, 20, 24, 22, 22, 22, 16

Mean = ________ Median = ________

5 Math test scores (in points):
100, 90, 72, 95, 85, 83, 89, 81, 86, 93, 98

Mean = ________ Median = ________

6 Goals per soccer game:
4, 3, 1, 1, 2, 2, 3, 3, 2

Mean = ________ Median = ________

7 Daily low temperatures (°F):
19, 20, 18, 19, 17, 30, 17, 19

Mode(s) = ________________

8 Marathon times (in hours):
3.0, 3.5, 3.75, 4.25, 4.0, 3.75, 4.25, 4.5

Mode(s) = ________________

9 Weekly babysitting earnings:
$25, $20, $25, $35, $27, $30

Mean = ________
Median = ________
Mode(s) = ________

10 Monthly electric bill:
$195, $207, $203, $245, $237, $211

Mean = ________
Median = ________
Mode(s) = ________

A newspaper reports the median house price is $250,000. From that standard, tell what you know about housing prices.

Name ______________________________ **Date** __________

Use the report on the right to find the mean, median, and mode of the test scores for each student.

Math Test Scores Report

Scott: 75, 52, 80, 88, 100

Olivia: 98, 92, 88, 92, 95

Gemma: 84, 92, 85, 73, 86

Chris: 88, 86, 93, 88, 90

1. Scott
   Mean = ________
   Median = ________
   Mode = ________

2. Olivia
   Mean = ________
   Median = ________
   Mode = ________

3. Gemma
   Mean = ________
   Median = ________
   Mode = ________

4. Chris
   Mean = ________
   Median = ________
   Mode = ________

Find the mean, median, and mode for each data set.

5. Monthly rainfall (in inches):
   1, 0, 2, 0.5, 0.25, 3, 0.25
   Mean = ________ Median = ________
   Mode(s) = ________

6. July 4th temperatures (°F):
   89, 94, 96, 99, 96, 97, 95, 92
   Mean = ________ Median = ________
   Mode(s) = ________

7. Baby sleep log (in hours):
   10, 8, 9, 8, 8.25, 9.25, 8.5
   Mean = ________ Median = ________
   Mode(s) = ________

8. Daily running log (in kilometers):
   3.5, 0, 2.5, 5, 2.5, 3, 4.5
   Mean = ________ Median = ________
   Mode(s) = ________

9. Reading log (in pages):
   21, 42, 25, 45, 37, 34, 30
   Mean = ________ Median = ________
   Mode(s) = ________

10. Monthly snowfall (in inches):
    0.5, 2, 5, 0.25, 1
    Mean = ________ Median = ________
    Mode(s) = ________

Look at your answers for Problems 1–4. Which measure best describes the students' test scores? Explain.

Name ______________________________ **Date** ________

Solve.

1. Sanjay has 6 math test scores. They are 83, 80, 88, 86, 88, 70. What is the median score?

2. For the first week of December, the daily low temperatures (°F) were 36, 40, 38, 41, 40, 32, 34. What was the mode?

3. Rachel ran 5 miles every day last week. Her running time was as follows: 39 min, 42 min, 41 min, 38 min, 39 min, 39 min, 42 min. What was her mean running time for 5 miles?

4. Ms. Krill's ten honor students scored the following grades on the pop quiz: 83, 90, 98, 96, 88, 98, 95, 97, 98, 100. What is the mode score?

5. On the bike trip, we rode 10 kilometers on Day 1, 18 kilometers on Day 2, 20 kilometers on Day 3, 15 kilometers on Day 4, and 18 kilometers on Day 5. What was the median distance we rode?

6. The rainfall for the second week in April was as follows (in inches): 1, 0, 2.5, 0.4, 0.8, 3, 0. What was the mean daily rainfall that week?

Circle the letter for the correct answer.

7. What is the mean of the data set 20, 12, 18, 25, 20?

   A 20
   B 19
   C 18
   D 13

8. What is the mean of the data set 112, 120, 114, 113, 118, 115, 113?

   A 113
   B 114
   C 115
   D 120

Unit 31 Mini-Lesson

Make and Interpret Dot Plots

Standard

Measurement and Data

6.12C (RS) Summarize numeric data with numerical summaries, including the mean and median (measures of center) and the range and interquartile range (IQR) (measures of spread), and use these summaries to describe the center, spread, and shape of the data distribution.

6.12D (RS) Summarize categorical data with numerical and graphical summaries, including the mode, the percent of values in each category (relative frequency table), and the percent bar graph, and use these summaries to describe the data distribution.

6.13A (RS) Interpret numeric data summarized in dot plots, stem-and-leaf plots, histograms, and box plots.

Model the Skill

- **Say:** *Today we are using data to make dot plots. A dot plot is like a line plot, but with dots instead of X's. Look at the data.* Explain how you could show this information. Draw the following dot plot and data on the board.

Class Survey

How many sports do you play?

0, 2, 1, 3, 1, 2, 0, 3, 2,
2, 1, 2, 1, 0, 2, 1

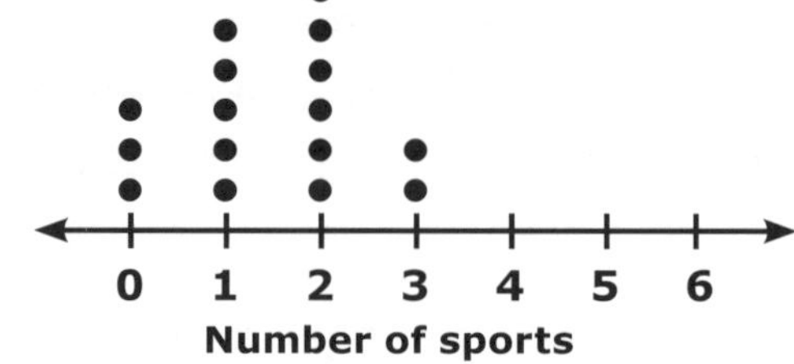

- Guide students to use the data to complete the dot plot. **Ask:** How is it useful to represent data in this way? (Shows results in a clear, organized, visual way)
- Assign students the appropriate practice page(s) to support their understanding of the skill.

Assess the Skill

Use the following problems to pre-/post-assess students' understanding of the skill.

- Ask students to conduct their own class survey asking questions such as shoe size, height, number of siblings, etc., and then use their survey result data to make a dot plot.

Name ______________________________ Date __________

Use the dot plot to answer each question.

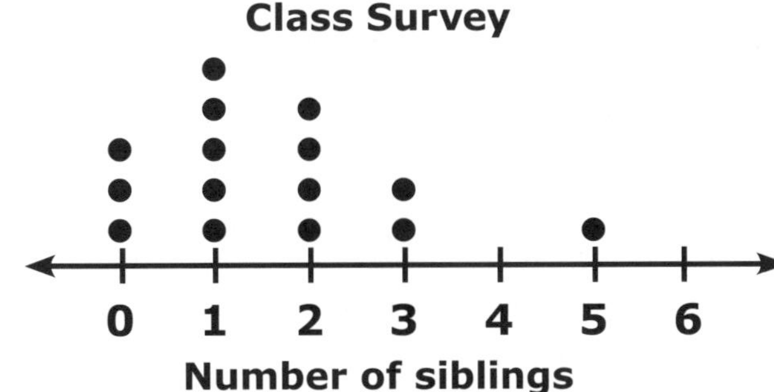

1. How many students participated in the survey? ________

   Think: Each dot represents one student.

2. What is the range of the data? ________

   Think: Subtract the least number from the greatest number (5–0). The difference is the range.

3. What is the mode of the data? ________

4. What is the median of the data? ________

Use the data to make a dot plot. Then answer each question.

5. **Class Survey**

   How many sports do you play?

   3, 2, 3, 4, 4, 1, 0, 2, 2,
   3, 0, 2, 1, 4, 2

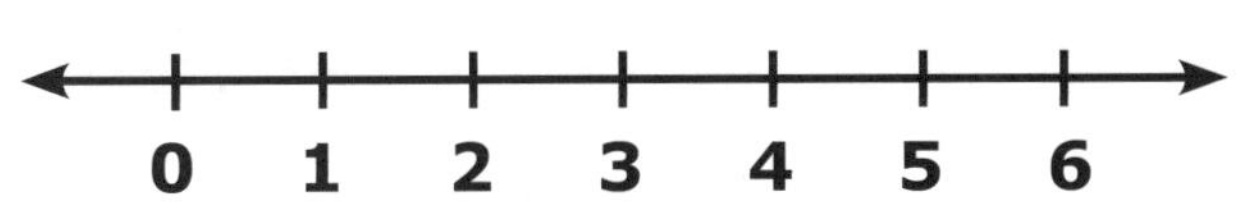

6. How many dots should you place above 3 on the number line? ________

7. What number occurs most frequently? ________

8. How many students participated in the survey? ________

9. What is the mean of the data? ________

Look at Problem 4. Tell how you found the median. Use the median to make a statement about the data: "The survey shows . . ."

Name ______________________________ Date ________

Use the dot plot to answer each question.

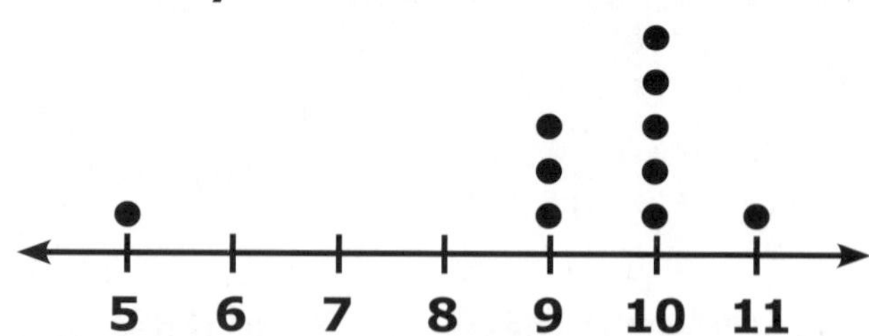

1. What is the range of the data?
   ____

2. What is the median of the data?
   ____

3. What is the mode of the data?
   ____

4. Of the three measures above, which describes the data best? Why?
   ____

Use the data to make a line plot. Then answer each question.

Class Survey

How many hours do you study?

6, 2, 5, 4, 4, 1, 2, 2,
3, 5, 2, 1, 5, 2

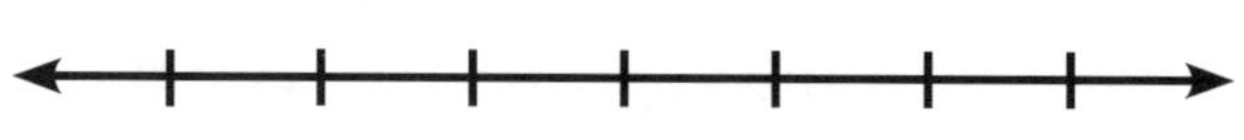

5. What number occurs most frequently?
   ____

6. What is the mode of the data? ________

7. What is the mean of the data? ________

8. What is the range of the data? ________

9. What is the median of the data?
   ____

10. Of the measures above, which describes the data best? Why?
    ____
    ____

What is the average number of hours spent studying according to the survey data at the top of the page? Explain how you found the mean.

Name ______________________________ **Date** __________

Solve. Use the dot plot.

Sam's Math Quiz Scores

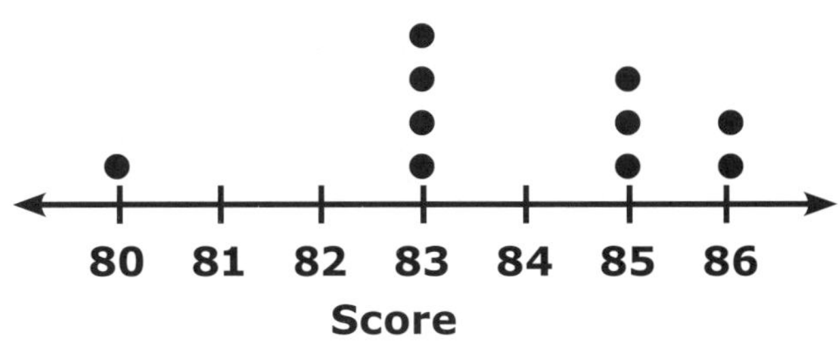

1. What is the range of scores on Sam's math quizzes? __________

2. What is the mode? __________

3. What is the median score? __________

Cedar Circle Household Size

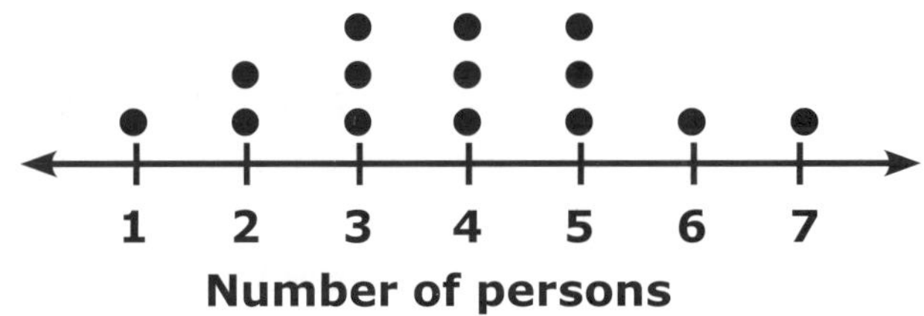

4. What is the mean household size on Cedar Circle? __________

5. What are the modes? __________

6. What is the median? __________

Circle the letter for the correct answer.

7. Which statement is true based on the data in the line plot?

22 23 24 25 26 27 28 29 30 31

Class size at Kennedy School

A Class size ranges from 22 to 31.

B Half of the classes have 26 students.

C The most common class size is 28.

D The median class size is 25.

8. Which statement is false based on the data in the line plot?

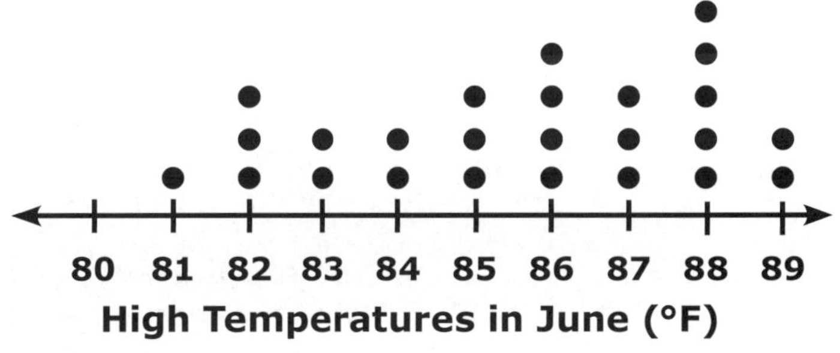

A The temperature in June ranges from 80 to 89.

B The least common temperature in June is 81.

C The most common high temperature is 88.

D The median temperature is 86.

Unit 32 Mini-Lesson

Make and Interpret Stem-and-Leaf Plots

Standard

Measurement and Data

6.12C (RS) Summarize numeric data with numerical summaries, including the mean and median (measures of center) and the range and interquartile range (IQR) (measures of spread), and use these summaries to describe the center, spread, and shape of the data distribution.

6.12D (RS) Summarize categorical data with numerical and graphical summaries, including the mode, the percent of values in each category (relative frequency table), and the percent bar graph, and use these summaries to describe the data distribution.

Model the Skill

Write the following data and draw a stem-and-leaf plot on the board.

Wellness Clinic
Baby weight at 12 months (lb)
17, 19, 20, 18, 18, 21, 19, 23, 21, 19, 22

Stem	Leaf
1	7 8 8 9
	9 9
2	

- **Say:** *Today we are going to use place value to create a stem-and-leaf plot. Here is some data from a health clinic about the weight of babies that the doctors saw one day.*
- **Ask:** *What does the stem represent?* (represents ten; the data has 2 digits) *What does the leaf represent?* (ones) *What number is 1 | 9?* (19)
- **Ask:** *What should we write for leaves for the stem 2?* (0, 1, 1, 2, 3) *What number is 2 | 0?* (20) Point out that the data is displayed in order by place value and from least to greatest, the last digit of the number being the leaf.
- **Say:** *It is easy to see the range of data, and the mode. We have to count to find the median.* Have students look at the plot and tell range (23 – 17 = 6), mode (19), and median (19), then interpret the data with those measures.
- Assign students the appropriate practice page(s) to support their understanding of the skill.

Assess the Skill

Use the following problems to pre-/post-assess students' understanding of the skill.

Have students create a stem-and-leaf plot with the following data, then tell range, median, and mode.

Test Scores

93, 90, 72, 85, 67, 85, 90, 98, 88, 87, 90, 75, 78, 89, 95

Name ______________________________ Date __________

Use the data to complete each stem-and-leaf plot. Then answer each question.

1

Points Scored				
TEAM RED				
34	12	15	28	7
15	22	25	15	30
12	27	26	32	15

Stem	Leaf
0	7
1	2 2 5
2	

2 How many points did Team Red score most often?

____

3 Did Team Red usually score more than 22 points? Explain.

____

4

Cookie Sales by Store			
Number of Boxes Sold in One Week			
205	215	217	209
220	216	225	207
213	220	223	

Stem	Leaf
20	5
21	
22	

5 How many stores are there?

____

6 What is the most common number of boxes sold?

____

7 Which sales figures are in the bottom half?

____

8 What is the range in sales?

____

Tell how you organize data in a stem-and-leaf plot.

Name ______________________________ Date __________

Display the data in a stem-and-leaf plot. Then answer each question.

1.

Mr. B's Math Class Final Exam Test Scores				
85	90	82	85	100
95	78	70	100	98
92	85	99		

Stem	Leaf

2. How many students took the exam?

____

3. What is the range in test scores?

____

4. What score was achieved by the greatest number of students? ____________

5. How many students scored above the median score? ____________

6. If the average score is 89, how many students scored above average?

____

7.

Mary Jo's Bagel Shop				
SUNDAY'S ORDERS, 6 A.M. – 7 A.M.				
12	6	12	13	18
24	6	6	12	12
12	13	12	8	6
12	8	6	10	24

Stem	Leaf

8. How many orders did the bagel shop get on Sunday between 6 and 7 A.M.?

____

9. Which amount represents the mode?

____

10. How many orders were greater than a dozen?

____

11. What was the range of the orders?

____

Tell how you find median and mode on a stem-and-leaf plot.

Name ________________________________ **Date** __________

Solve.

1 What is the range, median, and mode of the data?

Stem	Leaf
0	6 8
1	0 5 5 8
3	2 4 6

range __________
median __________
mode __________

2 Use the data to complete the stem-and-leaf plot.

Ms. T's Bus Route Trip Times (in minutes)		
25	27	28
30	22	31
32	27	25
28	28	40

Stem	Leaf

3 What is the range of the data?

4 What is the mode of the data?

5 What is the median of the data?

6 How many times did the bus trip take more than a half hour?

Circle the letter for the correct answer.

7 The stem-and-leaf plot below shows the points scored by the football team so far this season.

Stem	Leaf
0	7 7
1	2 4
2	1 1 1 4 7

Which statement is *not* supported by the information in the stem-and-leaf plot?

A Most frequently, the team scored 21 pounds

B The team never scored more than 20 points above its lowest score.

C The team won more games than it lost.

D The team has played 9 games so far this season.

8 Which stem-and-leaf plot accurately represents the data below?

Pecan Tree Height (feet)				
30	22	25	38	47
31	34	35	45	40
32	27	36	32	25

A

Stem	Leaf
2	2 5
3	0 1 2 5 6 8
4	0 5

B

Stem	Leaf
2	2 5 7
3	0 1 2 5 6 8
4	0 5

C

Stem	Leaf
2	2 5 7
3	0 1 2 2 5 6 8
4	0 5 7

D

Stem	Leaf
2	2 5 5 7
3	0 1 2 2 4 5 6 8
4	0 5 7

Unit 33 Mini-Lesson
Display and Interpret Data

Standard

Measurement and Data

6.1D (PS) Communicate mathematical ideas, reasoning, and their implications using multiple representations, including symbols, diagrams, graphs, and language as appropriate.

6.12A (SS) Represent numeric data graphically, including dot plots, stem-and-leaf plots, histograms, and box plots.

Model the Skill

- **Say:** *Today we are going to look at data and at various ways to display it. We have already made line plots and stem-and-leaf plots to show data.*
- **Say:** *A bar graph lets us compare data easily by looking at the length of each bar.* **Ask:** *What kind of data is best shown on a bar graph?* Discuss discrete data including length, area, height, weight, attendance, votes, etc.
- **Ask:** *What kind of data is best shown on a line graph?* Discuss data that shows change over time, including growth rates, temperature, sales, etc.
- **Ask:** *If I collect data on the height of a corn plant over 8 weeks, what kind of graph would I most likely use?* (line graph) *How could I best display data on the height of 8 varieties of corn at full growth?* (line plot, stem and leaf, or bar graph) Make up some data points for each scenario and sketch a line graph and a bar graph on the board. Discuss the different displays.
- Assign students the appropriate practice page(s) to support their understanding of the skill.

Assess the Skill

Use the following problems to pre-/post-assess students' understanding of the skill.

Have students answer questions about the data in the graph below.

What data does the graph show?

What is the range of the data?

What is the mode of the data?

What is the approximate mean of the data? How can you tell without calculating?

Which animal is taller, the ibis or the egret? How much taller in inches?

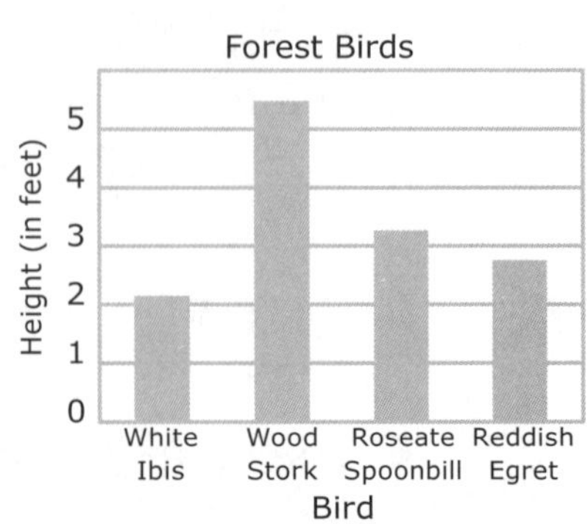

Name ______________________________ Date __________

Complete each graph or plot and answer the questions.

1.

Height of Tomato Plants in the Garden (inches)							
18	23	24	26	32	19	28	19
24	28	31	30	28	32	28	

Stem	Leaf
1	8
2	
3	

2. Which display of the data do you like better? Why?

____

3. What is the most common height of the tomato plants?

____

4. What is the range in height of the tomato plants?

____

5.

Students Who Take the Bus to School		
Grade	**Number of Boys**	**Number of Girls**
6	130	170
7	145	135
8	180	115

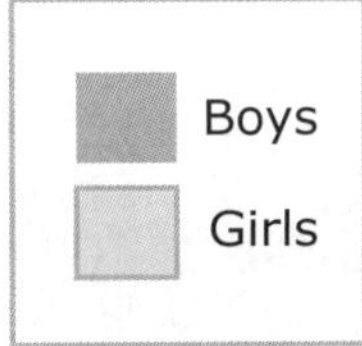

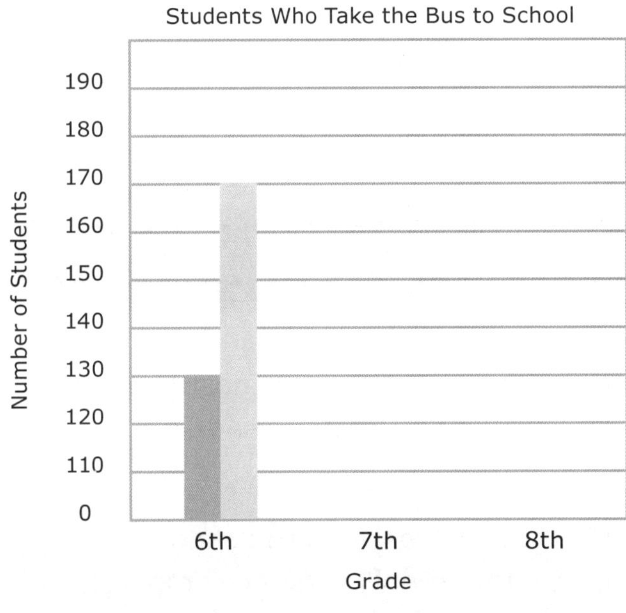

6. Which grade takes the bus more than any other group?

____

7. Which grade has the closest ratio of boys and girls riding the bus?

____

☆ **Tell why a double bar graph is a good choice to display the data in Problem 5.**

Name ____ Date __________

Make a graph or plot and answer the questions.

Cost of Car Insurance	
Year	**Annual Cost**
2012	$2,400
2010	$2,000
2008	$2,000
2006	$1,700
2004	$1,350

1. Which type of graph will best display the data? Choose among bar graph, line plot, or line graph. Explain your choice.

____

2. Make a graph to display the data.

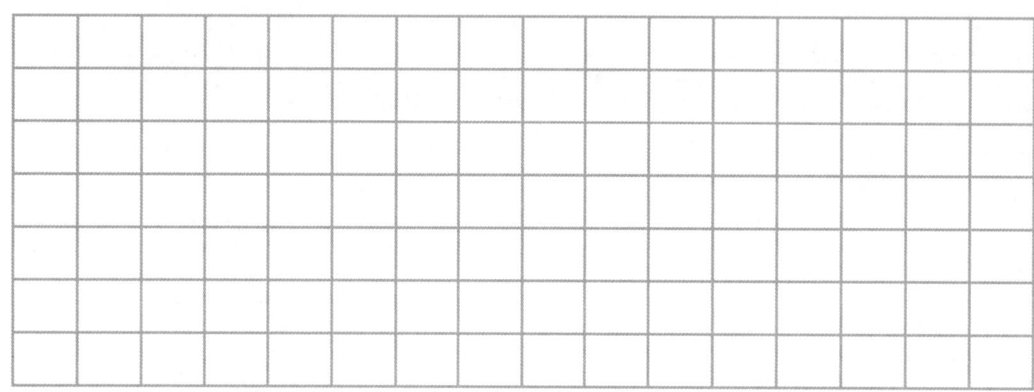

3. Title the graph at right.

____

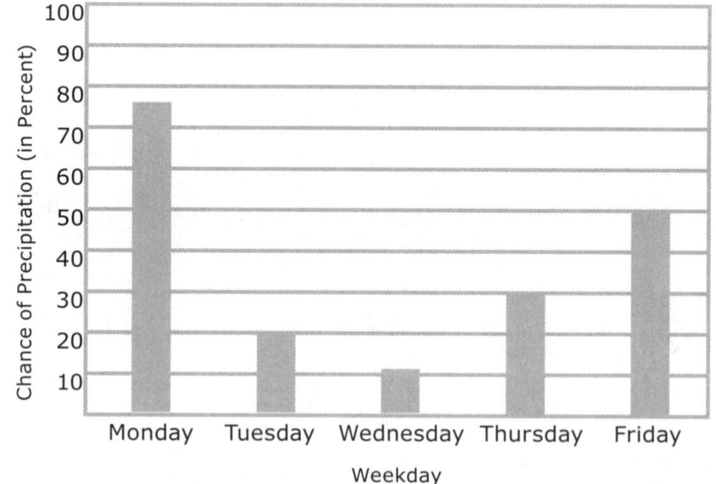

4. On which two days is it most likely that it will not rain, sleet, or snow?

5. How much greater is the chance of precipitation on Thursday compared to Wednesday?

6. In this five-day forecast, how many days show a 50% or greater chance of precipitation?

Tell how you used the graph to answer Problems 3 and 4.

Name ______________________________ **Date** __________

Solve.

1. The class voted on favorite ice cream flavors. Twenty-five students voted. Kyle wants to survey at least ten teachers for their favorite flavor. When he completes his survey, how should he display the data? Explain your answer.

____

____

2. Ana Laura is writing a science report on the atmosphere and wants to show the different percentage of elements that make up the air that we breathe. How should she display the data? Explain your answer.

____

____

Circle the letter for the correct answer.

3. The graph shows the daily high temperature recorded in July in Dallas.

Which statement is *not* supported by the information in the graph?

A The range of temperature in 2000 and 2012 is the same.
B The greatest difference in temperature between 2000 and 2012 for this period is 5 degrees.
C The high temperature stayed the same for 3 days in July 2000.
D The high temperature stayed the same for 3 days in July 2012.

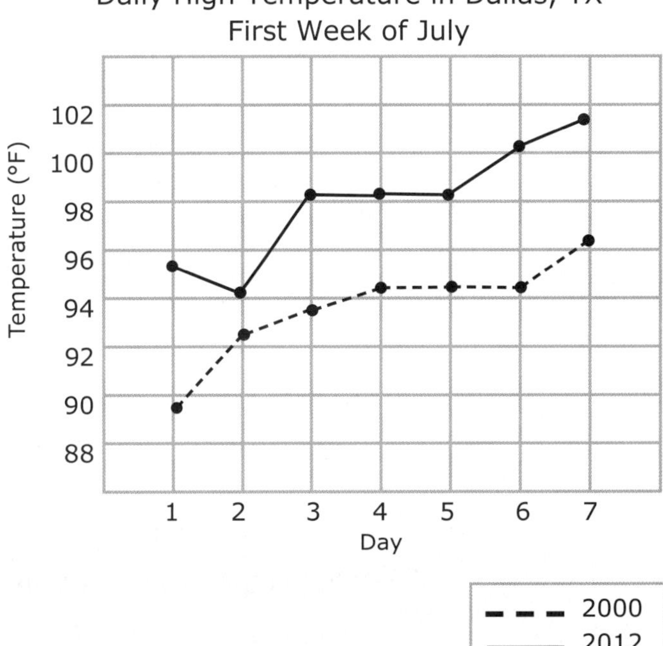

4. How many degrees hotter is the hottest day in 2012 than the hottest day in 2000?

A 2°F
B 3°F
C 4°F
D 5°F

Unit 34 Mini-Lesson

Box Plots

Standard

Probability and Statistics

6.13A (RS) Interpret numeric data summarized in dot plots, stem-and-leaf plots, histograms, and box plots.

Model the Skill

- **Say:** *We have recently studied mean, median, and mode. As a review, mean is the average of a set of numbers; median is the middle number of an ordered set of data; and mode is the number that occurs most often in a set of data.*
- **Say:** *Today we will study lower quartile and upper quartile and how those words help make a box plot, also known as a box-and-whisker plot.*
- **Ask:** *Can you tell me a word similar to* ***quartile****? What do you think* ***quartile*** *means?* (quart or quarter; *quartile* could mean "fourth")
- **Say:** *The lower quartile is the median of the lower half of the data set. The upper quartile is the median of the upper half of the data set.*
- Assign students the appropriate practice page(s) to support their understanding of the skill.

Assess the Skill

Use the following problems to assess the students' understanding of the skill.

Given the data set: 2 6 8 8 14 24 26 30 35

What is the mean, median, and mode?

What number is the smallest number?

What number is the largest number?

What is the range of this data set?

Name ______________________________ **Date** __________

A box plot is a graph or display that shows how the values in a data set are distributed. To make a box plot, or box-and-whisker plot, you need to find five values from the data set.

- the smallest or least value
- the lower quartile
- the median
- the upper quartile
- the largest or greatest value

Make a box plot. Use scores from your math tests.

93 83 97 92 87 92 90 85 82 80 98

1. Order the data from least to greatest.

2. What is the least number?

3. What is the greatest number?

4. What is the median?

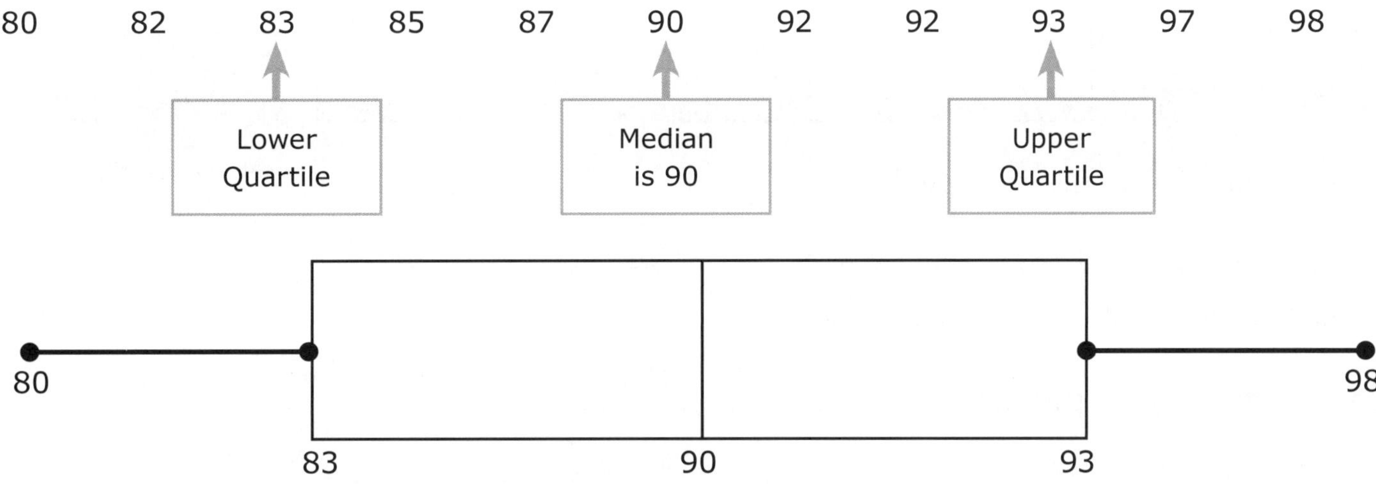

 **How do you find the upper quartile?**

Name ________________________________ **Date** __________

Use the box plots to answer the questions.

1

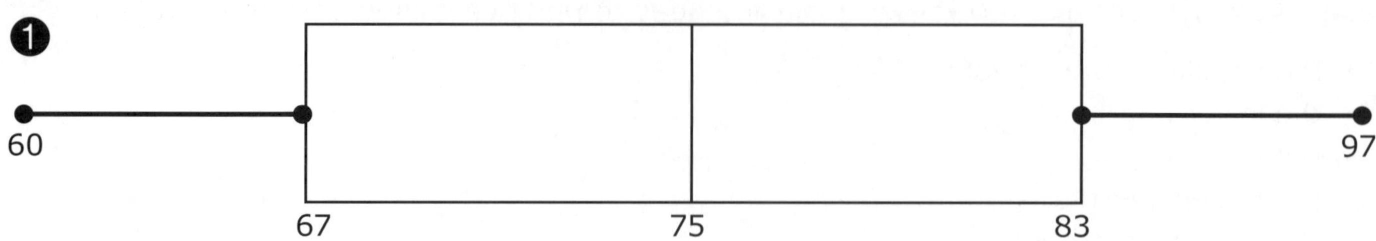

What is the median of the set of data? Explain. ______________________________

What is the smallest value? Explain. ______________________________

What is the largest value? Explain. ______________________________

What is the range of this set of data? Explain. ______________________________

What is the lower quartile? Explain. ______________________________

What is the upper quartile? Explain. ______________________________

2

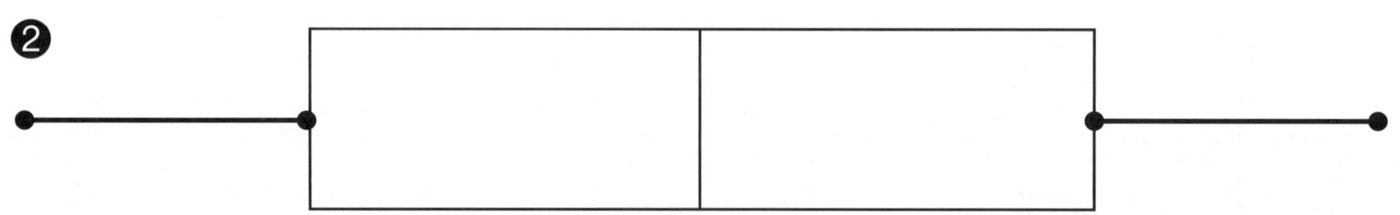

Put the following on the box plot above:

Median = 75 Lowest number = 60 Highest number = 97
Lower quartile = 67 Upper quartile = 83

What is the range of this data? ______________________________

 **How do you find the range in a data set?**

Name ____ **Date** ________

Make box plots.

1. The heights of students (in inches) in Miss Melendez's class are listed below. Make a box plot for the data set.

   48 52 45 46 56 58 46 47 57 52 48

2. The daily temperatures (°F) for Dallas is shown in the table below. Make a box plot for the data set.

   87 92 88 89 91 94 90

3. Maria recorded the number of students who attended the school dance. From the data set below, make a box plot to show the data set.

   34 26 42 21 32 39 25 30 26

4. Last week's rainfall (in inches) for Travis County is shown below. Make box plot from the data set.

   0.4 0 0.6 1.2 1.0 0.7 2.5

Unit 35 Mini-Lesson
Debit Cards vs. Credit Cards

Standard

Personal Financial Literacy

6.14B (SS) Distinguish between debit cards and credit cards.

Model the Skill

On the board, write the words *debit cards* and *credit cards*.

- **Say:** *A debit card is a plastic card that allows holders to purchase goods or services with funds that are deducted immediately from their checking or savings account.*
- **Ask:** *What do you think is an advantage of using a debit card?*
- **Say:** *A credit card is a plastic payment card often issued by a bank. It authorizes the delivery of goods and services in exchange for future payment with interest. Customers receive a monthly bill and may be charged a yearly fee.*
- **Ask:** *What do you think is an advantage of using a credit card?*
- Assign students the appropriate practice page(s) to support their understanding of the skill.

Assess the Skill

Use the following problem to assess the students' understanding of the skill.

What is 12% interest on $150?

Name ______________________________ **Date** __________

Credit cards and debit cards have many similarities, but there are also a number of differences. Discuss the advantages and disadvantages of each comparison.

1

Credit cards are used to borrow money.	Debit cards use funds from your own bank.

2

Credit cards often have interest charged.	Debit cards do not have interest charged.

3

With credit cards, you pay for your purchases over time.	With debit cards, you pay for your purchases immediately.

4

With credit cards, you often pay more than the sale price of the item.	With debit cards, you pay only the sale price of the item.

Name ______________________________ **Date** __________

Answer the questions and explain.

1. Miguel wants to purchase a new pair of shoes. He has the money in his checking account. Should Miguel use a credit card or a debit card? Explain.

2. Sabrina wants to purchase a new refrigerator for her home. She does not have enough money in her checking account or her savings account to purchase the refrigerator at this time. Should Sabrina use a credit card or a debit card? Explain.

3. While Paulette was driving to work, her gas pump went out on her car. Since she did not have enough money to pay for the gas pump to be replaced, Paulette used a card that would allow her to pay for the repairs later. Did Paulette use a credit card or a debit card? Explain.

4. William does not like to carry cash so he pays for his lunch with a plastic card. Each time William uses his card, the amount of money in his bank account decreases. Is William's plastic card a credit card or a debit card? Explain.

Name ______________________________ **Date** __________

Solve.

1. Dakota would like to purchase a new television for his room. The sale price on the television is $150. There is an 8% sales tax on the television.

   What is the total cost of the television including tax? ____________________

2. Dakota decided to use a credit card to purchase his new television. He decided pay $30 a month to pay for this television. Dakota's credit card company charges 1.25% per month on the unpaid balance. Complete the chart below.

End of Month	Unpaid balance	Interest on unpaid balance (0.0125)	Monthly Payment	Monthly Balance
1*	$162.00	$2.03	$30.00	$134.03
2	$134.03		$30.00	
3			$30.00	
4			$30.00	
5			$30.00	
6				$0.00

*Since the total amount borrowed was not paid off at the end of the first month, interest was calculated on the beginning balance.

3. What is the total amount of interest that Dakota paid for his television? ____________

4. Including tax and interest, how much did Dakota pay for his television? ____________

 **Which type of card will charge you interest on the unpaid balance?**

Unit 36 Mini-Lesson
Balancing a Checking Account

Standard

Personal Financial Literacy

6.14C (SS) Balance a check register that includes deposits, withdrawals, and transfers.

Model the Skill

On the board, write the words *checking account, deposits, withdrawals, transfers,* and *check register*.

- **Say:** *A checking account is an account set up in a bank or credit union where you keep your money.*
- **Say:** *Deposits are the amounts of money that you put into your checking account. Deposits are added to your balance.*
- **Say:** *Withdrawals are the amounts of money that you take out of your checking account. Withdrawals are subtracted from your balance.*
- **Say:** *Transfers are the amounts of money that you move or transfer from your savings account to your checking account or vice versa. Transfers may add or subtract from your balance.*
- **Say:** *A check register is a record of your bank account activity. This is where you keep track of your deposits, withdrawals, and transfers, as well as any bank fees.*
- Assign students the appropriate practice page(s) to support their understanding of the skill.

Assess the Skill

Use the following problem to assess the students' understanding of the skill.

Your bank account has a balance of $467.53. You make a withdrawal of $56.35. What is your new balance?

Name ______________________________ Date ________

Complete each of the following transactions.

1. Balance: $167.34
   Deposit: $45.78

   New Balance: ______________

2. Balance: $752.45
   Withdrawal: $152.65

   New Balance: ______________

3. Balance: $675.15
   Transfer from savings: $500.00

   New Balance: ______________

4. Balance: $2,753.50
   Transfer from savings: $1,500.00

   New Balance: ______________

5. Balance: $268.29
   Deposit: $175.00
   Withdrawal: $215.23

   New Balance: ______________

6. Balance: $1,586.50
   Deposit: $56.78
   Deposit: $158.50
   Withdrawal: $75.59
   Withdrawal: $578.65

   New Balance: ______________

What is the difference between a deposit and a withdrawal in your checkbook?

Name ______________________________ **Date** __________

A check register is used to keep track of transactions made to a bank account. Complete each of the following check registers.

Check #	Date	Transaction	Deposit		Withdrawal		Balance	
	1/31	Beginning Balance					$467	15
	2/01	Deposit (from Yard Sale)	$225	75				
3125	2/05	Rent			$375	00		
3126	2/06	Groceries			$156	35		
3127	2/07	Electricity/Water			$75	50		
	2/10	Transfer from Savings	$1000	00				
	2/20	ATM Withdrawal			$100	00		
3128	2/25	Car Repairs			$650	15		
3129	2/28	Clothes			$150	00		

At the end of the month, the bank sends you a statement with an account balance of $185.90. According to your check register, is this correct? Explain.

Check #	Date	Transaction	Deposit		Withdrawal		Balance	
	08/31	Balance					$1275	34
	09/01	Service Charge			$10	00		
	09/02	Deposit (Work)	$675	00				
7852	09/05	House Payment			$975	00		
7853	09/06	Telephone Payment			$75	60		
7854	09/07	Utilities			$135	78		
7855	09/15	Groceries			$156	34		
	09/20	Deposit (Baby Sitting)	$45	50				
7857	09/25	New Shoes			$45	75		
7858	09/30	Movie Tickets			$25	50		

At the end of the month, the bank sends you a statement with an account balance of $521.87. This does not match the balance in your check register. Can you find your error?

Name ______________________________ **Date** ________

Complete the chart and answer the questions.

❶ Fernandez had a balance of $956.89 at the end of May (05/31). He made deposits of $45.78, $67.87, $145.90, and $325.00. He made withdrawals of $157.34 (check #456 for groceries), $178.34 (check #457 for utilities), $850.15 (check #458 for rent), and $102.34 (check #459) for new clothes. Complete Fernandez's check register.

Check #	Date	Transaction	Deposit		Withdrawal		Balance	

❷ Why do you think it is important to keep a check register?

❸ Why do you think it is important to balance your register each month?

Grade 6 STAAR Mathematics Practice Assessment 1

Name ______________________________ **Date** __________

Centimeters 0 1 2 3 4 5 6 7 8 9 10 11 12 13 14 15 16 17 18 19 20

Inches 0 1 2 3 4 5 6 7 8

Reference Materials

LENGTH

Customary	Metric
1 mile (mi) = 1,760 yards (yd)	1 kilometer (km) = 1,000 meters (m)
1 yard (yd) = 3 feet (ft)	1 meter (m) = 100 centimeters (cm)
1 foot (ft) = 12 inches (in.)	1 centimeter (cm) = 10 millimeters (mm)

VOLUME AND CAPACITY

Customary	Metric
1 gallon (gal) = 4 quarts (qt)	1 liter (L) = 1,000 milliliters (mL)
1 quart (qt) = 2 pints (pt)	
1 pint (pt) = 2 cups (c)	
1 cup (c) = 8 fluid ounces (fl oz)	

WEIGHT AND MASS

Customary	Metric
1 ton (T) = 2,000 pounds (lb)	1 kilogram (kg) = 1,000 grams (g)
1 pound (lb) = 16 ounces (oz)	1 gram (g) = 1,000 milligrams (mg)

TIME

1 year = 12 months
1 year = 52 weeks
1 week = 7 days
1 day = 24 hours
1 hour = 60 minutes
1 minute = 60 seconds

PERIMETER			
Square			$P = 4s$
Rectangle			$P = 2l + 2w$
CIRCUMFERENCE			
Circle	$C = 2\pi r$	or	$C = \pi d$
AREA			
Triangle	$A = \frac{bh}{2}$	or	$A = \frac{1}{2}bh$
Square			$A = s^2$
Rectangle	$A = lw$	or	$A = bh$
Parallelogram			$A = bh$
Trapezoid	$A = \frac{(b_1 + b_2)h}{2}$	or	$A = \frac{1}{2}(b_1 + b_2)h$
Circle			$A = \pi r^2$
VOLUME			
Cube			$V = s^3$
Rectangular prism	$V = lwh$	or	$V = Bh$
ADDITIONAL INFORMATION			
Pi			$\pi \approx 3$

1 Pam took a survey of the students in her class. She asked them how they got to school this morning. The table below shows the results of her survey.

Transportation Survey

Kind of Transportation	Number of Students
Walk	39
Bike	9
Car	24
Bus	48

What decimal represents the fraction of students who rode a bike to school?

A 0.075

B 0.09

C 0.75

D 0.90

---

2 Samantha is a barista at a local coffee shop. She served three kinds of drinks this morning. The table below shows the drinks she served.

Drinks Served

Drink	Number Served
Coffee	61
Espresso Drink	23
Tea	16

What decimal represents the fraction of the drinks that were espresso drinks?

Record your answer and fill in the bubbles.
Be sure to use correct place value.

			.		
0	0	0		0	0
1	1	1		1	1
2	2	2		2	2
3	3	3		3	3
4	4	4		4	4
5	5	5		5	5
6	6	6		6	6
7	7	7		7	7
8	8	8		8	8
9	9	9		9	9

3 Kelly conducted a survey among her classmates on number and types of pets. The table below shows the results of her survey.

Pets Survey

Response	Number of Students
Have Only a Cat	**7**
Have Only a Dog	**4**
Have a Cat and a Dog	**3**
Have No Pets	**9**

What decimal represents the fraction of students in Kelly's class that have pets?

A 0.12

B 0.16

C 0.28

D 0.61

---

4 Paul is in charge of ordering the food for a large business meeting. The table below shows the meals he ordered for the meeting.

Meals Ordered

Meal	Orders
Grilled Cheese	**19**
Super Burger	**10**
Salmon Salad	**11**

What decimal represents the fraction of people in the meeting who requested the salmon salad?

A 0.11

B 0.275

C 0.51

D 0.725

5 The table below shows the members of the track team of a high school by grade.

Track Team by Grade

Grade	Runners
9th Grade	15
10th Grade	8
11th Grade	7
12th Grade	10

What decimal represents the fraction of members of the track team that are in tenth grade?

A 0.20

B 0.40

C 0.375

D 0.15

---

6 The table below shows the results of a dance competition.

Dance Competition Results

Dancer	Number of Votes
Alissa	24
Grover	18
Roger	51
Marta	27

What decimal represents the fraction of votes that the winner of the dance competition received?

A 0.375

B 0.425

C 0.51

D 0.575

7 Dex is $1\frac{1}{8}$ inches shorter than his sister Mallory. Mallory is $58\frac{3}{4}$ inches tall. How tall is Dex?

A $57\frac{1}{8}$ in.

B $57\frac{1}{4}$ in.

C $57\frac{1}{2}$ in.

D $57\frac{5}{8}$ in.

---

8 Timothy broke his record jump in the long jump by 1.25 meters. His new record is 8.8 meters. What was his old record?

A 7.35 m

B 7.55 m

C 7.65 m

D 7.75 m

---

9 The Smith family just had twin babies, Jess and Joss. Jess was born with a length of $20\frac{1}{4}$ inches. Joss was $\frac{3}{8}$ inch longer than his twin. How long was Joss?

A $19\frac{1}{8}$ in.

B $19\frac{3}{4}$ in.

C $19\frac{7}{8}$ in.

D $20\frac{5}{8}$ in.

10 Ruthie is a sculptor. She carved a marble statue that is 3.3 meters high. The statue rests on a marble stand that is 0.25 meters high. How tall are the statue and the stand together?

A 5.8 m

B 3.55 m

C 3.325 m

D 3.05 m

---

11 Jason competes in the high jump in track. His new record is $62\frac{1}{2}$ inches. This is $3\frac{1}{2}$ better than his previous record. What was his previous record?

A $59\frac{1}{4}$ in.

B $60\frac{1}{4}$ in.

C 59 in.

D 60 in.

---

12 Frank is signing autographs. He signs about 12 autographs every 10 minutes. There are 67 people in line to get autographs. Which is a good estimate for how long it will take Frank to give everyone an autograph?

A 60 minutes

B 75 minutes

C 85 minutes

D 90 minutes

---

13 Emily is writing thank-you cards for people who attended her wedding. There were 112 people in attendance. She writes cards at a rate of 15 cards per day. Based on this information, which of the following is a reasonable conclusion?

A She will have written less than half of the cards after 4 days.

B She will have written less than a third of the cards after 3 days.

C She will have written more than 50 cards after 3 days.

D She will write all thank-you cards within 8 days.

14 Matt took 411 pictures this year and submitted them to the yearbook committee. If they accept 10% of his photos, and the yearbook is 256 pages long, what percentage of the pages of the yearbook could contain Matt's photography?

A 10%

B $\frac{1}{16}$

C 16%

D 62%

---

15 Lanh is transcribing an interview. The interview is 112 minutes long. His transcribing rate is about 23 minutes per hour. Based on this information, which of the following statements is a reasonable conclusion?

A He will have transcribed less than half of the interview after 3 hours.

B He will have transcribed more than half of the interview after 3 hours.

C He will have transcribed more than 60 minutes of the interview after 2 hours.

D He will have transcribed fewer than 40 minutes of the interview after 2 hours.

---

16 Miguel is editing a batch of 112 photographs. He edits at a rate of 17 photographs per hour. Based on this information, after how many hours will he be at least halfway done?

A 3 hours

B 4 hours

C 5 hours

D 6 hours

17 Stephanie is going to read a 385-page book that she borrowed from the library. She wants to read roughly the same number of pages each day. The book is due in 10 days. Based on this information, how many pages should she try to read each day?

A 40 pages

B 50 pages

C 60 pages

D 65 pages

---

18 On any given day, 5 out of 7 yogis that come into Mitra Yoga studio are women. On Thursday, there were 26 men that came into the studio. Based on this information, how many people can you expect to have been at Mitra Yoga studio that day?

A 14

B 65

C 91

D 140

---

19 On any sunny day, Carla expects 3 out of every 5 people to wear sunglasses. On Thursday, it was sunny and there were 68 people at the park. Based on this information, how many people can you expect to have been wearing sunglasses that day?

Record your answer and fill in the bubbles.

Be sure to use the correct place value.

			.		
0	0	0		0	0
1	1	1		1	1
2	2	2		2	2
3	3	3		3	3
4	4	4		4	4
5	5	5		5	5
6	6	6		6	6
7	7	7		7	7
8	8	8		8	8
9	9	9		9	9

20 At a concert, the band expects that 1 out of every 8 people who attend will buy a T-shirt. If the band sold 24 T-shirts, how many people would you expect to have gone to the concert?

A 60

B 80

C 160

D 190

---

21 The chances of getting a prize in a Blue Burst Berry Flakes cereal box is 1 in 5. If there are 74 boxes of cereal at the grocery store, how many prizes can you expect to be in this grocery store?

A 15

B 20

C 25

D 30

---

22 Pam runs a lemonade stand. The table below shows how much money she earned, in dollars, based on how many hours she kept the stand open.

Lemonade Stand Earnings

Number of Hours	Earnings (in Dollars)
2	62
3	93
5	155
6	186
h	E

What expression could be used to find E, the earnings Pam would have if she kept the lemonade stand open for h hours?

A $31h$

B $31 + h$

C $62h$

D $62 + h$

23 Jeffrey's family owns a building. The table below shows how much money he collects, in dollars, based on how many apartment units pay rent.

Rent for the Building

Number of Units	Rent (in Dollars)
2	1,420
3	2,130
5	3,550
a	R

What expression could be used to find R, the amount of rent Jeffrey collects if he collects rent from a apartment units?

A $1{,}420a$

B $1{,}420 + a$

C $710a$

D $710 + a$

---

24 The table below shows the amount of calories Rob eats based on how many servings of potato chips he consumes.

Calories in Potato Chips

Number of Servings	Calories
2	310
3	465
5	775
s	C

What expression could be used to find C, the number of calories Rob consumes if he eats s servings of potato chips?

A $310s$

B $155 + s$

C $155 + 2s$

D $155s$

25 The table below shows the amount of calories Andy burns based on how many miles he runs.

Calories Burned Running

Miles Run	Calories
2	250
3	375
5	625
m	C

What expression could be used to find C, the number of calories Andy burns if he runs m miles?

A $125m$

B $125 + m$

C $125 + 2m$

D $250m$

---

26 Colin transcribed 80 minutes of an interview in 5 hours. He transcribed 15 minutes in each of the first 3 hours, and n minutes in the fourth hour. Which equation can be used to find m, the number of minutes of the interview Colin transcribed in the fifth hour?

A $m = 80 - (15 \bullet n)$

B $m = 80 - (15 \bullet n) - 3$

C $m = 80 - 3(15 + n)$

D $m = 80 - (15 \bullet 3) - n$

---

27 Hugo read 320 pages of a book in 7 days. He read 50 pages in each of the first 4 days, and t pages on each of the fifth and sixth days. Which equation can be used to find p, the number of pages of the book Hugo read on the seventh day?

A $p = 320 - (50 \bullet 2t)$

B $p = 320 - (50 \bullet 4) - 2t$

C $p = 320 - (50 \bullet 2) - 4t$

D $p = 320 - (6 \bullet t) - 50$

28 Hannah baked 86 cookies in 4 batches. She baked c cookies in each of the first 2 batches, and 15 cookies in the third batch. Which equation can be used to find b, the number of cookies Hannah baked in the fourth batch of cookies?

A $b = 86 - (15 \bullet 2c)$

B $b = 86 - (2 \bullet c) - 15$

C $b = 86 - 2(15 + c)$

D $b = 86 - (15 \bullet 2) - c$

---

29 For a census, Ian took surveys of 145 households in 5 days. He surveyed 38 households on each of the first 3 days, and h households on the fourth day. Which equation can be used to find g, the number of households Ian surveyed on the fifth day?

A $g = 145 - (38 \bullet 3) - 5h$

B $g = 145 - (3 \bullet h) - 38$

C $g = 145 - (38 + 3h)$

D $g = 145 - (38 \bullet 3) - h$

---

30 Which of the following could be the angle measurements for ΔDEF, if ΔDEF is an acute triangle?

A $m\angle D = 90^\circ$, $m\angle E = 30^\circ$, $m\angle F = 60^\circ$

B $m\angle D = 100^\circ$, $m\angle E = 50^\circ$, $m\angle F = 30^\circ$

C $m\angle D = 60^\circ$, $m\angle E = 40^\circ$, $m\angle F = 80^\circ$

D $m\angle D = 90^\circ$, $m\angle E = 45^\circ$, $m\angle F = 45^\circ$

---

31 Which of the following could be the angle measurements for quadrilateral $CDEF$, if $m\angle C = 30$?

A $m\angle D = 90^\circ$, $m\angle E = 90^\circ$, $m\angle F = 150^\circ$

B $m\angle D = 100^\circ$, $m\angle E = 50^\circ$, $m\angle F = 130^\circ$

C $m\angle D = 120^\circ$, $m\angle E = 150^\circ$, $m\angle F = 90^\circ$

D $m\angle D = 90^\circ$, $m\angle E = 90^\circ$, $m\angle F = 90^\circ$

32 The circumference of a circular fountain is 28 feet. Which of the following expressions represents the radius of the fountain?

A $\frac{28}{\pi}$

B $28 \bullet \pi$

C $28 \bullet 2\pi$

D $\frac{28}{2\pi}$

---

33 The radius of a circular rug is 8 feet. Which of the following expressions represents the circumference of the rug?

A $\frac{8}{\pi}$

B $8 \bullet \pi$

C $8 \bullet 2\pi$

D $\frac{8}{2\pi}$

---

34 The diameter of a circular garden is 9 feet. Which of the following expressions represents the circumference of the garden?

A $\frac{9}{\pi}$ 9

B $9 \bullet \pi$

C $9 \bullet 2\pi$

D $\frac{9}{2\pi}$

---

35 The circumference of a circular bird bath is 157 centimeters. What is the radius of the bird bath?

Record your answer and fill in the bubbles. Be sure to use correct place value.

			.		
0	0	0		0	0
1	1	1		1	1
2	2	2		2	2
3	3	3		3	3
4	4	4		4	4
5	5	5		5	5
6	6	6		6	6
7	7	7		7	7
8	8	8		8	8
9	9	9		9	9

36 There are 3 vertices of rectangle *ABCD* plotted on the coordinate grid below. The fourth vertex of the rectangle will be point *D*.

Which of the following ordered pairs best represents point *D*?

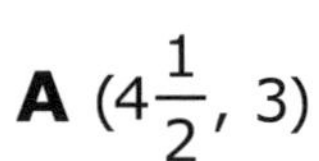

A $(4\frac{1}{2}, 3)$

B $(7\frac{1}{2}, 3)$

C $(3, 4\frac{1}{2})$

D $(4\frac{1}{2}, 7\frac{1}{2})$

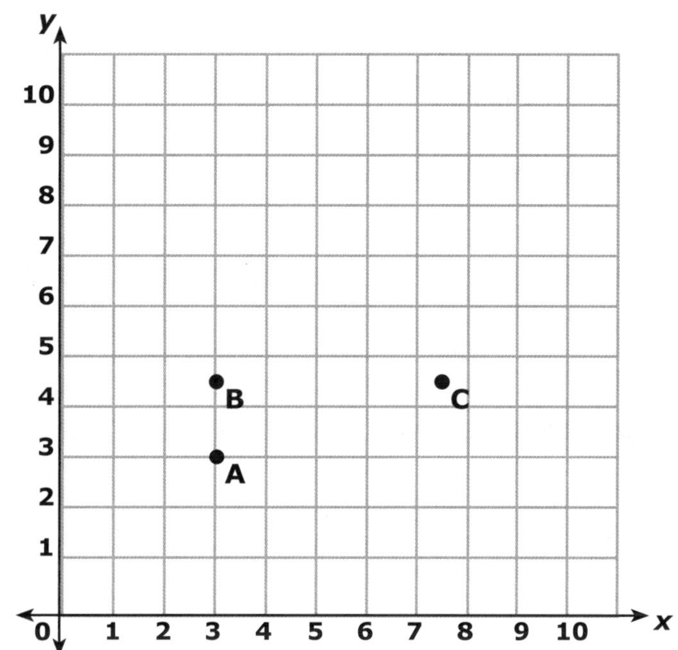

---

37 There are 3 vertices of rectangle *DEFG* plotted on the coordinate grid below. The fourth vertex of the rectangle will be point *G*.

Which of the following ordered pairs best represents point *G*?

A $(5\frac{1}{2}, 3\frac{1}{2})$

B $(2, 5\frac{1}{2})$

C $(2, 3\frac{1}{2})$

D $(8, 3\frac{1}{2})$

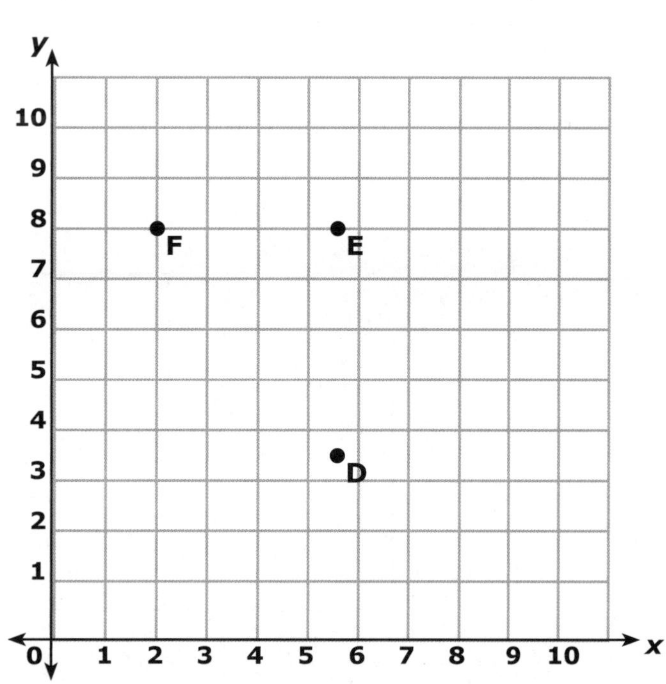

38 The figure below represents the floor of a building. Use a ruler to measure the dimensions of the figure to the nearest $\frac{1}{2}$ inch.

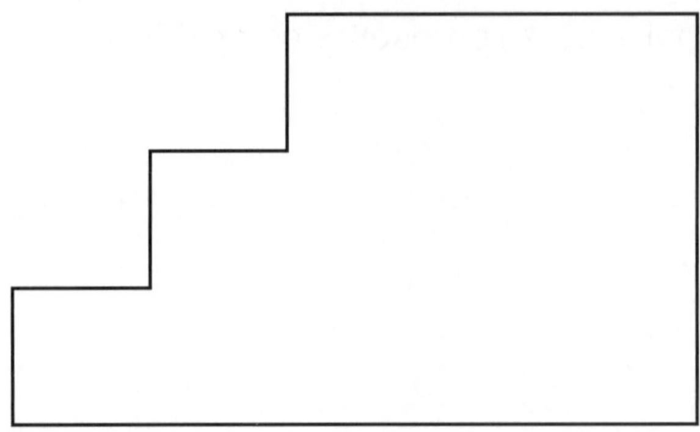

Scale
0.5 in. = 20 ft

Which is closest to the perimeter in feet of the floor of the actual building?

A 140 ft

B 160 ft

C 280 ft

D 320 ft

---

39 The figure below represents the floor of a room. Use a ruler to measure the dimensions of the figure to the nearest $\frac{1}{2}$ inch.

Which is closest to the perimeter in feet of the floor of the room?

A 80 ft

B 90 ft

C 8 ft

D 9 ft

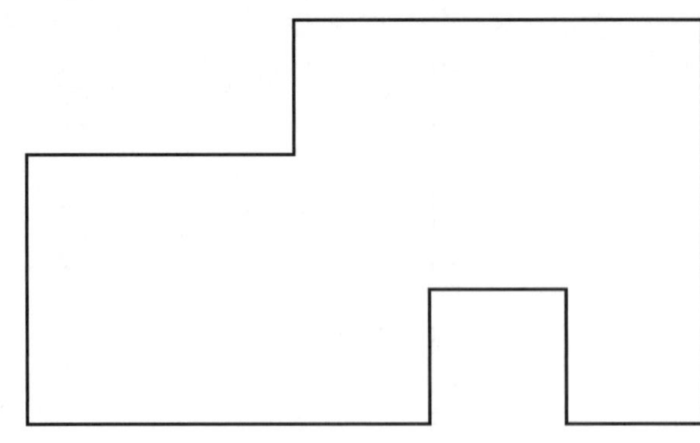

Scale
1.0 in. = 10 ft

40 The figure below represents a garden. Use a ruler to measure the dimensions of the figure to the nearest $\frac{1}{2}$ inch.

Which is closest to the perimeter in feet of the actual garden?

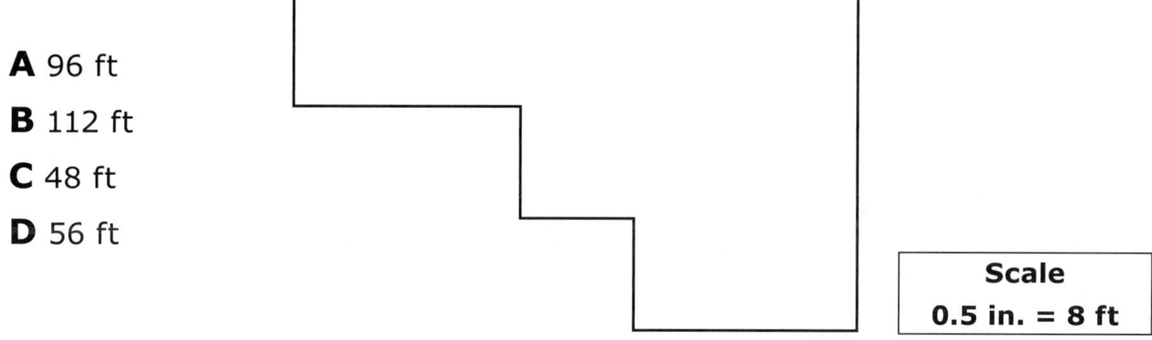

A 96 ft

B 112 ft

C 48 ft

D 56 ft

---

41 The figure below represents the plan for a porch. Use a ruler to measure the dimensions of the figure to the nearest $\frac{1}{2}$ inch.

Which is closest to the perimeter in feet of actual porch?

Record your answer and fill in the bubbles. Be sure to use the correct place value.

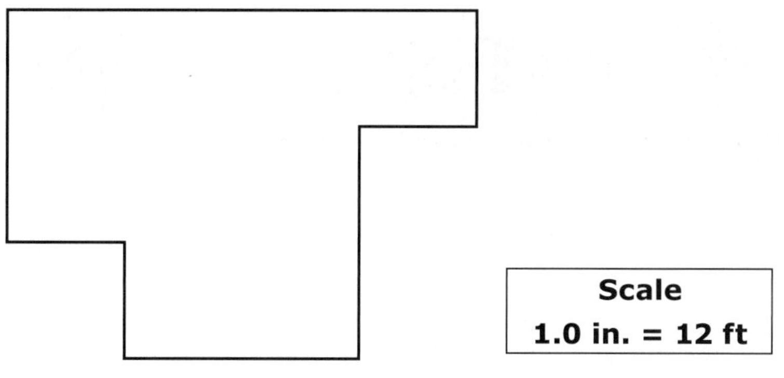

			.		
0	0	0		0	0
1	1	1		1	1
2	2	2		2	2
3	3	3		3	3
4	4	4		4	4
5	5	5		5	5
6	6	6		6	6
7	7	7		7	7
8	8	8		8	8
9	9	9		9	9

42 Olivia has $3\frac{1}{2}$ gallons of applesauce that she is distributing into 1-pint containers. How many containers can she fill with the applesauce?

A 28 containers

B 21 containers

C 14 containers

D 7 containers

---

43 George works at a hotel. He pours all the soap he has to fill 1-pint dispensers in each of 40 bathrooms in the hotel. How many gallons did George pour in all?

A 8

B 7

C 6

D 5

---

44 Amber is a chef who is pouring 4.5 gallons of olive oil into 1-quart containers. How many containers can she fill completely?

A 16

B 18

C 20

D 27

---

45 Patrick has 22 quarts of apple juice. How much apple juice is this measured in gallons?

A 4.5

B 5

C 5.5

D 6

46 Rene has 11 kittens. Four of the kittens are gray. The rest are black. If Rene selects a kitten at random, which expression represents the probability that she will select a black kitten?

A $1 - \frac{4}{7}$

B $1 + \frac{4}{7}$

C $1 - \frac{4}{11}$

D $1 - \frac{7}{11}$

---

47 Ryoko has 9 pairs of shoes. Of the pairs, 6 pairs are athletic. The rest of the shoes are dress shoes. If Ryoko selects a pair of shoes at random, which expression represents the probability that he will select dress shoes?

A $1 - \frac{3}{9}$

B $1 + \frac{3}{9}$

C $1 - \frac{3}{15}$

D $1 - \frac{6}{15}$

---

48 Debbie has 25 records. Of them, 19 are rock records. The rest are jazz records. If Debbie selects a record at random, which expression represents the probability that she will select a jazz album?

A $1 - \frac{6}{19}$

B $1 + \frac{6}{19}$

C $1 - \frac{6}{25}$

D $1 - \frac{19}{25}$

49 Matthew has 28 books. Of them, 20 are fiction. The rest are nonfiction. If Matthew selects a book at random, which expression represents the probability that he will select a book of nonfiction?

A $1 - \frac{8}{20}$

B $1 - \frac{8}{28}$

C $1 + \frac{8}{28}$

D $1 - \frac{20}{28}$

---

50 The graph below shows the number of participants in three games at a carnival.

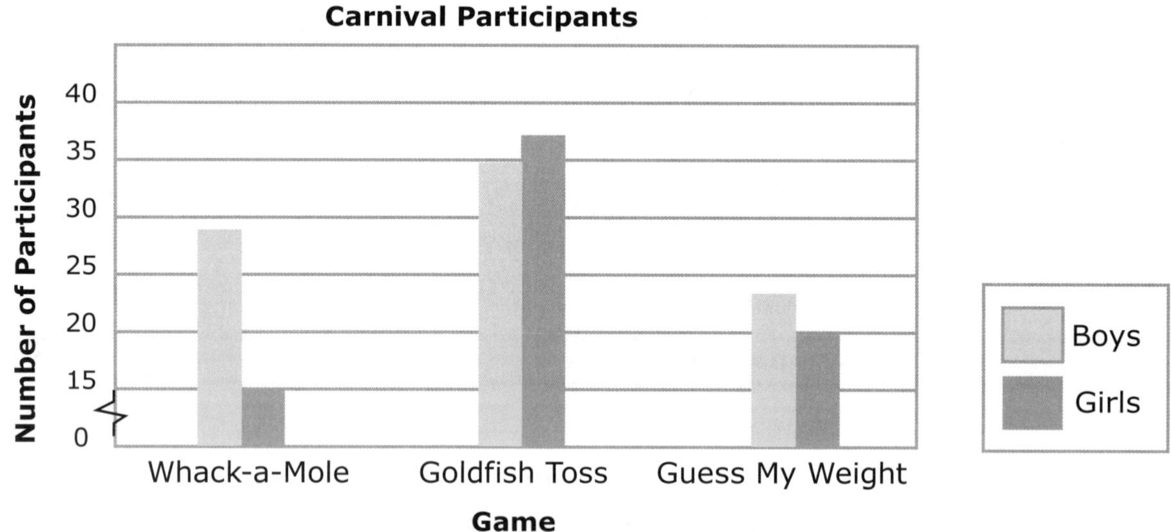

Which statement is NOT supported by the information on the graph?

A Goldfish Toss was the most popular game for girls.

B More boys than girls played every game.

C Goldfish Toss drew approximately 27 more participants than Guess My Weight.

D Whack-a-Mole and Guess My Weight drew about the same number of participants.

51 The graph below shows the number of tickets sold for three movies at a theater.

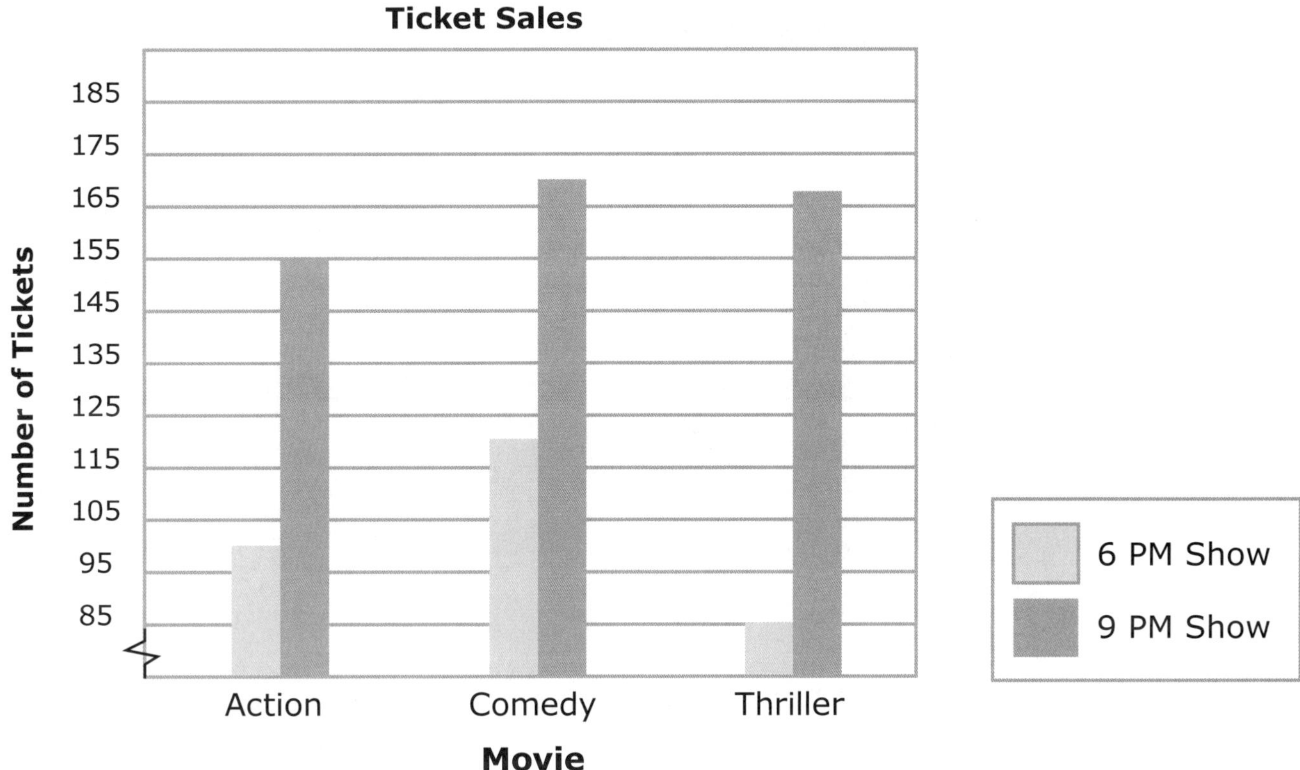

Which statement is NOT supported by the information on the graph?

A The number of tickets sold for 9:00 PM shows is double the number of tickets sold for 6:00 PM shows.

B The number of tickets sold for the 6:00 PM action movie is approximately 18 greater than the number of tickets sold for the 6:00 PM thriller.

C Approximately the same number of tickets were sold for the thriller as the action movie.

D Fifty more tickets were sold for the comedy show at 9:00 PM than the earlier comedy show.

52 The graph below shows the number of students who participated at the track meet on Thursday.

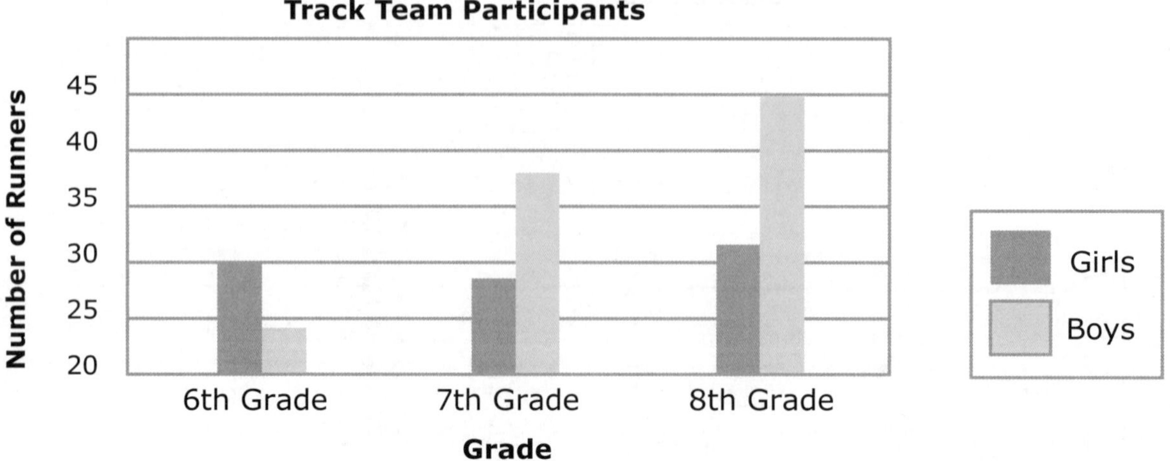

Which statement is NOT supported by the information on the graph?

A The seventh grade has 9 more boys than girls on the team.

B The eighth grade has approximately 22 more runners than the sixth grade has.

C There are more girl runners than boy runners.

D There are more female runners in the eighth grade than in the seventh grade.

Grade 6 STAAR Mathematics Practice Assessment 2

Name ______________________________ **Date** __________

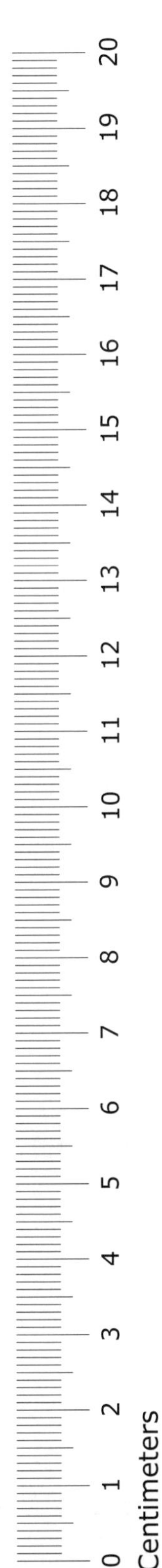

Reference Materials

LENGTH

Customary	Metric
1 mile (mi) = 1,760 yards (yd)	1 kilometer (km) = 1,000 meters (m)
1 yard (yd) = 3 feet (ft)	1 meter (m) = 100 centimeters (cm)
1 foot (ft) = 12 inches (in.)	1 centimeter (cm) = 10 millimeters (mm)

VOLUME AND CAPACITY

Customary	Metric
1 gallon (gal) = 4 quarts (qt)	1 liter (L) = 1,000 milliliters (mL)
1 quart (qt) = 2 pints (pt)	
1 pint (pt) = 2 cups (c)	
1 cup (c) = 8 fluid ounces (fl oz)	

WEIGHT AND MASS

Customary	Metric
1 ton (T) = 2,000 pounds (lb)	1 kilogram (kg) = 1,000 grams (g)
1 pound (lb) = 16 ounces (oz)	1 gram (g) = 1,000 milligrams (mg)

TIME

1 year = 12 months
1 year = 52 weeks
1 week = 7 days
1 day = 24 hours
1 hour = 60 minutes
1 minute = 60 seconds

PERIMETER			
Square			$P = 4s$
Rectangle			$P = 2l + 2w$
CIRCUMFERENCE			
Circle	$C = 2\pi r$	or	$C = \pi d$
AREA			
Triangle	$A = \frac{bh}{2}$	or	$A = \frac{1}{2}bh$
Square			$A = s^2$
Rectangle	$A = lw$	or	$A = bh$
Parallelogram			$A = bh$
Trapezoid	$A = \frac{(b_1 + b_2)h}{2}$	or	$A = \frac{1}{2}(b_1 + b_2)h$
Circle			$A = \pi r^2$
VOLUME			
Cube			$V = s^3$
Rectangular prism	$V = lwh$	or	$V = Bh$
ADDITIONAL INFORMATION			
Pi			$\pi \approx 3$

1 The table below shows enrollment in a foreign language program at a community college.

Foreign Language Enrollment

Language	Number of Students
French	90
Russian	45
Japanese	15

What decimal represents the fraction of these students that are enrolled in Russian class?

A 0.30

B 0.40

C 0.45

D 0.60

---

2 The table below shows the members of a high school choir by grade.

Choir Participants

Grade	Number of Singers
9th Grade	4
10th Grade	10
11th Grade	17
12th Grade	19

What decimal represents the fraction of the choir that is NOT in the twelfth grade?

Record your answer and fill in the bubbles. Be sure to use correct place value.

			.		
0	0	0		0	0
1	1	1		1	1
2	2	2		2	2
3	3	3		3	3
4	4	4		4	4
5	5	5		5	5
6	6	6		6	6
7	7	7		7	7
8	8	8		8	8
9	9	9		9	9

3 Rachel is a waitress at a breakfast place. The table below shows the different plates that customers ordered from Rachel on a Wednesday.

Breakfast Orders

Meal	Number Ordered
Eggs Benedict	4
Belgian Waffle	12
Fruit Salad	6
Egg on a Bagel	18

What decimal represents the fraction of customers that ordered the Belgian Waffle?

A 0.52

B 0.30

C 0.28

D 0.11

---

4 A town has a local singing contest. The table below shows the results of the voting in this contest.

Best Singer Contest Votes

Singer	Number of Votes
Gilligan	45
Ginger	39
Daisy	24
Eric	42

What decimal represents the fraction of votes that the second-place contestant, Eric, received?

A 0.45

B 0.42

C 0.30

D 0.28

5 Reggie is organizing the drinks for a morning meeting at a business conference. The table below shows the final drink order for the group.

Drinks for the Meeting

Drink	Number of Bottles
Apple Juice	12
Orange Juice	10
Water	18

What decimal represents the fraction of meeting participants that ordered water?

A 0.45

B 0.40

C 0.30

D 0.25

---

6 Christie broke her long jump record by 1.15 meters. Her new record is 7.3 meters. What was her previous record?

A 8.45 m

B 8.15 m

C 6.45 m

D 6.15 m

---

7 Kim's length when she was born was $1\frac{1}{2}$ inches less than the length of her sister Karol at birth. Karol was born $18\frac{3}{4}$ inches long. How long was Kim at birth?

A $16\frac{3}{4}$ in.

B $17\frac{1}{4}$ in.

C $19\frac{1}{4}$ in.

D $20\frac{1}{4}$ in.

8 Ashley competes in the shot put in track and field. On her first try, she threw the shot a distance of 18.5 meters. On her next try she threw it 0.75 meters further. What was the length of her second throw?

A 19.25 m

B 20.25 m

C 20.75 m

D 26.0 m

---

9 Teresa bought a set of curtains and hemmed the ends so that they were $1\frac{7}{8}$ inches shorter. Before she hemmed them, they were $63\frac{1}{2}$ inches long. How long were Teresa's curtains after she hemmed them?

A $60\frac{3}{4}$ in.

B $61\frac{3}{8}$ in.

C $61\frac{5}{8}$ in.

D $62\frac{3}{4}$ in.

---

10 Between December and the following July, Briana grew $2\frac{1}{2}$ inches. In December, she was $42\frac{3}{8}$ inches tall. How tall was she in July?

A $45\frac{1}{8}$ in.

B $44\frac{7}{8}$ in.

C $44\frac{4}{8}$ in.

D $45\frac{4}{10}$ in.

11 Lisa is $52\frac{7}{8}$ inches tall. She is wearing a pair of high-heeled shoes that make her $2\frac{1}{2}$ inches taller. How tall is Lisa when she wears this pair of shoes?

A $54\frac{3}{8}$ in.

B $54\frac{3}{10}$ in.

C $55\frac{3}{8}$ in.

D $56\frac{1}{8}$ in.

---

12 Amy is signing autographs. She can sign about 7 autographs every 5 minutes. There are 48 people in line to get autographs. Which is the best estimate for how long it will take Amy to give each person an autograph?

A 14 minutes

B 35 minutes

C 60 minutes

D 70 minutes

---

13 Casey wants to read a 318-page book that she borrowed from the library. The book is due 5 days from now. If she wants to read roughly the same number of pages each day, how many pages should she try to read each day?

A 50 pages

B 55 pages

C 60 pages

D 65 pages

14 Justin is transcribing an interview. The interview is 85 minutes long. His transcription rate is about 21 minutes per hour. Based on this information, which of the following statements is a reasonable conclusion?

A He will have transcribed more than half of the interview after 2 hours.

B He will have transcribed more than $\frac{1}{3}$ of the interview after an hour.

C He will have transcribed more than 60 minutes of the interview after 3 hours.

D He will have transcribed fewer than 40 minutes of the interview after 2 hours.

---

15 Gary is writing thank-you cards for people who came to his fund-raising event. There were 176 people in attendance. He writes cards at a rate of 20 cards per day. Based on this information, which of the following is a reasonable conclusion?

A He will have written more than half of the cards after 4 days.

B He will have written more than a third of the cards after 3 days.

C He will have written more than 120 cards after 5 days.

D He will have written fewer than 50 cards after 3 days.

---

16 Jeremy is archiving a batch of 147 historical photographs. He archives at a rate of 18 photographs per hour. Based on this information, after how many hours will he be at least halfway done?

A 3 hours

B 4 hours

C 5 hours

D 6 hours

17 On any given day, 4 out of 6 yogis that come to Sunny's Yoga Studio are women. On Thursday, 126 yogis came to the studio. Based on this information, how many men would you expect to have been at Sunny's Yoga Studio on that day?

A 42

B 21

C 63

D 100

---

18 At a concert, the band expects that 1 out of every 12 people will buy a CD. If there were 450 people at the concert last night, what is a good estimate for the number of CDs sold by the band?

A 37

B 45

C 54

D 120

---

19 On a cold day, Richard expects to see 3 out of every 7 people on the train wearing scarves. If there are 63 people on his train car this morning, how many of them does Richard expect to be wearing a scarf?

A 27

B 36

C 45

D 54

---

20 At an elementary school, 2 out of every 9 children wear eyeglasses. If there are 1,800 students at the school, how many of them can be expected to wear eyeglasses?

Record your answer and fill in the bubbles. Be sure to use correct place value.

			.		
⓪	⓪	⓪		⓪	⓪
①	①	①		①	①
②	②	②		②	②
③	③	③		③	③
④	④	④		④	④
⑤	⑤	⑤		⑤	⑤
⑥	⑥	⑥		⑥	⑥
⑦	⑦	⑦		⑦	⑦
⑧	⑧	⑧		⑧	⑧
⑨	⑨	⑨		⑨	⑨

21 Jin runs a car wash. The table below shows how much money he earned, in dollars, based on how many hours he kept the car wash open.

Car Wash Earnings

Number of Hours	Earnings (in Dollars)
2	84
4	168
5	210
h	*E*

What expression could be used to find E, the earnings Jin would have if he kept the car wash open for h hours?

A $84h$

B $84 + h$

C $42h$

D $42 + h$

---

22 Cathy's family owns a building. The table below shows how much money she collects, in dollars, based on how many apartment units pay rent.

Rent for the Building

Number of Units	Earnings (in Dollars)
2	1,040
3	1,560
5	2,600
a	*R*

What expression could be used to find R, the amount of rent Cathy collects if she collects rent from a apartment units?

A $520a$

B $520 + 2a$

C $1{,}040a$

D $1{,}040 + a$

23 The table below shows the amount of calories Amanda eats based on how many servings of jelly beans she consumes.

Calories in Jelly Beans

Number of Servings	Calories
2	82
4	164
5	205
b	C

What expression could be used to find C, the number of calories Amanda consumes if she eats b servings of jelly beans?

A $82b$

B $41 + b$

C $41 + 2b$

D $41b$

---

24 The table below shows the amount of calories Natasha burns based on how many miles she walks.

Calories Burned Walking

Miles Walked	Calories
2	170
4	340
5	425
m	C

What expression could be used to find C, the number of calories Natasha burns if she walks m miles?

A $170m$

B $85m$

C $85 + 2m$

D $85m + 170$

25 Zoe transcribed 115 minutes of an interview in 4 hours. She transcribed n minutes in each of the first 3 hours, and 45 minutes in the last hour. Which equation can be used to find m?

A $m = 115 - (45 \bullet 3n)$

B $m = 115 - (3 \bullet n) - 45$

C $m = 115 - 3(45 + n)$

D $m = 115 - (45 \bullet 3) - n$

---

26 Earl baked 65 cookies in 3 batches. He baked b cookies in each of the first 2 batches. Which equation can be used to find c, the number of cookies in the third batch?

A $c = 65 - 15$

B $c = 65 - (15 \bullet 2)$

C $c = 65 - (2 + b)$

D $c = 65 - (2 \bullet b)$

---

27 Kelly read 415 pages of a book in 5 days. He read 110 pages in each of the first 3 days, and t pages on the fourth day. Which equation can be used to find p, the number of pages Kelly read on the fifth day?

A $p = 415 - (110 \bullet 2) - t$

B $p = 415 - (110 \bullet 3) - t$

C $p = 415 - (110 \bullet 3t)$

D $p = 415 - (6 \bullet t) - 110$

---

28 For a census, Mickey took surveys of 130 households in 6 days. He surveyed 25 households on each of the first 4 days, v households on the fourth day, and $2v$ households on the fifth day. Which equation can be used to find w, the number of households Mickey surveyed on the sixth day?

A $w = 130 - (25 \bullet 4) - 3v$

B $w = 130 - (25 \bullet 4) - 2v$

C $w = 130 - (25 \bullet 4v)$

D $w = 130 - (3 \bullet v) - 25$

29 In ΔABC, $m\angle A = 30^\circ$. Which kinds of triangle could ΔABC be?

A Obtuse triangle or right triangle
B Right triangle or equilateral triangle
C Obtuse triangle or acute triangle
D Right triangle or acute triangle

---

30 Which of the following could be the angle measurements for ΔDEF, if ΔDEF is an obtuse triangle?

A $m\angle D = 30^\circ$, $m\angle E = 60^\circ$, $m\angle F = 90^\circ$
B $m\angle D = 60^\circ$, $m\angle E = 60^\circ$, $m\angle F = 60^\circ$
C $m\angle D = 120^\circ$, $m\angle E = 30^\circ$, $m\angle F = 30^\circ$
D $m\angle D = 90^\circ$, $m\angle E = 45^\circ$, $m\angle F = 45^\circ$

---

31 Which of the following could be the angle measurements for quadrilateral *CDEF*, if $\text{m}\angle C = 90$?

A $m\angle D = 85^\circ$, $m\angle E = 90^\circ$, $m\angle F = 95^\circ$
B $m\angle D = 100^\circ$, $m\angle E = 50^\circ$, $m\angle F = 130^\circ$
C $m\angle D = 80^\circ$, $m\angle E = 115^\circ$, $m\angle F = 95^\circ$
D $m\angle D = 100^\circ$, $m\angle E = 90^\circ$, $m\angle F = 110^\circ$

---

32 The circumference of a circular garden is 40 feet. Which of the following expressions represents the radius of the garden?

A $\frac{40}{\pi}$
B $40 \bullet \pi$
C $\frac{40}{2\pi}$
D $40 \bullet 2\pi$

33 The radius of a circular fountain is 13 feet. Which of the following expressions represents the circumference of the fountain?

A $13 \bullet 2\pi$

B $13 \bullet \pi$

C $\frac{13}{\pi}$

D $\frac{13}{2\pi}$

---

34 There are 3 vertices of rectangle ABCD plotted on the coordinate grid below. The fourth vertex of the rectangle will be point D.

Which of the following ordered pairs best represents point D?

A $(2\frac{1}{2}, 6)$

B (6, 5)

C (5, 6)

D $(6, 2\frac{1}{2})$

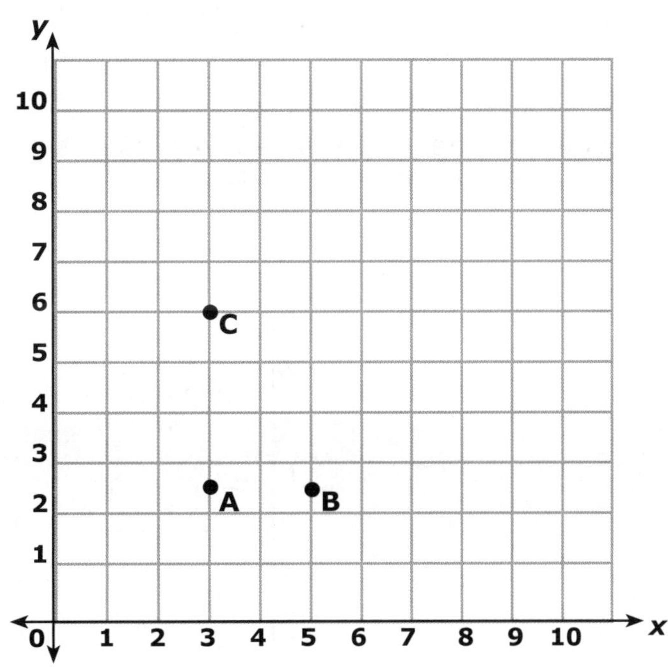

35 There are 3 vertices of rectangle DEFG plotted on the coordinate grid below. The fourth vertex of the rectangle will be point G.

Which of the following ordered pairs best represents point G?

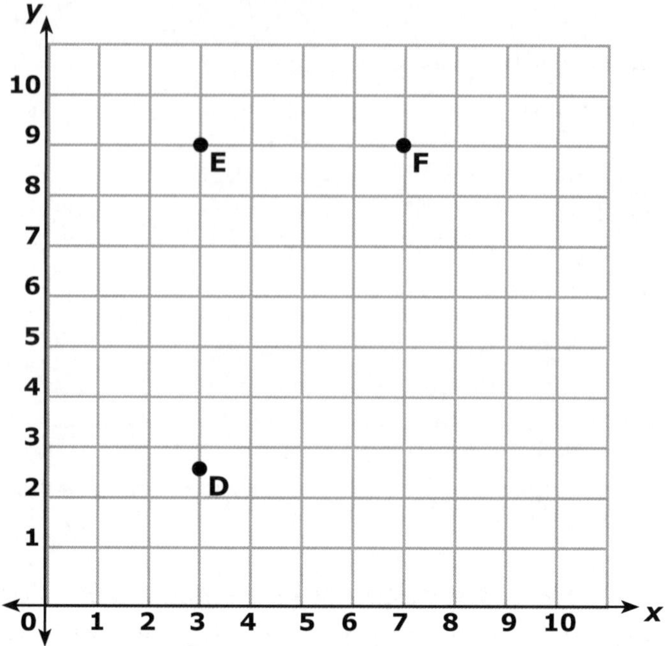

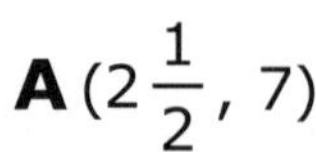

A $(2\frac{1}{2}, 7)$

B $(2, 7\frac{1}{2})$

C $(7\frac{1}{2}, 2)$

D $(7, 2\frac{1}{2})$

---

36 There are 3 vertices of rectangle KLMN plotted on the coordinate grid below. The fourth vertex of the rectangle will be point N.

Which of the following ordered pairs best represents point N?

A $(2\frac{1}{2}, 8)$

B $(8, 2\frac{1}{2})$

C $(5, 2\frac{1}{2})$

D $(2\frac{1}{2}, 5)$

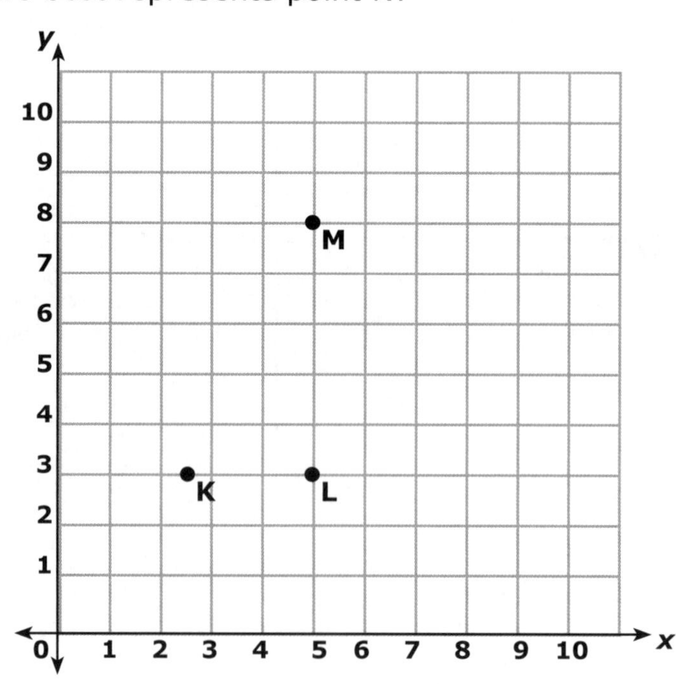

37 The figure below represents the floor of a building. Use a ruler to measure the dimensions of the figure to the nearest $\frac{1}{2}$ inch.

Which is closest to the perimeter in feet of the floor of the actual building?

A 216 ft

B 192 ft

C 108 ft

D 81 ft

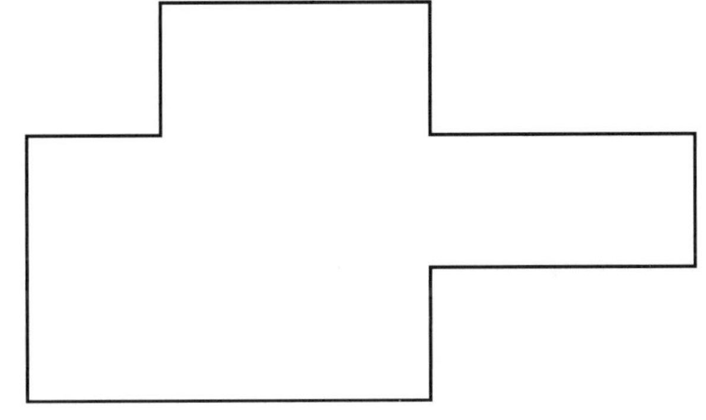

Scale
0.5 in. = 12 ft.

38 The figure below represents the plan for a garden. Use a ruler to measure the dimensions of the garden to the nearest $\frac{1}{2}$ inch.

Which is closest to the perimeter in feet of the actual garden?

A 60 ft

B 70 ft

C 240 ft

D 280 ft

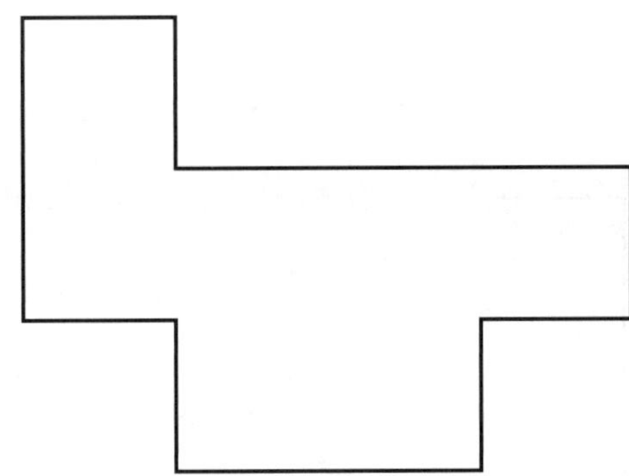

Scale
1.0 in. = 40 ft.

39 The figure below represents the floor of a room. Use a ruler to measure the dimensions of the figure to the nearest $\frac{1}{2}$ inch.

Which is closest to the perimeter in feet of the floor of the actual room?

A 160 ft

B 140 ft

C 80 ft

D 70 ft

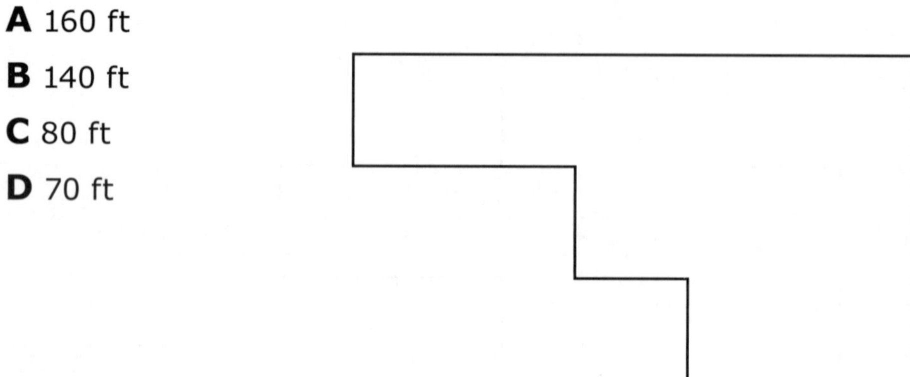

Scale
0.5 in. = 10 ft.

---

40 The figure below represents the floor of a building. Use a ruler to measure the dimensions of the figure to the nearest $\frac{1}{2}$ inch.

What is closest to the perimeter in feet of the floor of the actual building?

Record your answer and fill in the bubbles.
Be sure to use correct place value.

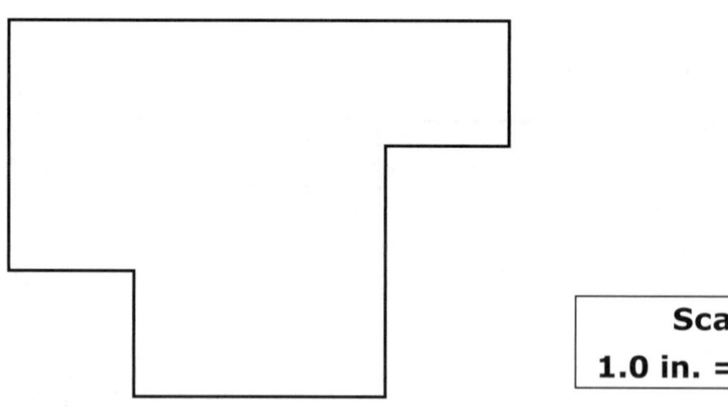

Scale
1.0 in. = 15 ft.

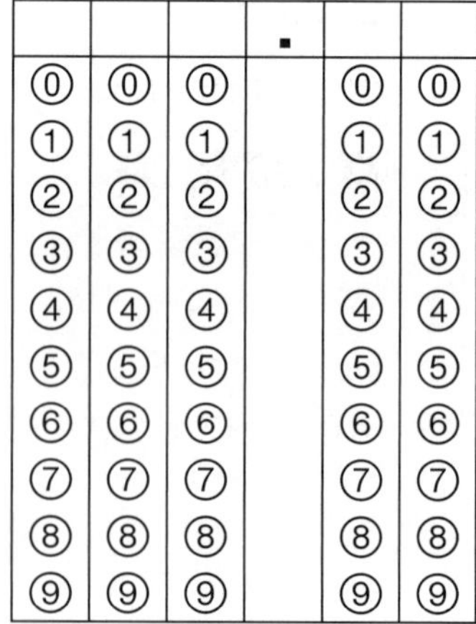

41 Meryl has 6.25 gallons of apple juice. How much apple juice is this measured in pints?

A 25

B 35

C 50

D 75

---

42 Josh works in a kitchen. He pours all the dish soap he has to fill 1-quart containers. He fills 4.75 gallons. How many containers did Josh fill?

A 20

B 19

C 18

D 15

---

43 Ned filled 36 1-pint containers of applesauce. How many gallons of applesauce did he have in all?

Record your answer and fill in the bubbles.

Be sure to use correct place value.

			.		
⓪	⓪	⓪		⓪	⓪
①	①	①		①	①
②	②	②		②	②
③	③	③		③	③
④	④	④		④	④
⑤	⑤	⑤		⑤	⑤
⑥	⑥	⑥		⑥	⑥
⑦	⑦	⑦		⑦	⑦
⑧	⑧	⑧		⑧	⑧
⑨	⑨	⑨		⑨	⑨

---

44 Amanda is a chef who is pouring 7.25 gallons of olive oil into 1-quart containers. How many containers can she fill completely?

A 15

B 20

C 29

D 30

45 At the clothing store where Elise works, there are 7 different kinds of sweaters. Of these sweater types, 3 have pockets. If any customer brings a sweater to checkout at random, which expression represents the probability that it will not have pockets?

A $1 + \frac{4}{7}$

B $1 - \frac{4}{7}$

C $1 - \frac{3}{11}$

D $1 - \frac{3}{7}$

---

46 Sean took 25 photos. Of these photos, 19 were in portrait layout. The rest were in landscape. If Sean chooses a photo at random, which expression represents the probability that it will be in landscape layout?

A $1 - \frac{6}{19}$

B $1 - \frac{6}{19}$

C $1 - \frac{19}{25}$

D $1 - \frac{6}{25}$

---

47 Ethan has written in 6 notebooks out of the 10 he owns. If Ethan chooses a notebook at random, which expression represents the probability that it will be empty?

A $1 - \frac{6}{10}$

B $1 - \frac{2}{6}$

C $1 - \frac{4}{6}$

D $1 - \frac{4}{10}$

48 Graham works at a bicycle shop, where he recently sold 17 bicycles. Of them, 12 were the men's model bicycles and the rest were women's model bicycles. If Graham chooses a receipt at random from this group of sales, which expression represents the probability that it will be for a women's-model bicycle?

A $1 - \frac{5}{17}$

B $1 - \frac{5}{12}$

C $1 - \frac{12}{17}$

D $1 - \frac{7}{12}$

---

49 The graph below shows the number of participants in three games at a carnival.

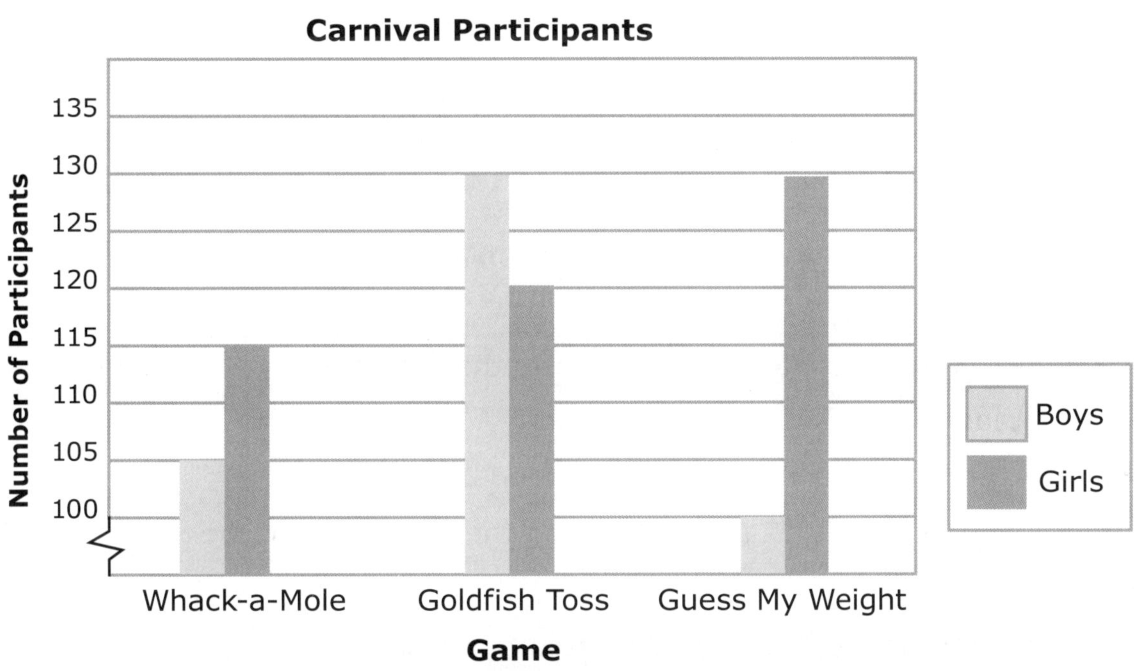

Which statement is NOT supported by the information on the graph?

A The number of girls who played Goldfish Toss is greater than the number of boys who played Whack-a-Mole.

B Approximately 220 children played Whack-a-Mole.

C Goldfish Toss drew approximately 20 more participants than Guess My Weight.

D The number of boys that played Goldfish Toss is approximately 30 more than the number of girls who played Goldfish Toss.

50 The graph below shows the number of students in three grades at a middle school.

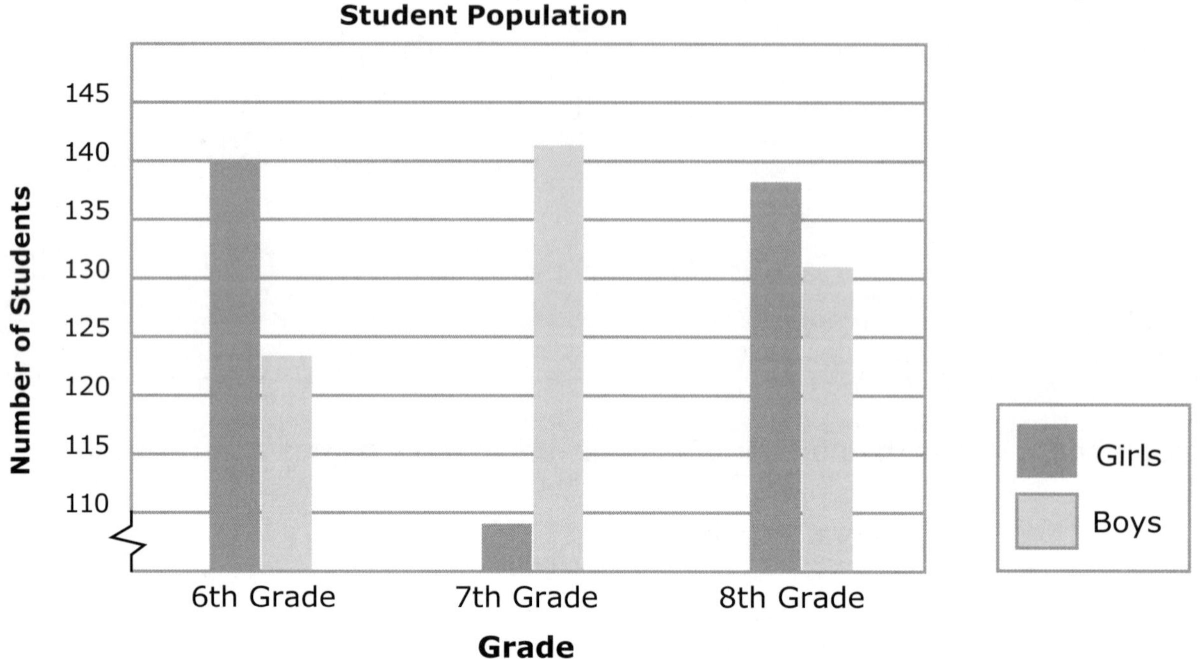

Which statement is NOT supported by the information on the graph?

A The number of girls in sixth grade is greater than the number of boys in seventh grade.

B There are approximately 400 girls that attend the school.

C There are approximately 32 more girls than there are boys in the seventh grade.

D The largest class is the eighth grade class.

51 The graph below shows the number of tickets sold for three movies at a theater.

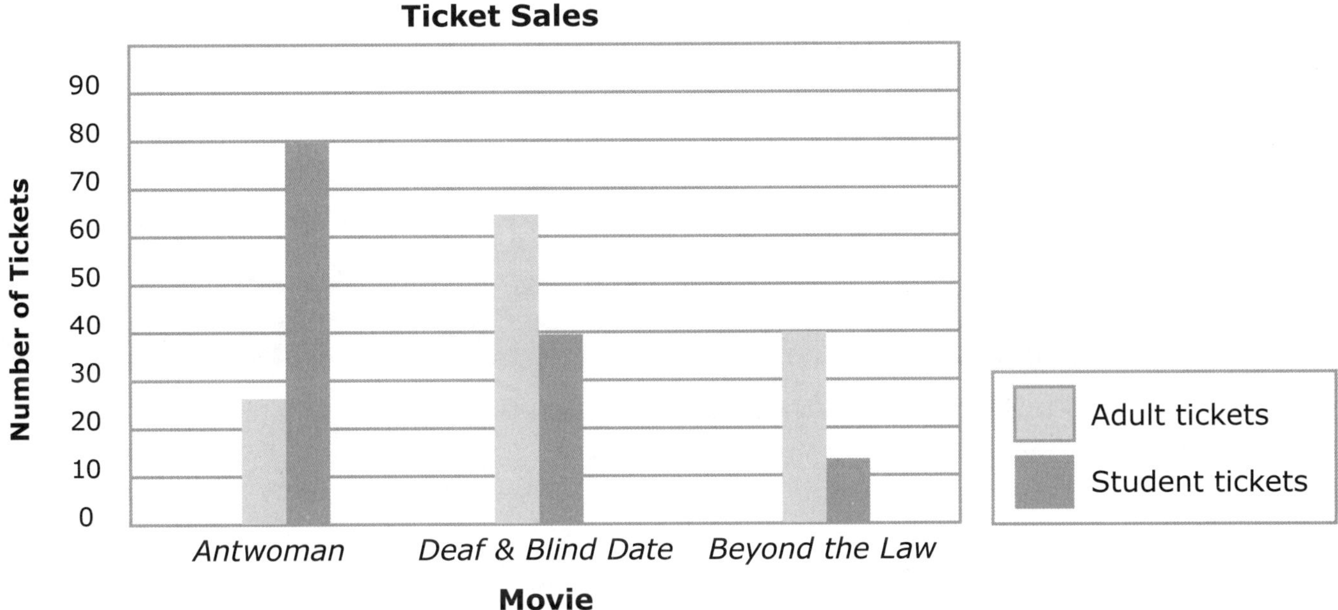

Which statement is NOT supported by the information on the graph?

A There were 5 more adult tickets sold than student tickets.

B More adult tickets were sold for *Deaf & Blind Date* than were sold student tickets for *Antwoman*.

C The number of adult tickets sold for *Beyond the Law* is equal to the number of student tickets sold for *Deaf & Blind Date*.

D More student tickets were sold for *Deaf & Blind Date* than were sold adult tickets for *Antwoman*.

52 The graph below shows the number of runners from each grade on the track team.

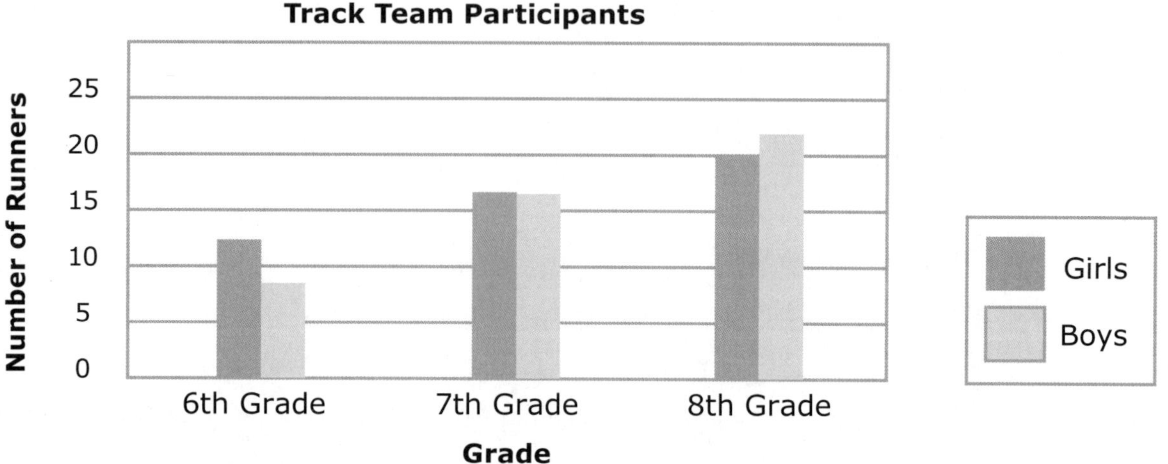

Which statement is NOT supported by the information on the graph?

A The eighth grade has 3 more boys than girls on the team.

B The eighth grade has approximately 22 more runners than the 6th grade has.

C There are more boy runners than girl runners.

D There are more female runners in the 8th grade than in the 7th grade.

Notes:

Notes: